Data Forecasting and Segmentation Using Microsoft Excel

Perform data grouping, linear predictions, and time series machine learning statistics without using code

Fernando Roque

BIRMINGHAM—MUMBAI

Data Forecasting and Segmentation Using Microsoft Excel

Copyright © 2022 Packt Publishing

Publishing Product Manager: Heramb Bhavsar
Senior Editor: David Sugarman
Content Development Editor: Sean Lobo
Technical Editor: Rahul Limbachiya
Copy Editor: Safis Editing
Language Support Editor: Safis Editing
Project Coordinator: Aparna Ravikumar Nair
Proofreader: Safis Editing
Indexer: Hemangini Bari
Production Designer: Sinhayna Bais
Marketing Coordinator: Priyanka Mhatre

First published: June 2022

Production reference: 1130522

Published by Packt Publishing Ltd.
Livery Place
35 Livery Street
Birmingham
B3 2PB, UK.

ISBN 978-1-80324-773-1

www.packt.com

To Sesi: I hope that someday you help to protect our natural biodiversity by looking at the North star, the pyramids, and the numbers.

Thanks to Philly, Peter de la Union, and Mercedes Thaddeus for your continuous assistance.

Contributors

About the author

Fernando Roque has 24 years of experience in working with statistics for quality control and financial risk assessment of projects after planning, budgeting, and execution. In his work, Fernando applies Python k-means and time series machine learning algorithms, using **Normalized Difference Vegetation Index (NDVI)** drone images to find crop regions with more resilience to droughts. He also applies time series and k-means algorithms for supply chain management (logistics) and inventory planning for seasonal demand.

About the reviewer

Ashwini Badgujar is a machine learning engineer at Impulselogic Inc. She has been involved in the machine learning domain for the last 3 years. She has research experience in Natural Language Processing and computer vision, specifically neural networks. She has also worked in the earth science domain, working on a number of earth science projects in collaboration with machine learning. She has worked at NASA in data processing and fire project analysis in calculating mixing heights, and at Comcast, where she worked on optimizing machine learning models.

Antonio L. Amadeu is a data science consultant, who is passionate about artificial intelligence and neural networks. He researches and applies machine learning and deep learning algorithms in his daily challenges, solving all types of issues in various business industries. He has worked for big companies such as Unilever, Lloyds Bank, TE Connectivity, Microsoft, and Samsung. As an aspiring astrophysicist, he does some research on astronomy object classification, using machine and deep learning techniques and **International Virtual Observation Alliance** (**IVOA**). He also participates in research at the Institute of Astronomy, Geophysics, and Atmospheric Sciences at Universidade de São Paulo.

Table of Contents

Part 2 – Grouping Data to Find Segments and Outliers

4

An Introduction to Data Grouping

5

Finding the Optimal Number of Single Variable Groups

6

Finding the Optimal Number of Multi-Variable Groups

7

Analyzing Outliers for Data Anomalies

Part 3 – Simple and Multiple Linear Regression Analysis

8
Finding the Relationship between Variables

9
Building, Training, and Validating a Linear Model

10

Building, Training, and Validating a Multiple Regression Model

Part 4 – Predicting Values with Time Series

11

Testing Data for Time Series Compliance

12

Working with Time Series Using the Centered Moving Average and a Trending Component

13
Training, Validating, and Running the Model

Index

Other Books You May Enjoy

Preface

This book is about giving you basic statistical knowledge to work with machine learning using complex algorithms to classify data, such as the K-means method. You will use an included add-in for Excel to practice the concepts of grouping statistics without the need for a deep programming background in the R language or Python.

The book covers three topics of machine learning:

- Data segmentation
- Linear regression
- Forecasts with time series

Data segmentation has many practical applications because it allows applying different strategies depending on the segment data ranges. It has applications in marketing and inventory rotation to act accordingly to the location and season of the sales.

The linear regression statistical concepts in this book will help you to explore whether the variables that we are using are useful to build a predictive model.

The time series model helps to do a forecast depending on the different seasons of the year. It has applications in inventory planning to allocate the correct quantities of products and avoid stalled cash flow in the warehouses. The time series depends on statistical tests to see whether the present values depend on the past, so they are useful to forecast the future.

Who this book is for

This book is for any professional that needs to analyze the data generated by the industry or academic scope using machine learning principles and algorithms. This book can help to better understand the different groups of data to apply a different approach to each one. Then, you can use the statistical tests of this book to see the most relevant variables that affect your performance using projections with linear regression. You will be able to link these variables with the time and season and use time series analysis to build a forecast that could help you to improve your planning in your professional scope.

What this book covers

Chapter 1, Understanding Data Segmentation, looks at how classifying the data of similar values is an approach for planning a strategy depending on the characteristics of the range of values of the groups. This strategy is more important when you deal with a problem with several variables, for example, finding the different groups of revenues for each season of the year and the quantities delivered for logistics demand planning.

Chapter 2, Applying Linear Regression, shows that the target of linear regression is to use related variables to predict the behavior of the values and build scenarios of what could happen in different situations, using the regression model as a framework for foreseeing the situations.

Chapter 3, What is Time Series?, examines how a time series model could do a forecast of the data, taking into account the seasonal trends based on the past time values.

Chapter 4, An Introduction to Data Grouping, delves into the importance of finding a different approach for each group. In complex multivariable problems, we need the assistance of machine learning algorithms such as K-means to find the optimal number of segments and the group's values range.

Chapter 5, Finding the Optimal Number of Single Variable Groups, shows how running an add-in for Excel that uses the K-means algorithm can help to get the optimal number of groups for the data that we are researching. In this case, we will start with a problem of just one variable to explain the concepts.

Chapter 6, Finding the Optimal Number of Multi-Variable Groups, demonstrates how to use the Excel add-in to do the grouping of problems of several variables, for example, the classification of quantity, revenue, and season of the inventory rotation.

Chapter 7, Analyzing Outliers for Data Anomalies, delves into another approach to data segmentation: researching what happens with the values that have a long-distance separation of all the groups. These values are anomalies, such as very short value expenses happening at non-business hours that could indicate evidence of possible fraud attempts.

Chapter 8, Finding the Relationship between Variables, shows how we have to do statistical tests of the relationship of the variables to check whether they are useful to design a predictive model before building a linear model.

Chapter 9, Building, Training, and Validating a Linear Model, talks about what happens after the relationship of the variables is statistically tested as useful to build a predictive model; we will use a portion of the data (regularly 20%) to test the model and see whether it gives a good sense of results similar to the known data.

Chapter 10, Building, Training, and Validating a Multiple Regression Model, discusses multiple regression, which involves three or more variables. We will see how to apply the statistical tests to see the most useful variables to build the predictive model. Then, we will test the regression with 20% of the data and see whether it makes sense to use the model to build new scenarios with unknown data.

Chapter 11, Testing Data for Time Series Compliance, shows how the time series forecast relies on the relationship of the present values to the past values. We will apply statistical methods to find whether the data is useful for a forecast model.

Chapter 12, Working with Time Series Using the Centered Moving Average and a Trending Component, explores the forecast model's dependence on two components: the centered moving average (which gives the seasonal ups and downs variations) and the linear regression (which gives the positive or negative orientation of the trend). Once we have these calculations, we will be able to test and use the model.

Chapter 13, Training, Validating, and Running the Model, covers the statistical tests time series and then models with 80% of the data. Then, we will test the time series with the remaining 20% and see whether the model returns results that make sense depending on our experience. Finally, we will use the model to do forecasts.

To get the most out of this book

To better understand this book, you must have a basic knowledge of statistical concepts such as average and standard deviation. You must also be able to use statistical functions in Excel to mark the cells' ranges input for calculations.

If you are using the digital version of this book, we advise you to type the code yourself or access the code from the book's GitHub repository (a link is available in the next section). Doing so will help you avoid any potential errors related to the copying and pasting of code.

Download the example code files

You can download the example code files for this book from GitHub at `https://github.com/PacktPublishing/Data-Forecasting-and-Segmentation-Using-Microsoft-Excel`. If there's an update to the code, it will be updated in the GitHub repository.

We also have other code bundles from our rich catalog of books and videos available at `https://github.com/PacktPublishing/`. Check them out!

Download the color images

We also provide a PDF file that has color images of the screenshots and diagrams used in this book. You can download it here: `https://static.packt-cdn.com/ downloads/9781803247731_ColorImages.pdf`.

Conventions used

There are a number of text conventions used throughout this book.

`Code in text`: Indicates code words in text, database table names, folder names, filenames, file extensions, pathnames, dummy URLs, user input, and Twitter handles. Here is an example: "Mount the downloaded `WebStorm-10*.dmg` disk image file as another disk in your system."

A block of code is set as follows:

```
html, body, #map {
  height: 100%;
  margin: 0;
  padding: 0
}
```

When we wish to draw your attention to a particular part of a code block, the relevant lines or items are set in bold:

```
[default]
exten => s,1,Dial(Zap/1|30)
exten => s,2,Voicemail(u100)
exten => s,102,Voicemail(b100)
exten => i,1,Voicemail(s0)
```

Any command-line input or output is written as follows:

```
$ mkdir css
$ cd css
```

Bold: Indicates a new term, an important word, or words that you see onscreen. For instance, words in menus or dialog boxes appear in **bold**. Here is an example: "Select **System info** from the **Administration** panel."

> **Tips or Important Notes**
> Appear like this.

Get in touch

Feedback from our readers is always welcome.

General feedback: If you have questions about any aspect of this book, email us at customercare@packtpub.com and mention the book title in the subject of your message.

Errata: Although we have taken every care to ensure the accuracy of our content, mistakes do happen. If you have found a mistake in this book, we would be grateful if you would report this to us. Please visit www.packtpub.com/support/errata and fill in the form.

Piracy: If you come across any illegal copies of our works in any form on the internet, we would be grateful if you would provide us with the location address or website name. Please contact us at copyright@packt.com with a link to the material.

If you are interested in becoming an author: If there is a topic that you have expertise in and you are interested in either writing or contributing to a book, please visit authors.packtpub.com.

Share Your Thoughts

Once you've read *Hands-On Financial Modeling with Microsoft Excel 365*, we'd love to hear your thoughts! Scan the QR code below to go straight to the Amazon review page for this book and share your feedback.

https://packt.link/r/1-803-23114-9

Your review is important to us and the tech community and will help us make sure we're delivering excellent quality content.

Part 1 – An Introduction to Machine Learning Functions

Learn the basic concepts of statistics and machine learning topics in this book, with practical applications in market segmentation, sales, and inventory.

This part includes the following chapters:

1
Understanding Data Segmentation

Machine learning has two types of algorithms depending on the level of adjustments that you require to give a response:

- Supervised
- Unsupervised

Supervised algorithms need continuous improvement in the form of the data used to train them. For example, a supervised machine learning function of a linear model needs a starter group of data to train and generate the initial conditions. Then, we have to test the model and use it. We need continuous surveillance of the results to interpret whether they make sense or not. If the model fails, we probably need to train the model again.

Unsupervised algorithms do not require any previous knowledge of the data. The unsupervised machine learning process takes data and starts analyzing it until it reaches a result. Contrary to supervised linear regression and time series, this data does not need a test to see whether it is useful to build a model. That is the case with the **K-means** algorithm, which takes unknown and untested data to classify the values of the variables and returns the classification segments.

In this book, we will cover three different topics of machine learning:

- Grouping statistics to find data segments
- Linear regression
- Time series

For grouping statistics, we will use an add-on for Excel that will do the classification automatically for us. This add-on is included with the book, and we will learn how to use it throughout this book. For linear regression, we will use Excel formulas to find out whetherthe data can be used to make predictions with regression models and forecasts from the time series.

We need a machine learning algorithm to classify and group data for the following reasons:

- A large amount of data is difficult to classify manually.
- Segmentation by observing a 2D or 3D chart is not accurate.
- Segmenting multiple variables is impossible because it is not possible to do a chart of multiple dimensions.

Before we do group segmentation using K-means clustering, we need to find the optimal number of groups for our data. The reason for this is that we want compact groups with points close to the average value of the group. It is not a good practice to have scattered points that do not belong to any group and that could be outliers that do not perform like the rest of the data, as they could be anomalies that deserve further research.

The K-means function will also help to get the optimal number of groups for our data. The best-case scenario is to have compact groups with points near their center.

We will review the basic statistical concepts to work with data grouping. These concepts are as follows:

- Mean
- Standard deviation

In the data grouping segment, the **mean** is the center, or centroid, of the group. The best case is that the values are compact and close to the segment's centroid.

The level of separation of the values within a group from its centroid is measured by the **standard deviation**. The best case is to have compact groups with values close to the group's mean point with a low standard deviation for each group.

When we have values and segments that are scattered with a large standard deviation, that means they are outliers. **Outliers** are data that behaves differently from the majority of other segments. It is a special kind of data because it requires further research. Outliers could indicate an anomaly that could grow and cause a problem in the future. Practical examples of outliers that require attention are as follows:

- Values that are different from the normal transaction amounts in sales and purchases. These could indicate a system test that could lead to a bigger issue in the future.

- A timeline of suspicious system performance. This could indicate hacking attempts.

In this chapter, we will cover the following topics:

- Segmenting data concepts
- Grouping data in segments of two and three variables

Segmenting data concepts

Before explaining data segments, we have to review basic statistical concepts such as mean and standard deviation. The reason is that each segment has a mean, or central, value, and each point is separated from the central point. The best case is that this separation of points from the mean point is as small as possible for each segment of data.

For the group of data in *Figure 1.1*, we will explain the mean and the separation of each point from the center measured by the standard deviation:

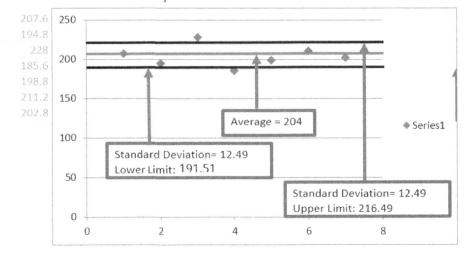

Figure 1.1 – Average, standard deviation, and limits. The data on the left is represented in the chart

The mean of the data on the left of the chart is 204. The group's centroid is represented by the middle line in *Figure 1.1*.

The standard deviation for this data is 12.49. So, the data upper limit is 216.49 and the lower limit is 191.51.

The standard deviation is the average separation of all the points from the centroid of the segment. It affects the grouping segments, as we want compact groups with a small separation between the group's data points. A small standard deviation means a smaller distance from the group's points to the centroid. The best case for the data segments is that these data points are as close as possible to the centroid. So, the standard deviation of the segment must be a small value.

Now, we will explore four segments of a group of data. We will find out whether all the segments are optimal, and whether the points are close to their respective centroids.

In *Figure 1.2*, the left column is sales revenue data. The right column is the data segments:

revenue	segment		
4	1	18.775	Average
8	1	15.069319	Standard Deviation
27.2	1		
6	1		
26	1		
39.2	1		
39.6	1		
0.2	1		
207.6	2	204.11	Average
194.8	2	12.492218	Standard Deviation
228	2		
185.6	2		
198.8	2		
211.2	2		
202.8	2		
174.8	3	152.35	Average
119.6	3	17.7374604	Standard Deviation
171.2	3		
159.2	3		
158.8	3		
138.8	3		
136.4	3		
160	3		
92.4	4	74.3	Average
62.4	4	12.051141	Standard Deviation
78	4		
64.4	4		

Figure 1.2 – Segments, mean, and standard deviation

We have four segments, and we will analyze the mean and the standard deviation to see whether the points have an optimal separation from the centroid. The separation is given by the standard deviation.

Figure 1.3 is the chart for all the data points in *Figure 1.2*. We can identify four possible segments by simple visual analysis:

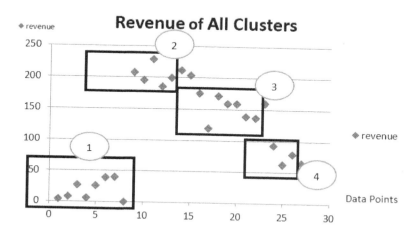

Figure 1.3 – Data segments

We will analyze the centroid and the separation of the points for each segment in *Figure 1.3*. We can see that the group between 0 and 60 on the *y* axis is probably an outlier because the revenue is very low compared with the rest of the segments. The other groups appear to be compact around their respective centroid. We will confirm this in the charts of each segment.

The mean for the first segment is 18.775. The standard deviation is 15.09. That means there is a lot of variation around the centroid. This segment is not very compact, as we can see in *Figure 1.4*. The data is scattered and not close to the centroid value of 18.775:

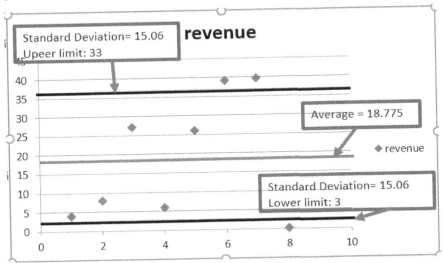

Figure 1.4 – Segment 1, mean and standard deviation

The centroid of this segment is 18.775. The separation of the points measured by the standard deviation is 15.06. The points fall in the range of 3 to 33. That means the separation is wide and the segment is not compact. An explanation for this type of segment is that the points are outliers. They are points that do not have normal behavior and deserve special analysis to research. When we have points that are outside the normal operation values, for example, transactions with smaller amounts than normal at places and times that do not correspond to the rest of the data, we have to do deeper research because they could be indicators of fraud. Or, maybe they are sales that occur only at specific times of the month or year.

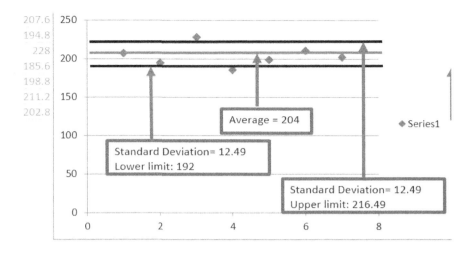

Figure 1.5 – Segment 2, mean and standard deviation

The second segment is more compact than the first one. The mean is 204 and there's a small standard deviation of 12.49. The upper limit is 216 and the lower limit is 192. This is an example of a good segmentation group. The distance from the data points to the centroid is small.

Next is segment number three:

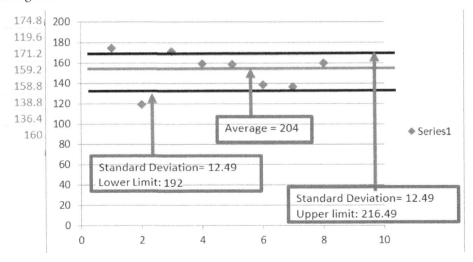

Figure 1.6 – Segment 3, mean and standard deviation

The mean is 204, the upper limit is 216, and the lower limit is 192. By the standard deviation of the points, we also conclude that the segment is compact enough to give reliable information.

The points are close to the centroid, so the behavior of the members of the group or segment is very similar.

Segment number four is the smallest of all. It is shown in *Figure 1.7*:

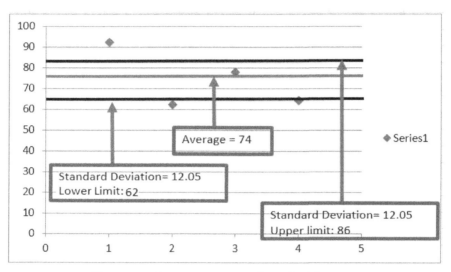

Figure 1.7 – Segment 3, mean and standard deviation

The limits are 62 and 86 and the mean is 74. *Figure 1.3* shows that segment four is the group with the second-lowest revenue after segment one. But segment one is scattered with a large standard deviation, so it is a not compact group, and the information is not reliable.

After reviewing the four segments, we conclude that segment number one is the lowest revenue group. It also has the highest separation of points from its centroid. It is probably an outlier and represents the non-regular behavior of sales.

In this section, we reviewed the basic statistical concepts and how they relate to segmentation. We learned that the best-case scenario is to have compact groups with a small standard deviation from the group's mean. It is important to follow up on the points that are outside the groups. These outliers (with very different behavior compared with the rest of the values) could be indicators of fraud. In the next section, we will apply these concepts to multi-variable analysis. We will have groups with two or more variables.

Grouping data in segments of two and three variables

Now, we are going to segment data with two variables. Several real-world problems need to group two or more variables to classify data where one variable influences the other. For example, we can use the month number and the sales revenue dataset to find out the time of the year with higher and lower sales. We will use online marketing and sales revenue. *Figure 1.8* shows the four segments of the data and the relationship between online marketing investment and revenue. We can see that segments **1**, **2**, and **4** are relatively compact. The exception is segment **3** because it has a point that appears to be an outlier. This outlier will affect the average and the standard deviation of the segment:

Marketing	Revenue	Cluster
3.27999992	92.4	4
2.76000004	62.4	4
1.2	4	1
4.8	207.6	2
4.24000015	174.8	3
4.72000008	194.8	2
3.24	119.6	3
3.07999992	78	4
1.31999998	8	1
1.96000004	27.2	1
6.95999985	228	2
4.2	171.2	3
4.52000008	185.6	2
1	6	1
1.87999992	26	1
1.83999996	39.2	1
2.2	159.2	3
2.87999992	64.4	4
4.15999985	158.8	3
4.6	198.8	2
4.92000008	211.2	2
1.11999998	39.6	1
1.23999996	0.2	1
3.84	138.8	3
3.92000008	136.4	3
4.8	202.8	2
2.8	160	3

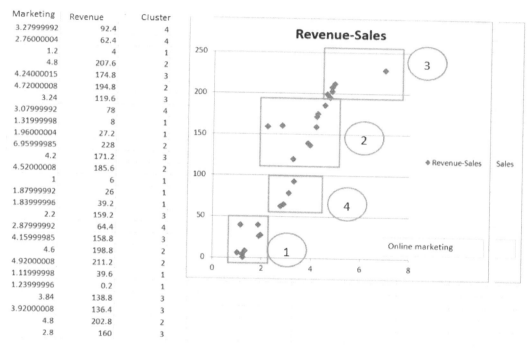

Figure 1.8 – Grouping with two variables

Segment **4** appears to have the smallest standard deviation. This group looks compact. Segment **2** also appears to be compact and it has a high value of revenue.

In *Figure 1.9*, we will find out the mean and the standard deviation of segment **2**:

Marketing	Revenue	Cluster		
4.8	207.6	2	5.04	Average Online mark.
4.72000008	194.8	2	1.53664354	standard deviation online mark.
6.95999985	228	2	204.11	Average Revenue
4.52000008	185.6	2	76.6370978	standard deviation revenue
4.6	198.8	2		
4.92000008	211.2	2		
4.8	202.8	2		

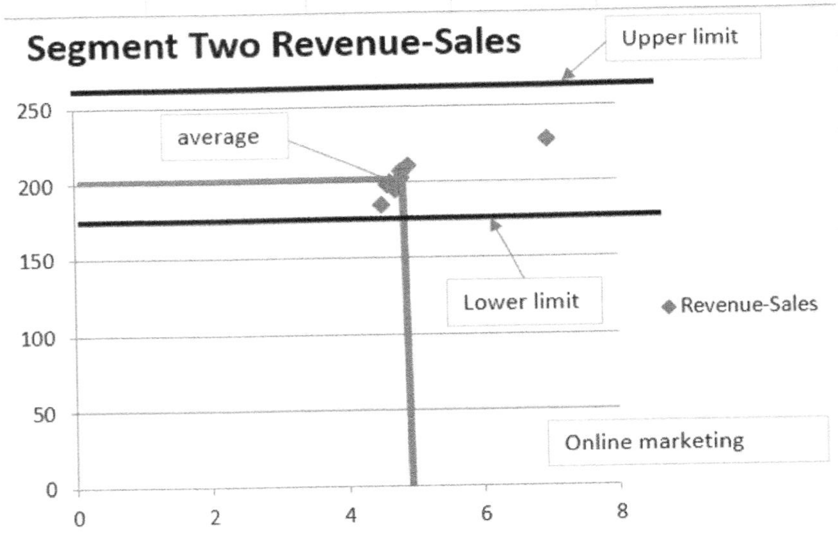

Figure 1.9 – Segment two mean and standard deviation

As we are analyzing two variables, the centroid of the segment has two coordinates: the online marketing spend and the revenue.

The mean has the following coordinates:

- Online marketing: 5.04

- Revenue: 204.11

In *Figure 1.9*, the centroid is at these coordinates.

The standard deviation of online marketing is 1.53, and for revenue, it is 76.63.

The limits of the revenue are the black lines. They are 160 and 280. So, segment two is not compact because the majority of points are between 160 and 210 with an outlier close to 280.

When we analyze data with three variables, the mean and the standard deviation are represented by three coordinates. *Figure 1.10* shows data with three variables and the segment that each of them belongs to:

Material	Online market	Revenue-Sales	segment
204.8	3.24	119.6	1
136.8	2.2	159.2	1
181.2	4.15999985	158.8	1
184.4	3.84	138.8	1
152.8	3.92000008	136.4	1
206.8	2.8	160	1
117.6	3.27999992	92.4	2
92.8	2.76000004	62.4	2
138.8	3.07999992	78	2
78.4	2.87999992	64.4	2
111.2	1.11999998	39.6	2
59.6	1.2	4	3
84.8	1.31999998	8	3
40.8	1.96000004	27.2	3
65.2	1	6	3
67.2	1.87999992	26	3
60.4	1.83999996	39.2	3
56.8	1.23999996	0.2	3
240	4.8	207.6	4
226.8	4.24000015	174.8	4
228.4	4.72000008	194.8	4
315.2	6.95999985	228	4
230.8	4.2	171.2	4
214	4.52000008	185.6	4
207.2	4.6	198.8	4
246	4.92000008	211.2	4
236	4.8	202.8	4

Figure 1.10 – Segments with three variables

The mean and standard deviation have three coordinates. For example, for segment three, these are the coordinates:

	Material Rotation	Online Marketing	Revenue
Average	62.11	1.49	15.8
Standard Deviation	12.19969889	0.360770146	13.7375398

Figure 1.11 – Mean and standard deviation coordinates with three variables

The standard deviation of revenue is large, 13.73. This means the points are widely scattered from the centroid, 15.8. This segment probably does not give accurate information because the points are not compact.

Summary

In this chapter, we learned why it's important to find the optimal number of groups before we conduct K-means clustering. Once we have the groups, we analyze whether they are compliant with the best-case scenario for segments having a small standard deviation. Research outliers to find out whether their behavior could lead to further investigation, such as fraud detection.

We need a machine learning function such as K-means clustering to segment data because classifying by simple inspection using a 2D or 3D chart is not practical and is sometimes impossible. Segmentation with three or more variables is more complicated because it is not possible to plot them.

K-means clustering helps us to find the optimal number of segments or groups for our data. The best case is to have segments that are as compact as possible.

Each segment has a mean, or centroid, and its values are supposed to be as close as possible to the centroid. This means that the standard deviation of each segment must be as small as possible.

You need to pay attention to segments with large standard deviations because they could be outliers. This type of value in our dataset could mean a preview for future problems because they have a random and irregular behavior outside the rest of the data's normal execution.

In the next chapter, we will get an introduction to the linear regression supervised machine learning algorithm. Linear regression needs statistical tests for the data to measure its level of relationship and to check whether it is useful for the model. Otherwise, it is not worth building the model.

Questions

Here are a few questions to assess your learning from this chapter:

1. Why is it necessary to know the optimal number of groups for the data before running the K-means classification algorithm?

2. Is it possible to use K-means clustering for data with four or more variables?

3. What are outliers, and how do we process them?

Answers

Here are the answers to the previous questions:

1. Having the optimal number of groups helps to get more compact groups and prevents us from having a large number of outliers.

2. Yes, it is possible. It is more difficult to visualize the potential groups with a chart, but we can use K-means clustering to get the optimal number of groups and then do the classification.

3. These are points that do not have the same behavior as the rest of the groups. It is necessary to do further research on them because it could lead to finding potential fraud or system performance degradation.

Further reading

To further understand the concepts of this chapter, you can refer to the following sources:

*   *Eight databases supporting in-database machine learning*:

    https://www.infoworld.com/article/3607762/8-databases-supporting-in-database-machine-learning.html

*   *Creating a K-means model to cluster London bicycle hires dataset with Google BigQuery*:

    https://cloud.google.com/bigquery-ml/docs/kmeans-tutorial

2
Applying Linear Regression

Linear regression requires the variables to have a relationship among them to be useful to build a predictive model. We will learn, in this and the following chapters, several statistical techniques to approve the data for a regression model. We will use a portion of the data to design and build the regression. Then, we will apply the other portion of the data to the model for testing. The final step is to load the model for prediction, and we are going to use our experience to see whether the regression is returning results that make sense for the purposes of our experiment or application. Linear regression is a supervised machine learning algorithm, as it needs continuous surveillance to verify that it continues to give results that make sense. If it does not, the algorithm needs a training update.

Linear regression has the following machine learning requirements:

- Defining the model from known data

- Training the model to see whether it is giving the expected results

- Testing the model with a reserve of around 20% of the sample data. Verifying that it gives the expected results

Before using the dataset to predict the linear model, we have to validate the dataset by charting the points and using our experience to judge whether the data has variables with relationships that could be useful for a prediction model. After that, we can use statistical tests to probe whether the variables have a relationship among them or not.

Use the model to generate predictions. Review to check whether the results make sense based on your experience.

The linear model uses the possible relationship between the variables called **predictors** and the result variable.

The steps before using the data to define a predictive model involve checking that the variables have a relationship. The predictors need a strong influence over the result variable to build a predictive model.

To check this requirement, we can use the following statistical tools:

- Visually confirm the variable's relationship with a 2D or 3D chart. With these charts, we can visualize whether the slope of the regression line is not zero, meaning that there is a relationship between the variables.

- Check the percentage of influence of the predictors over the results with the coefficient of correlation and coefficient of determination.

- Reject the null hypothesis that the slope is equal to zero with t-statistics or the p-value. **f-statistics** is a test to reject the hypothesis that the slope is equal to zero, meaning that there is no relationship between the regression variables, so the data is not useful to build a prediction model. The `p-value` also tests the relationship between the regression variables.

You have to keep in mind the importance of understanding the error separation of the predictive model to the expected results. This concept is the **sum of squares error** (SSE) or unexplained variation. This term is important to all the statistical tests to see whether the data has enough significance to build a predictive model.

In this chapter, we will cover the following topics:

- Understanding the influence of variables in linear regression
- Projecting values from predictor variables

Understanding the influence of variables in linear regression

The goal of linear regression is to build a model useful to predict future values based on evidence in the present data. To achieve this objective, we have two types of variables:

- The predictor variables determine the value of a variable for which we want to know the possible future values.
- The result variable is affected by the predictor variables.

The model accuracy depends on the statistical relevance of the relationship between the variables. To test this relevance, we can probe the model's data relationships. Examples of probes include the following:

- Coefficient of determination, or R-squared
- Coefficient of correlation
- t-statistics and p-value
- f-statistics

The statistical tests are necessary to prove that the variables have a relationship that could be useful to build a predictor model. The four probes previously mentioned are used to test the alternate hypothesis that there is a relationship between variables, meaning that the slope of the variables is not zero.

Once we are sure that the predictor model is useful, we apply the following machine learning steps to use the model:

1. Train and generate the model with 80% of the known data.
2. Test the model with the remaining 20% of the known data.
3. Use the model to predict new future values.

Figure 2.1 shows the parts of a linear regression predictor model:

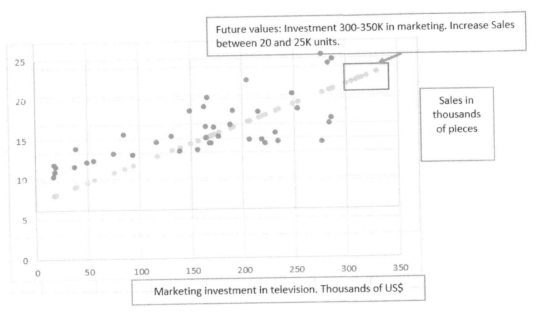

Figure 2.1 – Predictive regression model

The dots are the points of the marketing investment influence over sales of inventory pieces. The model predicts the number of sales based on the level of investment in marketing. The straight line is enclosed in the red box.

The previous example is a simple linear model. It involves only one predictor and a result variable. It is also possible to have multiple linear models with several predictor variables and one result. Using multiple variables is better, as it allows us to discover which are the most influential to use them to build the prediction regression model.

In *Figure 2.2*, we have the sales revenue as the result variable, and several possible predictor variables of sector sales, kilometers to store competition, and material rotation:

Sales Revenue	Hours out of service	Material rotation	Online marketing	Sectos Sales	Kms. to store competion
92.4	1.2	117.6	3.279999924	3.279999924	4.4
62.4	0.880000019	92.8	2.760000038	1.639999962	4.8
4	0.2	59.6	1.2	1.720000076	6
207.6	2.2	240	4.8	6.440000152	0.4
174.8	1.760000038	226.8	4.240000152	5.640000152	2
194.8	1.920000076	228.4	4.720000076	5.079999924	1.6
119.6	1.239999962	204.8	3.24	4.040000152	4
78	1	138.8	3.079999924	3.36	4.8
8	0.480000019	84.8	1.319999981	0.839999962	6
27.2	0.24000001	40.8	1.960000038	1.879999924	3.2
228	2.160000038	315.2	6.959999848	4.920000076	0.4
171.2	1.679999924	230.8	4.2	5.6	2.8
185.6	1.879999924	214	4.520000076	6	1.2
6	0.24000001	65.2	1	1	5.6
26	0.480000019	67.2	1.879999924	1.319999981	4.4
39.2	0.64000001	60.4	1.839999962	1.080000019	4
159.2	1.720000076	136.8	2.2	6.4	1.6
64.4	1.039999962	78.4	2.879999924	2.520000076	5.2
158.8	1.519999981	181.2	4.159999848	5.559999848	2.8
198.8	2.120000076	207.2	4.6	6.519999696	0.4
211.2	2.239999962	246	4.920000076	6.4	0
39.6	0.320000005	111.2	1.119999981	2.6	5.6
0.2	0.44000001	56.8	1.239999962	0.64000001	4.8
138.8	1.439999962	184.4	3.84	4.520000076	2.4
136.4	1.4	152.8	3.920000076	4.6	2
202.8	2.039999962	236	4.8	6.279999924	0
160	3.44	206.8	2.8	4.8	3.2

Figure 2.2 – The revenue-sales result variable and possible predictor variables

Using data from *Figure 2.2*, we will apply statistical tests to find out which variables are more useful to build a predictor model.

For this example, we use the p-value to find these variables. We will explain the details of this method in *Chapter 8, Finding the Relationships between Variables*. For now, we look for a p-value of less than 0.01 to find useful variables.

In *Figure 2.3*, we can see the results of the regression function in Excel:

SUMMARY OUTPUT

Regression Statistics	
Multiple R	0.996583914
R Square	0.993179497
Adjusted R Square	0.991555568
Standard Error	7.059696658
Observations	27

ANOVA

	df	SS	MS	F	ignificance F
Regression	5	152406.2	30481.24613	611.5904	5.4E-22
Residual	21	1046.626	49.8393169		
Total	26	153452.9			

	Coefficients	andard Err	t Stat	P-value	Lower 95%	Upper 95%	ower 95.0%	pper 95.0%
Intercept	-7.543765663	12.06009	-0.625514812	0.538372	-32.6241	17.53656689	-32.6241	17.53657
Hours out of service	16.20157356	3.544437	4.570986073	0.000166	8.830513	23.57263445	8.830513	23.57263
Material Rotation	0.174635154	0.057606	3.031540961	0.006347	0.054837	0.294433531	0.054837	0.294434
Online marketing	11.52626903	2.532103	4.55205324	0.000174	6.260472	16.79206611	6.260472	16.79207
Sector Sales	13.5803129	1.770457	7.670514392	1.61E-07	9.898447	17.26217897	9.898447	17.26218
Kms. To store competion	-5.31097141	1.705427	-3.114160174	0.005249	-8.8576	-1.764342766	-8.8576	-1.76434

Figure 2.3 – The revenue-sales result variable and possible predictor variables

Material rotation and online marketing are the variables with a p-value less than 0.05. We use both as predictors of the sales revenue to build the regression model.

We plot both the material rotation and online marketing variables against sales revenue to examine the relationship and confirm that they are useful to predict values. The plots of both variables are shown in *Figure 2.4*:

Figure 2.4 – Influence of the online marketing and inventory rotation variables on sales revenue

We can visually confirm the influence of inventory rotation and online marketing on the sales revenue variable. These multiple regression model variables are useful to predict future values.

We can plot a 3D chart with these three variables to see the linear regression model, as shown in *Figure 2.5*:

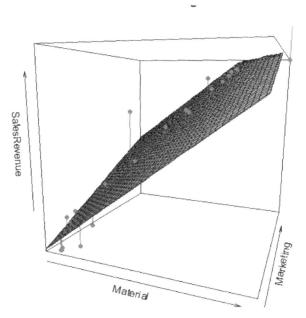

Figure 2.5 – 3D chart showing the influence of material rotation and online marketing on sales revenue

The 3D plane represents the predictor multi-linear model. Review the relationship of the predictor variables of the sales revenue.

We can use the same statistical methods to build multiple regression models with more than three variables. But, we can't do a plot of four or more dimensions; we can only see the results in the regression table in these higher-dimensional cases.

In the next section, we will learn the basics of statistical methods to test the relationships between variables and confirm that they are useful to generate a predictor equation.

Projecting values from predictor variables

As we saw in the previous section, the first task when building a predictor model is to test whether the predictor variables have a close relationship with the result variable. In this section, we will learn the introductory concepts of statistical tests for relationships between variables. Linear model accuracy is represented by the concepts displayed in *Figure 2.6*:

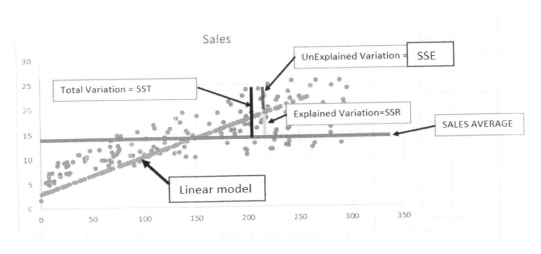

Figure 2.6 – Elements involved in calculating the model confidence

The visual elements of the statistical methods to measure the variables' relationships are as follows:

- The sales average is the horizontal line near **15** on the *y* axis.

- The linear model is shown by the diagonal line. This line predicts the future values.

- Unexplained variation (the SSE) is the distance between the expected value and the linear model.

- Explained variation (the **sum of squares regression (SSR)**) is the distance from the linear model to the average of the result variable – in this case, the average of sales revenue.

- Total variation (the **sum of squares total (SST)**) is the sum of the unexplained and explained variations. Also known as the distance between the expected value and the average of the result variable.

From the linear regression formula, we get the following coefficients to build the linear model:

- Intercept
- Slope

The linear formula is as follows:

```
Y = B0 (intercept)  + B1 (Slope) X
```

The results of the linear regression model are shown in *Figure 2.7*:

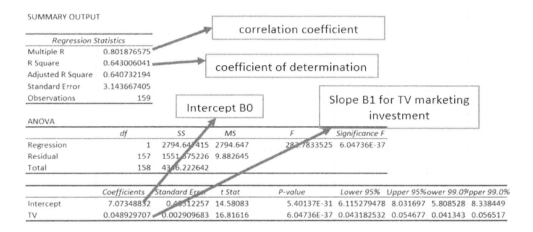

Figure 2.7 – Response output for the linear regression function

The formula for the linear model of *Figure 2.7* created from the Excel regression function is as follows:

```
B0 (intercept)= 7.07
B1 (slope)     = 0.0489
Y = 7.07   + 0.0489 *  X
```

The first statistical test for the relationship between the marketing influence variable over sales is the coefficient of determination. It is a factor of the explained variation SSR with respect to the total variation SST. Refer to *Figure 2.4* to see the relationship between these two terms.

In *Figure 2.5*, the coefficient of determination is **R Square = 0.64**. This means that the linear model fits the expected values of 64%. This factor is acceptable for use in a predictive model.

The correlation coefficient has this formula:

$$r_{xy = sign \ of \ b1 \ \sqrt{Coefficient \ of \ determination}} = sign \ of \ b1\sqrt{r^2}s$$

It determines whether the slope is positive or negative. A positive slope means that the relationship is directly correlated: if the X value grows, the Y value also grows. A negative slope indicates a negative correlation where if X declines, Y grows.

According to *Figure 2.5*, the correlation coefficient is 0.8 with a positive slope. This means that the linear model fits 80% of the expected values. It is, therefore, acceptable for use in a predictive model.

Charting the relationship between sales (Y) and marketing (X) allows us to determine that the slope is not zero and whether it is positive or negative. A slope equal to zero means that there is no relationship between the variables. The t-statistics test is used to confirm or reject whether the slope equals zero. We will implement the t-statistics test step by step in *Chapter 8, Finding the Relationship between Variables. Figure 2.8* shows the types of slopes seen in the first approach of data analysis. It gives us an idea of whether the variables are linked or not:

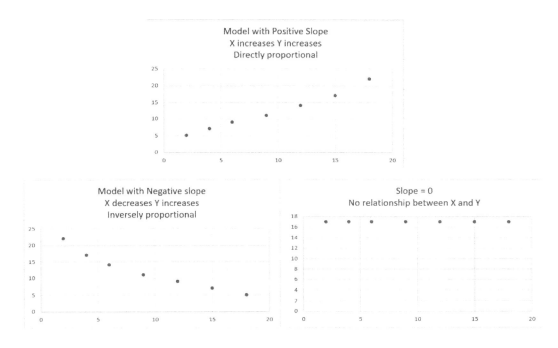

Figure 2.8 – Types of slopes

The t-statistics test probes the evidence to reject the null hypothesis that says the slope is equal to zero. The objective is to accept the alternate hypothesis that the slope is *not* equal to zero. This probes the relationship between the variables.

We will see details throughout this book on how to find the critical value of t-statistics to reject or accept the hypothesis about the slope.

For the following example, the t-statistics value is 16.82. It falls in the rejection area of the null hypothesis, so the slope is *not* equal to zero.

The p-value is *6.04E-37*. It is lower than the *alpha = 0.05*. So, the p-value also rejects the null hypothesis. The slope is not zero. The existence of a relationship between the variables is, therefore, confirmed statistically.

Once we have probed the existence of a relationship between the variables, we can use them to predict values. *Figure 2.9* shows the prediction values of the linear model:

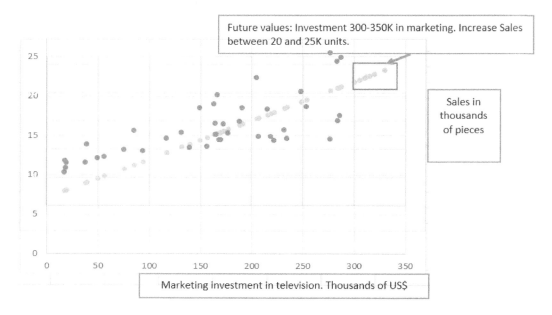

Figure 2.9 – Prediction values from the linear model

The linear model predicts the sales figures achieved with future investments above US$300K in marketing. The predicted values are enclosed in the box in the top right of *Figure 2.9*.

In our work through the previous sections, we have seen that the relationship between variables has to be tested with statistical methods before we can use the data to predict new values.

Summary

To produce a predictive model with linear regression, we have to be sure that the variables involved have a strong relationship.

Linear regression is a supervised machine learning algorithm because it needs known data for training and testing. Even after the model is in production, we need to keep checking whether the model needs an update with new data.

Before we design a model, we have to use statistical methods to probe the relationship between the variables. These methods include the coefficients of correlation and regression, t-statistics, and p-values. The machine learning models are defined and trained on a portion of the data. Then, we test the model with the remaining data, and finally, use the model to make predictions. We have to use our judgment and experience to decide whether the model is accurate or not. Build a chart with predictive values from the model to see whether the values make sense based on your experience.

In the next chapter, we will be introduced to another type of prediction. It is a forecasting method to predict the values that have seasonal behavior during different years. We will learn how to test whether the data is useful by checking for autocorrelation, where past data influences the present values.

Questions

Here are two questions to assess your learning from this chapter:

1. What test is necessary before designing a linear model?
2. What is the meaning of a negative slope?

Answers

Here are the answers to the previous questions:

1. Do a test for correlation, a p-value or f-test, to see whether the variables have a relationship and are, therefore, useful to make predictions.
2. It indicates that the variables have an inverse relationship.

Further reading

To further understand the concepts of this chapter, you can refer to the following sources:

*   *Build regression models with Amazon Redshift ML*: `https://aws.amazon.com/blogs/machine-learning/build-regression-models-with-amazon-redshift-ml/`

*   *Using BigQuery ML to predict penguin weight*: `https://cloud.google.com/bigquery-ml/docs/linear-regression-tutorial`

3
What is
Time Series?

Time series prediction involves collecting data on an event over time. That means the data is oscillating in a relatively continuous way. It is useful for predicting problems that don't have a linear progression with continuously growing or decreasing results. Some have season-dependent behavior. For example, the demand for inventory rotation items can change depending on the season of the year. Time series analysis could help to optimize the planning of purchase orders to avoid overstocking warehouses. The inventory in the warehouse needs rotation to keep the cash flow moving, pay the providers, and get more stock to sell. Another application is to analyze the passenger traffic in transportation in order to plan the seasonal allocation of the service equipment.

In the same way that linear regression models need statistical analysis to discover the relationships between the variables, time series models need data that has an autocorrelation. **Autocorrelation** means the present and future values are dependent on the past values. The Durbin-Watson statistical test examines the alternate hypothesis that data has a time-dependent relationship and is useful for predictions. We will learn that, like any other prediction, a forecast just gives an idea of what the future values could be, based on the past evidence of the data.

In this chapter, we will learn about the following:

- Understanding time series data
- Designing a time series data model
- Doing a forecast

Technical requirements

Download the Excel file for this chapter here: `https://github.com/` `PacktPublishing/Data-Forecasting-and-Segmentation-` `Using-Microsoft-Excel/blob/main/Chapter03/` `chapterThreeTimetoUPLOADSeries.xlsx`.

Understanding time series data

The objective of a *time series machine learning* algorithm is to forecast values and effectively plan the use of resources, such as inventories, seasonal-demand equipment allocation, and agriculture production, for example.

As a regression model needs a statistically significant relationship between the variables, a time series model needs autocorrelated data to be useful for a predictive model. In the following figure, we can see that the regression model variables' relationship is tested by statistical methods such as *f-statistics* and *p-value*:

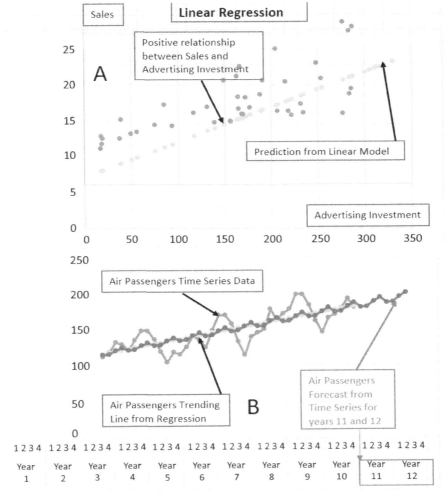

Figure 3.1 – A: Linear regression and B: Air passenger time series

Figure 3.1 shows the prediction model for four trimesters of years 11 and 12 from air passenger time series data from the past 10 years. To build a useful predictive model, the air passenger data from years 1 to 10 needs to autocorrelate. This means that each value is dependent on prior data. Looking at the air passenger time series data in *Figure 3.1*, it appears to have a cycle, meaning that future data can be predicted from past data. To be sure, we will show how to do a Durbin-Watson statistical test to examine the autocorrelation of the data and our confidence in it in order to build a predictive design. Additionally to the time series data, we need the trending line given by the regression model represented in *Figure 3.1*. With these two inputs, we will calculate the forecast for years 11 and 12.

The Durbin-Watson statistical test examines whether the time series data is autocorrelated. This test finds the autocorrelation, meaning the past data determines the present data, so we can use it to build a forecast. In *Figure 3.2*, we see the chart of errors or the residuals of the linear regression model of the air passenger data in *Figure 3.1*:

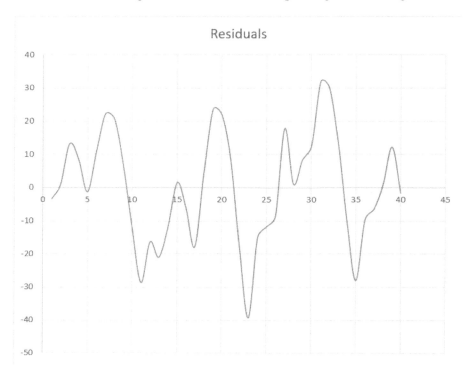

Figure 3.2 – Residuals of the air passenger time series data

In *Figure 3.2*, we can see that the chart has a repeating cycle, suggesting that future data depends on past data. This information will be confirmed by the Durbin-Watson test by rejecting the null hypothesis that no autocorrelation is present in the data, and accepting the alternate hypothesis confirming the autocorrelation.

In this section, we learned that we can use an algorithm to forecast time-dependent data. In the same way that linear regression has a variable dependency prerequisite in order to forecast future values, time series data needs to have an autocorrelation relationship. We can examine this autocorrelation by plotting the data and applying the Durbin-Watson statistical test. In the next section, we will learn how to build a model with test data to forecast future time series values.

Designing the time series data model

We are going to explain the general steps to building a time series model using training data. Use your judgment and experience to discern from the chart whether the data is autoregressive before applying the Durbin-Watson statistical test.

The sequential steps required to build the predictive model with time series machine learning are as follows:

1. Plot the data to inspect the possible autocorrelation relationship.
2. Use the Durbin-Watson statistical test to see whether the data is autocorrelated.
3. Calculate the **centered moving average** of each period lag of the data.
4. Determine the separation between the data and the centered moving average. This is known as **seasonal irregularity**.
5. Get the trending component of the time series using the regression model line.
6. Multiply the seasonal irregularity value by the trending result to make the forecast.

We use the centered moving average to smooth or to take the general trend of the data average. We need to extract this trend because the periodic average generally has big jumps or peaks that make it difficult to make a forecast. This trend gives the seasonal component of the data, indicating how it changes over time. The linear regression of the data gives the trending direction of the data through the time series.

These steps will be explained using charts to show the method's general idea.

Analyzing the air passenger 10-year data chart

We are going to make a 2-year forecast using the 10-year passengers' flight occupancy data. The following chart shows the 10-year passenger data:

Figure 3.3 – Flight passengers' 10-year data (trimester lag)

In the preceding chart, we can observe that the data is probably autocorrelated because we can see a cycle. This cycle shows that past values influence the next values. Note that there is a peak in demand in the third trimester. The peak of demand is not regular for all years, but it is the first point of inspection to apply our experience in the data.

We will use the Durbin-Watson test to garner statistical evidence that the data is autocorrelated and can be used to build a forecast model.

Conducting a Durbin-Watson test on our 10-year data

We will explain in *Chapter 11, Testing Data for Time Series Compliance*, how to conduct the Durbin-Watson test. For now, see *Figure 3.2*, the residuals from the linear regression of the 10-year data, and analyze that they have a cycle. That means the past values influence future values. When we run the Durbin-Watson test, we get a value of 0.75. This value falls on the rejection region of the hypothesis that no correlation is present in the data.

We will smooth the chart data using the centered moving average for each time lag.

Computing the centered moving average of each period lag of the data

Calculate the centered moving average for each trimester of the air passenger data. This is shown in *Figure 3.4*. The centered moving average is a method of smoothing out the oscillations in the data to ease the calculation of the forecast:

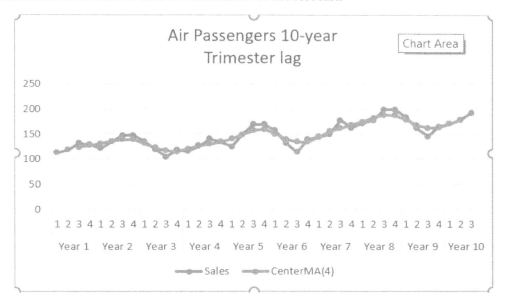

Figure 3.4 – Centered moving average

In the preceding chart, see how the centered moving average smooths the peaks and troughs of years 5 and 6. The objective is to prevent the higher peaks and deeper troughs from affecting the forecast calculation. The separation factor between the centered moving average and the data is the seasonal irregularity. This separation value is useful to calculate the forecast because it converts the cyclical data into a straighter trending line.

Analyzing the seasonal irregularity

To calculate the seasonal irregularity, divide each data point by its distance from the centered moving average. You can see these distances in the following chart:

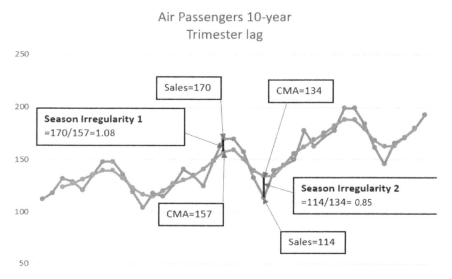

Figure 3.5 – Seasonal irregularity: the distance from the data to the centered moving average

In the preceding chart, we can see that *Season Irregularity 1* divides the data (sales = 170) by the centered moving average (value 157) and we get a result of 1.08. This means that the centered moving average is 8% above the data. In another example, *Season Irregularity 2* divides the data (sales = 114) by the centered moving average (value 134) with a result of 0.85. This means that the data (sales) is 15% below the center of the moving average.

With this information, we have a factor of the cyclical movement of the data. Next, we will get the trending component with the regression model line.

Trending component of the time series

Each time series could have an increasing or decreasing trending line as well as cyclical or seasonal data. We can get this trending line by calculating the regression model of the data. The regression is shown in the following chart:

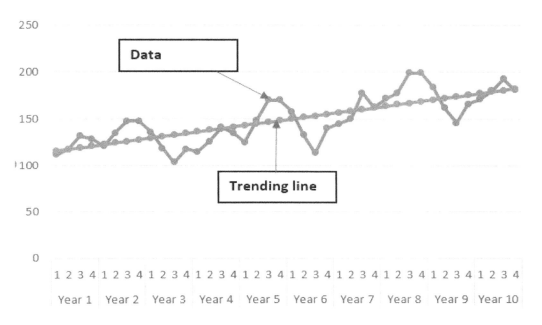

Figure 3.6 – Trending component of our time series

In the preceding figure, we see the chart of the time series data and its trending line given by the regression model. If we have a case where the trend is zero, with a slope also equal to zero, that means the seasonal cycling data is neither increasing nor decreasing. It would be a perfect sinusoidal chart. In that case, we would use only the intercept element of the regression to do the forecast.

The trending line multiplied by the seasonal irregularity gives us the direction of the line to help us do the cyclical forecast of the time series. We will do this calculation to predict the future time series data in the next section.

Doing the forecast

To calculate the forecast of a time series, we have to multiply the seasonal irregularity by the trending data of the regression model. With this, we will have the ups and downs of the seasonal irregularity in our forecast. These results are explained in the following figure:

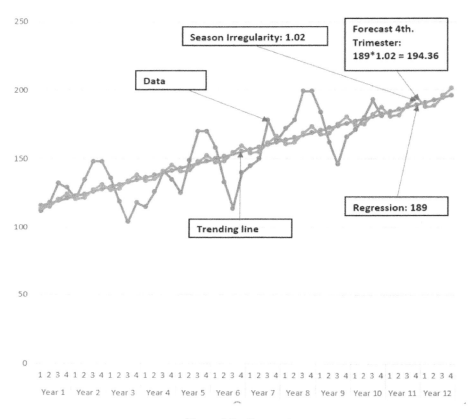

Figure 3.7 – Forecast

The preceding figure shows the components of the forecast of our time series. We have the seasonal or cycling data with the up-trending line to do a forecast of the multiplication of the seasonal irregularity trend that we discussed before.

Like the regression model, the time series forecast just gives us an idea of what could happen in the future; it is not an exact prediction. For example, we can see that for the fourth semester of year 11, we will see a growth in passenger demand. This makes sense with the past data showing an increased passenger demand in the fourth trimesters of almost all the past years. The relatively low increment in the forecast could be explained by the fact that in years 3, 4, 6, and 9, the sales fell much more compared with the other years. The low increment in the forecast is taking into account these steep troughs.

The other example of sales (in *Figure 3.8*) shows that the seasonal data is regular. The forecast has a clear trend for years 11 and 12:

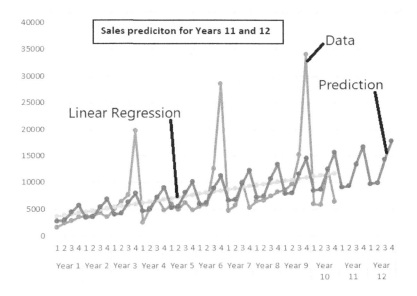

Figure 3.8 – Sales forecast

In the preceding chart, we can see the forecast for years 11 and 12. The seasonal or cyclical data is more regular than the previous data because here we have just three high peaks of demand in the fourth trimester of the years 3, 6, and 9. That is an explanation of why the forecast has a more defined prediction.

In this section, we learned how to do a forecast using the trending line of the regression model, adjusted up or down by the seasonal irregularities. With every prediction, we learned that the time series forecast gives us an idea of the future, but it is not an exact prediction.

Summary

In this introduction to time series forecasting, we learned that we need the data to autocorrelate to be useful for predictions. We have to plot the data and see whether it has seasonal or cyclical trends to learn whether past data influences the next period of data. Then, we need to use the Durbin-Watson statistical test to prove that the data is autocorrelated.

The forecast calculation uses the trending line of the regression model multiplied by the seasonal irregularity factor. This factor gives us the direction of the trending line based on the cyclical information of the past data. Use your experience to analyze whether the forecast returned by the model makes sense with the past data.

In the next chapter, we will start studying grouping statistics.

Questions

Here are a few questions and their answers to assess your learning from this chapter:

1. What is the requisite of the time series data in order to build a forecast?
2. How do you get the cyclical trend of the forecast from the trending line?
3. Why do we need the centered moving average in forecasting?
4. What elements of the regression model are used for the Durbin-Watson test?

Answers

Here are the answers to the previous questions:

1. The data needs autocorrelation. We use the chart and the Durbin-Watson statistical test to prove it.
2. We multiply the trending line of the regression model by the seasonal irregularity.
3. To smooth the cyclical seasonal data movements. With this value, we can calculate the cycling season of the trending line.
4. Use the elements of the error to research whether the data has a cyclical trend that could indicate an autocorrelation relationship.

Further reading

To further understand the concepts of this chapter, you can refer to the following sources:

- *Excel time series forecasting*: `https://www.youtube.com/watch?v=kcfiu-f88JQ`

- *Durbin-Watson tests*: `https://www.youtube.com/watch?v=gaOAFFb3q_Q`

Part 2 –
Grouping Data
to Find Segments
and Outliers

Traditional business intelligence analysis focuses on finding only the best information from big data. Grouping big data helps us to break it down into different segments for better analysis and prediction. This part focuses on grouping data, finding the optimal number for single and multiple variables, and analyzing data anomalies.

This part includes the following chapters:

- *Chapter 4, An Introduction to Data Grouping*
- *Chapter 5, Finding the Optimal Number of Single Variable Groups*
- *Chapter 6, Finding the Optimal Number of Multi-Variable Groups*
- *Chapter 7, Analyzing Outliers for Data Anomalies*

4
Introduction to Data Grouping

Data grouping is a **machine learning** application to segment large amounts of data into assigned groups for data points with similar behavior. It is necessary to use the **K-means** machine learning algorithm because it is very difficult to visualize a large amount of data on a business intelligence chart. Furthermore, when the number of variables is greater than four, we can't make a chart.

The best-case scenario for groups is compact data with a small standard deviation. If we have groups with a large standard deviation, it could mean that they are outliers. Outliers have different behaviors compared with the other groups and could indicate possible suspicious activity such as fraud or poor system performance, which could affect the entire operation in the near future.

The K-means algorithm is the best known of the grouping methods. There are others that could be better than K-means depending on the data. Four examples of classification algorithms are as follows:

- Mean-shift clustering
- Density-based spatial clustering of applications with noise – **Expectation-Maximization (EM)**
- Clustering using Gaussian mixture models
- Agglomerative hierarchical clustering

The advantage of **mean-shift clustering** is that it does not need a pre-defined number of groups. The drawback of **density-based spatial clustering** is when clusters are scattered and are separated one from another. **Agglomerative hierarchical clustering** is the most efficient algorithm and does not need a pre-defined number of groups. In this book, we use K-means because it is easier to explain and does not need many memory resources to execute it with a personal computer.

In this chapter, we will cover the following topics:

- Grouping with the K-means machine learning function

- Finding groups of multiple variables

- Understanding outliers

Technical requirements

Download the Excel file for this chapter here: `https://github.com/ PacktPublishing/Data-Forecasting-and-Segmentation- Using-Microsoft-Excel/blob/main/Chapter04/ IntrodDataGroupingChapterFour.xls`.

Grouping with the K-means machine learning function

We need a machine learning classification algorithm because classifying a large amount of data is very difficult using traditional business intelligence tools such as **pivot tables** and **charts**. We will review and analyze two cases of a large amount of data:

- Sales in multiple countries and regions

- Absentees in the office due to different diseases in human resources

We'll inquire about the results of grouping this data with the classification and grouping algorithm, K-means. Then, we will look at the basic concepts of grouping for single- and multiple-variable classifications. This knowledge is important because we will apply these terms to calculate the groups using the Excel add-in K-means function in the next chapter.

As it is difficult to classify large amounts of data, the following segregations are used:

- Revenue per country

- Absent hours per disease and month

The challenges of doing effective grouping statistical analysis and understanding the segments' behavior are as follows:

- Knowing the optimal number of groups
- Establishing the value ranges for each group

We will analyze this data using K-means to probe the utility of using machine learning to segment the data and plan a strategy for each group:

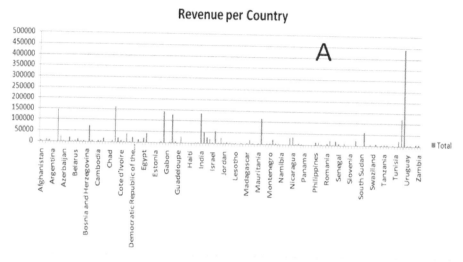

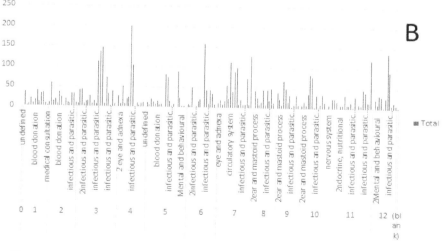

Figure 4.1 – A: Revenue per country, and B: Absent hours per disease and months

We need a quantitative method to find the different revenue ranges to classify the revenue per country. Using just our eyes and intuition is not enough.

We apply the *group statistics method* to this data and the algorithm returns four revenue groups for sales revenue per country. These four groups and their ranges are shown in *Figure 4.2*. The K-means grouping statistical algorithm does several iterations to find the centroids (average value) of each group and assigns the points that belong to each segment.

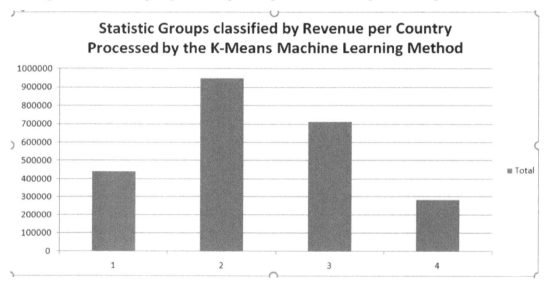

Figure 4.2 – Groups by revenue per country

By doing this analysis, we know that the top revenue group is number *2* with a revenue of around *950,000*, and the lowest revenue group is number *4* with less than *300,000* in revenue.

With the group index classification, we can use business intelligence, such as pivot tables and charts, to get the countries that belong to each group. With this information, we can plan a segmentation strategy for each group. Note that without this arrangement, it is not easy to plan how to improve the sales in each segment because they are different markets and probably have different income population levels.

In *Figure 4.3*, we see the countries that belong to *Group 2* with the highest revenue performance. *Group 3* has the countries with the lowest revenue. Note that they belong to different geographic zones of the world:

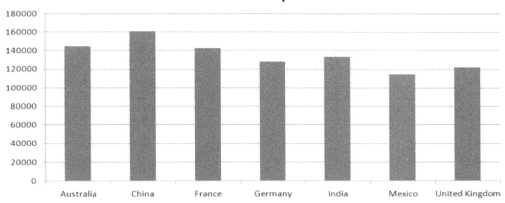

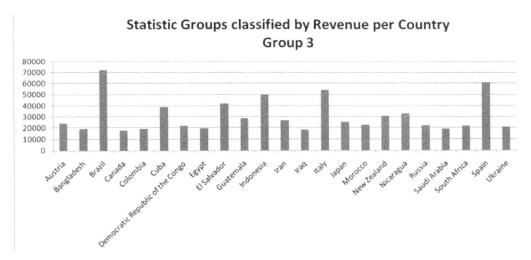

Figure 4.3 – Groups 2 and 3 after K-means classification

By analyzing the high-revenue *Group 2*, we see that it is focused on *Europe* and has a low number of countries, while the lower-revenue *Group 3* has a large number of countries. These regions have different economic situations, so we have to plan a distinct strategy for each one. The best approach is to run the K-means algorithm just on *Group 3* to get a more accurate classification of the low-revenue countries.

The next case is the number of absent hours due to diseases in human resources. After running the K-means algorithm on the large amount of data on hours and diseases in *Figure 4.1 (B)*, we get these results:

- The optimal number of groups and ranges
- The disease associated with each group

With this information, we can plan a preventive method for the kinds of sicknesses that are affecting our human resources. This information is depicted in *Figure 4.4*:

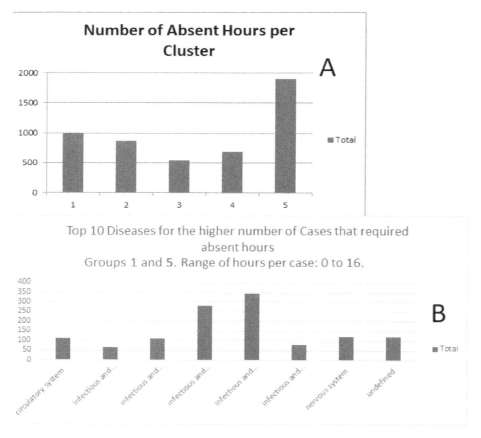

Figure 4.4 – A: Value ranges for absent hours, and B: Disease for groups 1 and 5

After applying the K-means algorithm, we get *Figure 4.4 (A)* with the classification of absent hours per disease. We see that K-means returned that the optimal number of groups is five and that groups *1* and *5* have the highest number of absent hours. Then, we use business intelligence to find out the diseases involved in these groups. We see that *circulatory system*, *infectious*, and *nervous system* diseases are the main causes of absent hours of human resources.

In this section, we reviewed practical applications of the K-means classification algorithm and the need for machine learning to get the optimal number of segments and ranges. Doing these calculations by charting the data using pivot charts or business intelligence is practically impossible.

In the next section, we will look at the basic concepts of K-means:

- Centroids or the average of each group
- Minimal standard deviation to calculate the optimal number of groups

K-means works to classify data of one or more variables. Visualizing the probable segments in one, two, or three dimensions is relatively easy. But, with more than three variables, it is not possible to see a chart of the groups. However, we need the K-means machine learning algorithm to classify data with more than three variables as, without K-means, it is not possible to see a chart of the groups.

Finding groups of multiple variables

The basic concepts of the K-means algorithm to calculate group segments are as follows:

- **Centroid**: This is the average value of each segment.
- **The optimal number of segments**: The K-means algorithm computes the optimal number of groups, calculating the minimal standard deviation or the distance of the members of the group from its centroid.

We'll check them out in depth in the following sections.

Calculating centroids and the optimal number of segments for one variable

The first case is the numbers in *Figure 4.5*, in which we have to find the optimal number of segments and the members of each of them:

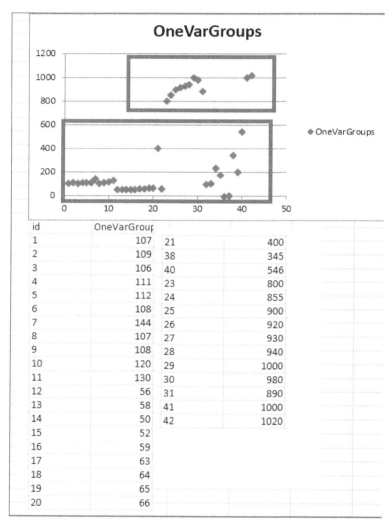

id	OneVarGroup		
1	107	21	400
2	109	38	345
3	106	40	546
4	111	23	800
5	112	24	855
6	108	25	900
7	144	26	920
8	107	27	930
9	108	28	940
10	120	29	1000
11	130	30	980
12	56	31	890
13	58	41	1000
14	50	42	1020
15	52		
16	59		
17	63		
18	64		
19	65		
20	66		

Figure 4.5 – Chart of data to classify into segments. The boxes represent the potential groups

The case data in the chart in *Figure 4.5* suggests that we have two possible groups, but we need the **K-means statistical process** to get the optimal number of groups before running the algorithm to get the group classification. K-means generates a chart called an **elbow chart**. We choose the optimal number of groups by looking at the K-means elbow chart and select the number where the curve starts to flatten. The elbow chart for this case is present in *Figure 4.6*:

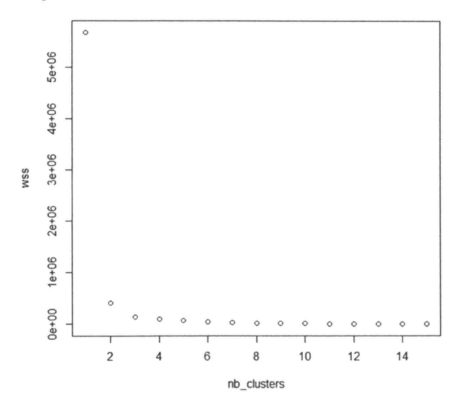

Figure 4.6 – Elbow chart for the data in Figure 4.5

From the K-means elbow chart of *Figure 4.6*, we see that the optimal number of groups for the data in *Figure 4.5* is three.

After we run the K-means algorithm with the number of groups equal to three, we get the classification of the chart in *Figure 4.7*:

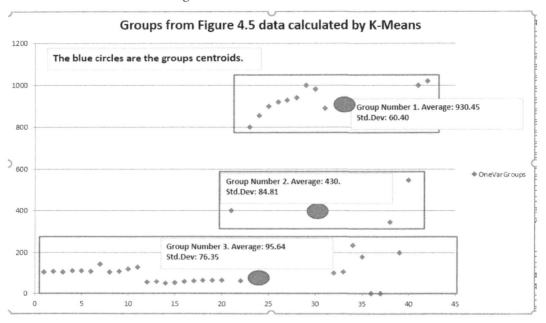

Figure 4.7 – K-means group classification of data from Figure 4.5. The circles are the groups' centroids

Analyzing the results, we can review the following facts about each group:

- *Group Number 1* has a range between *800* and *1,020*. It is a very compact group because its average, or centroid, is *930.45*, and the standard deviation is *60.40*. So, the points are a short distance from the centroid. The centroid is the blue circle.

- *Group Number 2* has an average, or centroid, of *430*, with a standard deviation of *84.81*. This group has relative separation and is small and not as compact as *Group Number 1*.

- *Group Number 3* is not compact. It has an average, or centroid, of *95.64* and a standard deviation of *76.35*. So, the points have a large separation from the group's centroid, as you can see in *Figure 4.7*. A group with scattered points like this could suggest outlier behavior. That means it does not have the same characteristics as the other groups and it needs more research.

We can do business intelligence analysis with a pivot chart of the K-means results to visualize the members of each group. These representations are shown in *Figure 4.8*:

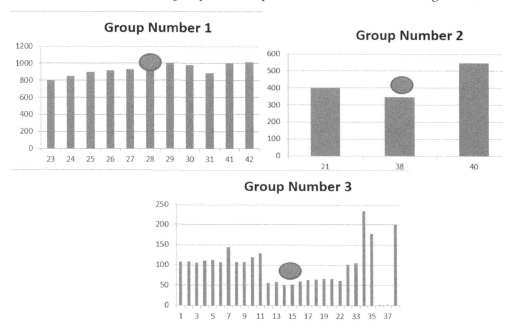

Figure 4.8 – Business intelligence pivot charts. The centroids are the big circles

With the business intelligence pivot chart, we have a clearer idea of the groups' classification ranges. The most compact and defined group is *Number 1*, while *Number 3* is very scattered, with a range between *0* and *240*. We noted, from the chart for this group data, outliers such as numbers *36* and *37*, which have zero values.

Calculating centroids and the optimal number of segments for two or more variables

Having introduced centroids and having an optimal number of groups for K-means with one variable, we are going to work with two or more variables.

Figure 4.9 shows the groups calculated by K-means for two variables, *X* and *Y*. The K-means algorithm elbow chart returned that the optimal number of groups is four:

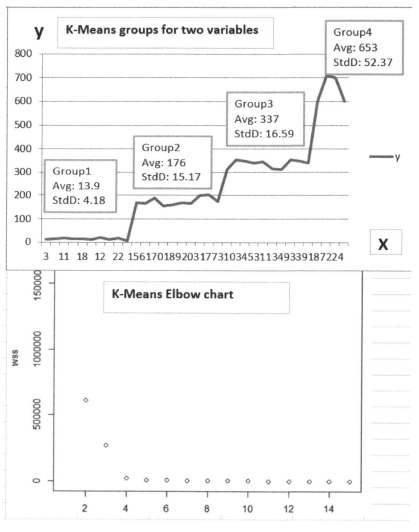

Figure 4.9 – Groups returned by K-means for two variables, X and Y

In *Figure 4.9*, we can see that the four groups are compact and have a short standard deviation. The segmentation is well formed and there are no possible outliers that require further investigation.

The next case is with three variables. Look at *Figure 4.10* and notice that with three variables, it is more complicated to calculate the average and the standard deviation, because we have a three-variable intersection:

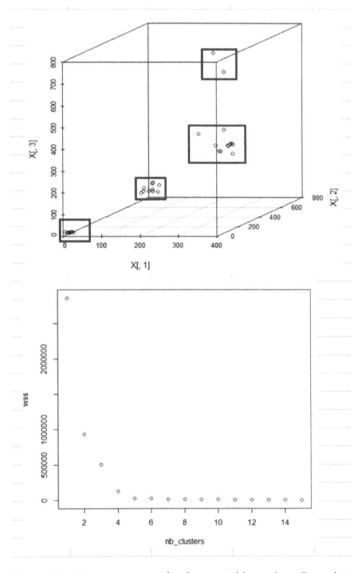

Figure 4.10 – K-means groups for three variables and an elbow chart

The K-means elbow chart says that the optimal number of groups is four. This result makes sense because the 3D chart also reflects that there are four different groups.

Since it is difficult to do calculations such as average and standard deviation, we depend on business intelligence charts to better understand the data points of each group. Look at *Figure 4.11* to see the three variable data points assigned to each group:

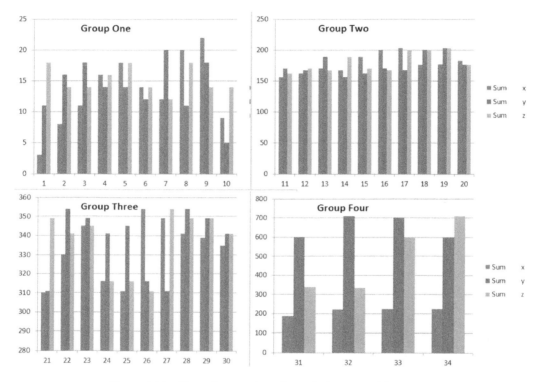

Figure 4.11 – Pivot chart analysis for each three-variable group

In *Figure 4.11*, we can visualize that *Group Four* is probably an outlier because it has much fewer elements than the other three groups.

The next case is the most complex of all. It involves four variables: *X*, *Y*, *Z*, and *W*. It is not possible to do a four-dimension chart, so we depend on the K-means group assignment and the business intelligence pivot chart analysis to explore the results and see whether there are outliers.

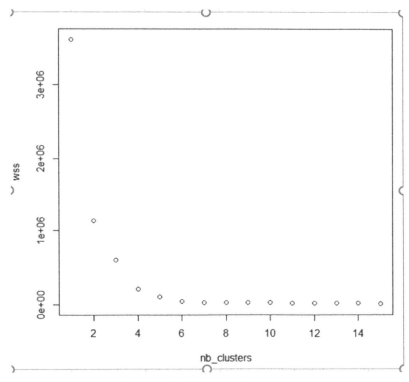

Figure 4.12 – K-means elbow chart

Figure 4.12 shows the K-means elbow chart, which shows that the optimal number of segments for the four variables is four.

After the K-means processing, the business intelligence results are shown in *Figure 4.13*:

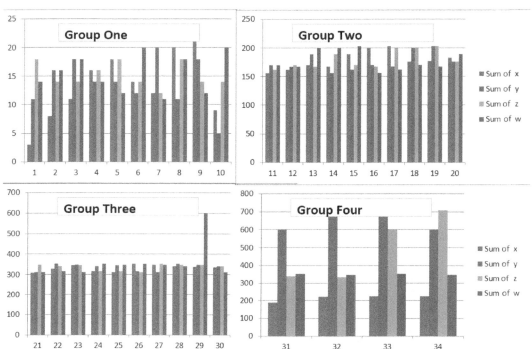

Figure 4.13 – Pivot chart analysis for each four-variable group

In the business intelligence pivot chart results, we have the bars of the variables *X*, *Y*, *Z*, and *W* in order from first to fourth place.

We can see that the probable outlier of the analysis is *Group Four* because it has fewer elements (it has just four) and also the *X* variable has a lower value than in the other groups (less than 200).

In this section, we reviewed how to segment two or more variables using K-means. Notice that with four or more variables, it is not possible to do a chart, so we depend on the pivot chart analysis to review the behavior of each variable. In the next section, we will see what happens with the values that fall far away from the centroid or the median of the group. The group with a large standard deviation is probably an outlier.

Understanding outliers

Many data points are far away from the group centroid or average, affecting the value of the standard value. Remember that the optimal case is to have a compact group with a small standard value. These data points are outliers that don't comply with the characteristics of the group or the general data. These outliers deserve further investigation because they could have suspicious behavior (for example, fraud or peaks in demand) that could affect the performance of the system, such as network traffic. Look at *Figure 4.14* to examine the outliers of the groups of one variable and the outliers of the 3D chart:

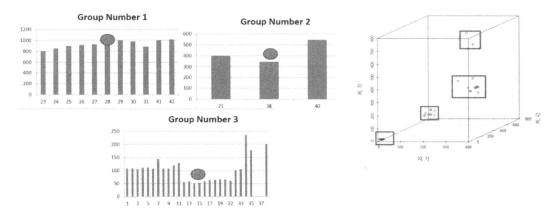

Figure 4.14 – Outliers for one variable and three variables

Group Number 3 is the outlier of the one-variable classification. Notice that the points have a large separation from the centroid. The standard deviation has a large amplitude. This group has different behavior compared with the other two, which are compact and close to their respective centroids.

In the three-variables chart, the outliers are the bottom and the top squares. This data is separated from the rest of the points, so it has different behavior compared to the others.

In this section, we had an introduction to outliers. These points (with a big separation from the centroid and the other groups) indicate that they have different, special behavior that demands further research. An outlier could indicate a malfunction that could affect the rest of the operation in the near future. In the next chapter, we will learn how to use the Excel add-in function of K-means to process data groups.

Summary

In this chapter, we learned that K-means helps us to classify large amounts of data that is very difficult to classify with a simple view or with business intelligence.

We discussed the application of segment groups in business sales and to research diseases that cause days of absence in human resources. We learned about K-means terms such as centroid, or the average of the group. The optimal group classification is compact and with a small standard deviation. The K-means elbow chart indicates the optimal number for group classification.

The K-means function does group classification for one or more variables. It is very difficult to visualize the probable classification of four or more variables because it is not possible to do a chart of the data. We also learned about outliers – points that have different behavior from the rest of the groups and could lead to fraud or system problems in the near future. In the next chapter, we will learn how to calculate groups using the Excel K-means add-in function.

Questions

Here are a few questions to assess your learning from this chapter:

1. What is the group centroid?
2. What is the best-case scenario for a group?
3. What situations could indicate an outlier?
4. How do you know how many groups K-means has to process?
5. How can we visualize the results of a four-variable grouping?

Answers

Here are the answers to the previous questions:

1. It is the average value of the group.
2. Its data points are compact and close to the group's centroids. They have a small standard deviation.
3. An outlier has different behavior compared with the rest of the groups. It could indicate fraud or a system performance problem that could lead to a crisis in the near future.

4. The K-means elbow chart displays the optimal number of groups. Choose the number where the curve starts to flatten.

5. Do K-means classification, then run the pivot chart analysis per group to review the segmentation of the variables' values.

Further reading

Partitional Clustering In R: The Essentials:

```
https://www.datanovia.com/en/lessons/K-means-clustering-in-r-
algorith-and-practical-examples/
```

5
Finding the Optimal Number of Single Variable Groups

In this chapter, we will learn that we have to preprocess data to find the optimal number of groups for the values. It is not an arbitrary number and is very difficult to determine with just a visual inspection of the data chart. We will work with just one variable in this chapter, and then, in the next chapter, we will use more than two variables to segment the data, which demands a more automatic process with K-means. In this chapter, we will also learn how to install and use the K-means Excel add-in included in this book and on GitHub. We have to use an R function for K-means in Excel because it is very difficult to do an automatic segmentation by hand in Excel.

The topics we will cover in this chapter are as follows:

- Finding an optimal number of groups for one variable
- Running the K-means function to get the centroids or group average
- Finding the groups and centroids of one-variable data with K-means and Excel

We will use pivot tables and charts to find the range of values for each group using the maximum, minimum, and average to see whether the group has scattered data that could be outliers or needs another K-means process to find subgroups.

Technical requirements

The following are the prerequisites of this chapter:

- Download the Excel file for this chapter here: `https://github.com/PacktPublishing/Data-Forecasting-and-Segmentation-Using-Microsoft-Excel/blob/main/Chapter05/kmeansClustersChapter4_5_6_7.xlsm`.

- Create and include the function in this code to calculate the optimal number of groups. Download the code from here: `https://github.com/PacktPublishing/Data-Forecasting-and-Segmentation-Using-Microsoft-Excel/blob/main/Chapter05/kmeanselbow.r`.

- Download the K-means function to group the data into segments from here: `https://github.com/PacktPublishing/Data-Forecasting-and-Segmentation-Using-Microsoft-Excel/blob/main/Chapter05/kmeansworking01.r`.

- The Kaggle data source for products, quantity, and profits to analyze the statistical groups included in the Excel file can be found at this link: `https://www.kaggle.com/tanmaygangurde/global-superstore-ml/notebook`.

Finding an optimal number of groups for one variable

The first task to solve grouping statistics is to find out the optimal number of groups for our data. Remember these facts by looking at *Figure 5.1*. Minimize the distance of each group point to its centroid or group average.

The optimal distance is a small standard deviation result of the group data. Data that is at a large distance from the group centroid is an outlier. This means that we need to further research these points because they could represent risky behavior.

Knowing these facts, look at *Figure 5.1* and see how difficult it is to decide, at a glance, how many groups have the optimal sales per product and the number of absent hours due to sickness for a human resources case study:

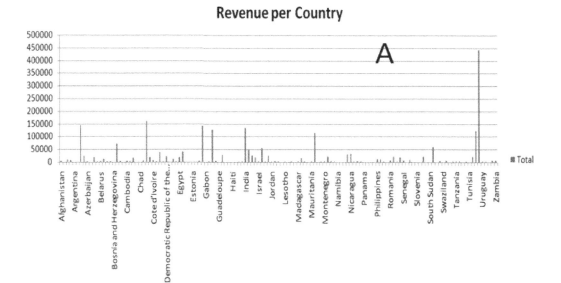

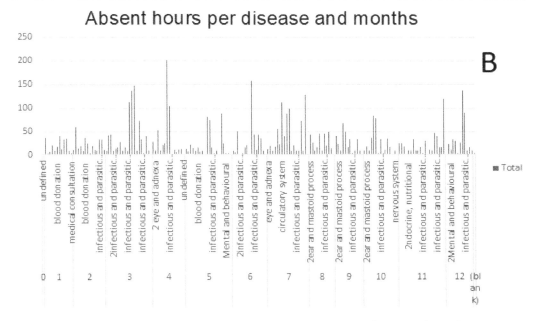

Figure 5.1 – A: Revenue per country, B: Absent hours per disease and month

To get the optimal number of groups, we need the K-means elbow algorithm chart. Choose the number where the curve starts to get flat. Before we develop the complex examples of sales per product and absent days due to sickness, we are going to learn how to calculate the optimal number of groups for the data example shown in *Figure 5.2*:

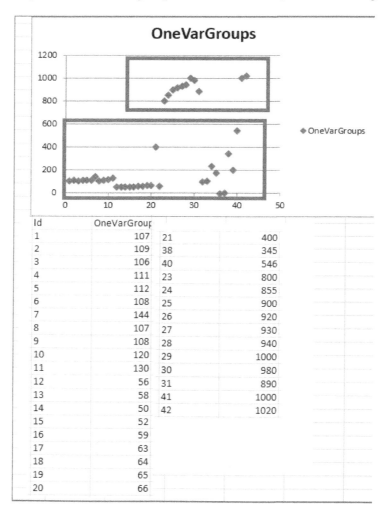

Id	OneVarGroup		
1	107	21	400
2	109	38	345
3	106	40	546
4	111	23	800
5	112	24	855
6	108	25	900
7	144	26	920
8	107	27	930
9	108	28	940
10	120	29	1000
11	130	30	980
12	56	31	890
13	58	41	1000
14	50	42	1020
15	52		
16	59		
17	63		
18	64		
19	65		
20	66		

Figure 5.2 – Chart of data to classify in segments. The red boxes highlight the visual probability groups

In *Figure 5.2*, there are two groups in the data outlined by the red squares. We need to run the K-means elbow function to confirm that we have two groups in this initial approach.

Instructions to run the required add-in in Excel

To calculate the optimal number of groups and then the grouping statistics, we need to run the K-means add-in for Excel included in this chapter. We will dedicate this section to explaining how to install the add-in for Excel to run K-means.

R functions require the best software package to run. The steps to install the K-means add-in for Excel are as follows:

1. Download and install BERT on your computer.

    You can download the BERT tool from here: `https://bert-toolkit.com/`.

2. Open complements in Excel and check that BERT is installed.

    Once installed, go to the upper tools of Excel and click the **Complements** option. Then, click on **BERT Console** to open the R editor. We are going to create the elbow and K-means functions here using the code in the GitHub repository.

3. Include the three functions to chart the data in 3D, get the optimal number of groups, and run the K-means to get the members of each group.

Running K-means elbow to get the optimal number of groups

Use the following steps to get the optimal number of groups:

1. Open the kmeanselbow R function from **Complements | Bert Console**.

2. Go to the top menu of Excel and click on **Complements**, then click on **BERT Console** to open the kmeanselbow R function. See *Figure 5.3* for general instructions:

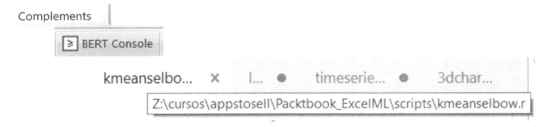

Figure 5.3 – Opening the kmeanselbow R function

The `kmeanselbow` R function receives the data input from Excel and calculates the optimal number of groups.

Do the same procedure to open the K-means function. Details to open and run the functions are in this chapter.

Passing the data values to the K-means elbow function

We will analyze the data, as shown in *Figure 5.4*, in the Excel sheet range of B2 to B43. So, we'll write these parameters in the elbow function in the line with this sentence:

```
rng <- EXCEL$Application$get_Range( "B2:B43" )
```

The following figure shows this step in detail:

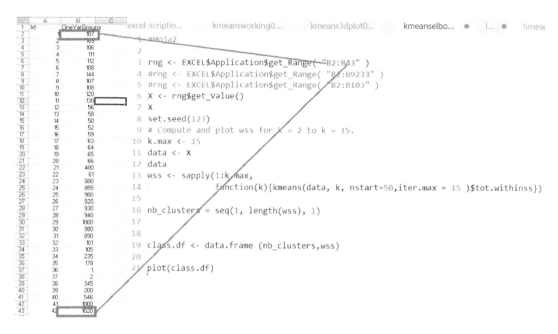

Figure 5.4 – Excel data range to calculate the optimal number of groups

The K-means elbow function will calculate the optimal number of groups and display a chart. We will identify the value at which the curve starts to flatten. The data range of B2 to B43 of the datasheet is shown in *Figure 5.4*. It explains how to pass the parameters and write them in the function.

Executing and interpreting the resulting chart of the optimal number of groups

Execute the function by right-clicking and choosing to execute the entire buffer. See *Figure 5.5* to understand the step and see the results. The elbow function analyzes the data and returns a curve chart, also shown in *Figure 5.5*. The idea is to choose the value where the curve starts to flatten. However, you have to use your judgment of what the best value to choose is:

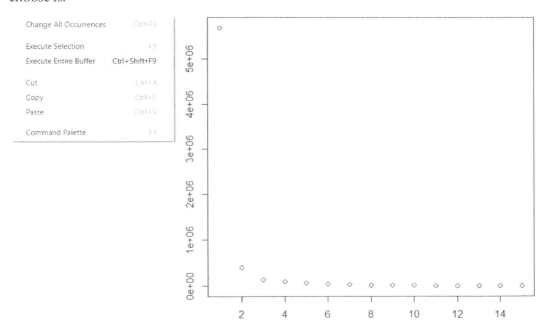

Figure 5.5 – Excel data range to calculate the optimal number of groups

Examine the results of the chart and see that the curve starts to flatten at value 3. Remember that, in our visual inspection of the data in *Figure 5.1*, we decided to choose only two groups. However, the function says that the optimal number of groups is three.

In this section, we explained how to use the K-means elbow function to get the optimal number of groups. We reviewed the case studies of product revenue and absent days due to sickness in *Figure 5.1* and understood the difficult task of choosing the optimal number of groups. We learned how to install the BERT Console add-in for Excel to run R functions that calculate the optimal number of groups, and how to execute the K-means group segmentation function. We learned how to identify the value where the optimal number of groups chart starts to flatten. This number of groups is a parameter to execute the K-means function to do the group segmentation. This is the topic of the next section.

Running the K-means function to get the centroids or group average

Now, we'll pass a parameter for the number of groups we want to process with K-means. This is a parameter in cell C1:1 for the function. Also, we include the range of input values and the range where the function will insert the group assignment values.

To execute the K-means function, take the following steps (and also see *Figure 5.6*):

1. Insert the number of groups to apply segmentation.
2. Define the Excel sheet data input range.
3. Specify the Excel sheet range to store the group segmentation results.

With the results, we will do a pivot analysis to understand the group assignment to every value of the data input.

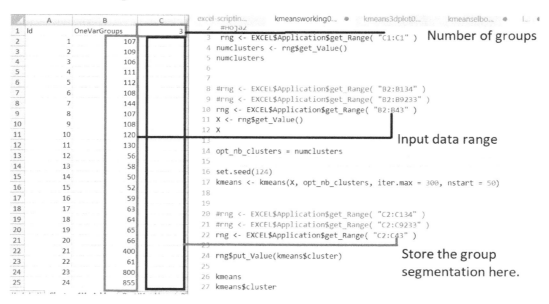

Figure 5.6 – Parameters to execute K-means

Figure 5.6 shows how we specify the parameters of the K-means function. We can explain this process step by step as follows:

1. Insert the number of groups to apply segmentation.

    The first parameter is the optimal number of groups we want to process. The elbow function returned 3. Write this value in cell C1:1 of Excel. See **Number of groups** in *Figure 5.6*. Also, write this value in this function sentence:

    ```
    rng <- EXCEL$Application$get_Range ( "C1:C1" )
    ```

2. Define the Excel sheet data input range.

    Write the input data range in the K-means function sentence. This is the range of the data we want to process. See **Input data range** in *Figure 5.6*. In this example, the range is B2:B43:

    ```
    rng <- EXCEL$Application$get_Range ( "B2:B43" )
    ```

3. Specify the Excel sheet range to store the group segmentation results.

    Finally, we specify the range where the function will store the group's assignment to every value of the input data. See **Store the group segmentation here** in *Figure 5.6*. In our example, the range is C2:C43. Write this value in the function sentence:

    ```
    rng <- EXCEL$Application$get_Range ( "C2:C43" )
    ```

Then, execute the function by right-clicking on the code canvas and choosing to execute the entire buffer, as we did with the elbow function.

After running the entire buffer, we get the results shown in *Figure 5.7*. The function calculates the group assignment for every value of the data and writes the result in the specified range of C2 : C43:

	A	B	C
1	Id	OneVarGroups	Group assigment
2	1	107	3
3	2	109	3
4	3	106	3
5	4	111	3
6	5	112	3
7	6	108	3
8	7	144	3
9	8	107	3
10	9	108	3
11	10	120	3
12	11	130	3
13	12	56	3
14	13	58	3
15	14	50	3
16	15	52	3
17	16	59	3
18	17	63	3
19	18	64	3
20	19	65	3
21	20	66	3
22	21	400	2
23	22	61	3
24	23	800	1
25	24	855	1

Figure 5.7 – Group assignment returned by the K-means function

The results returned by the K-means group segmentation function are shown in *Figure 5.7*. In the preliminary analysis, we see that group number three has a value range of 66 to 107. Group number two has at least one value of 400. Group number one has value examples of 800 and 855. We are going to do a pivot analysis to explore these ranges of values for each group in the next section.

In this section, we learned how to pass the parameters to the K-means function. We need to pass the number of groups we want to classify, the range of the input data, and where to store the groups' assignment results returned by the K-means function. We explored the value range assigned to each group by reading the maximum and minimum values for each group. In the next section, we will do a pivot analysis for every segment to get the centroid and the value range for every group, and start understanding what values the outliers could be.

Finding the groups and centroids of one-variable data with K-means and Excel

After we process the data, we can use pivot tables to research the group members and value ranges, the centroids and upper/lower values, and the possible outliers of the data.

With the pivot chart analysis, we will explore the following segment information:

- Assigning values for every group
- Calculating the centroid or the average point for every group
- Exploring the range of values for each segment

This information will give us a complete picture of how the segment values range. With this information, we can plan a different strategy for each group. We will likely see that we have to create a subsegment of a group because it has a large standard deviation or many scattered points at a distance from its centroid. We will also identify the possible outliers for each group.

Assigning values for every group

We'll build a pivot table with the ID, OneVarGroups (data values), and Group assignment source fields. See *Figure 5.8*. From here, move Sum of OneVarGroups to the Values square. Then, move Cluster (groups) and ID to the Categories square:

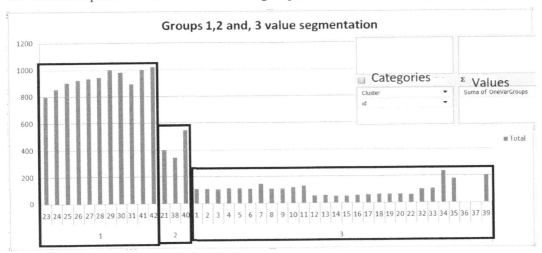

Figure 5.8 – Group assignment returned by the K-means function

After we move `Cluster` and `ID` to the `Categories` square, and `Sum of OneVarGroups` to the `Values` square, we get the results shown in *Figure 5.8*.

We see that group one has the largest values, above 800. Group two has intermediate values, between 400 and 600. Group three has the lowest values, below 200. Note that IDs 36 and 37 of group three have a value of 0. These values are probably outliers because they don't have a similar behavior compared with the rest of the group. They have a large distance from the average or the centroid.

Calculating the centroid or the average point for every group

To get the centroids for every group using the pivot table, move the `Cluster` field to the `Categories` square. Then, choose `Average calculation of OneVarGroups` in the `Values` square. See *Figure 5.9* to analyze the centroids for each group:

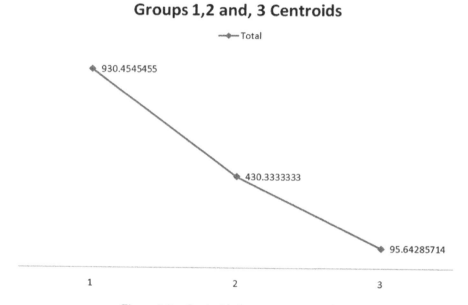

Figure 5.9 – Centroids for groups 1, 2, and 3

From *Figure 5.9*, we can conclude that group three has two outliers because IDs 36 and 37 have a value of 0. Zero has a large distance from the average or centroid, or the group with a value of 95.

Exploring the range of values for each segment

To get the range of values and the centroid for every group, move the minimum, maximum, and average fields to the Values square in the pivot fields. With this information, we can visually detect whether the groups have a large standard deviation and see the possible outliers. See *Figure 5.10* to understand how scattered the data of each group is:

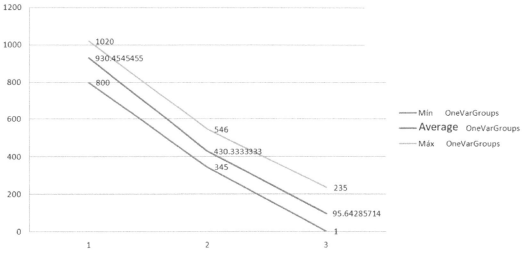

Figure 5.10 – Value ranges and centroid for each group

From *Figure 5.10*, we can see that groups one and two are relatively compact because their maximum and minimum values are close to the group's centroid. The difference is with group three because it has a large distance between the minimum value of 1 and the centroid, with a value of 95. This group has outliers that need more research to see whether they could affect results in the near future.

In the next step, we will run the elbow and K-means functions to analyze the groups of product categories and revenue. This analysis will give us an idea of how to plan a strategy for bestselling products and for others that need to improve. We will learn how the region affects the profits of the product. The source for this data is in the downloads from GitHub at the beginning of the chapter.

Finding the segments for products and profits

This analysis has a large database of products, regions, and profits. We are going to use the `ProductsOneVar` sheet of the `kmeansClusterChapter4_5_6_7.xlsm` Excel file.

The value dimension is profit. The classifications are the product category and the market location. One of the goals is to identify the categories with the most profitable market location.

It is very difficult to do a profit segmentation for the products because it is a large data file, as you can see in *Figure 5.11*:

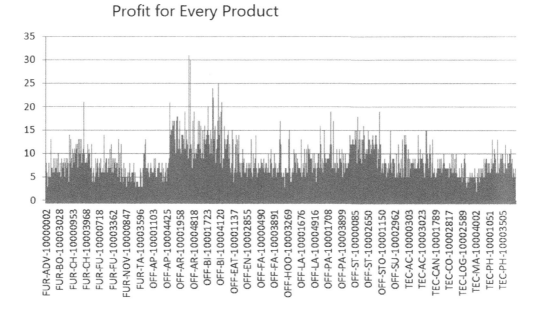

Figure 5.11 – Chart of profits for every product

As you can see from *Figure 5.11*, it is almost impossible to classify what the different segments of the products' profits are. We probably know what the top 20 bestselling products are but the rest of the portfolio does not have a strategy because it is very difficult to analyze the different segments that are in the medium-to-low selling products.

The steps to do this market segmentation research are as follows:

- Find the optimal number of groups using the K-means elbow function.
- Run the K-means function to do the group segmentation.

- Do a pivot analysis of the results to get the ranges of profit for each group and the corresponding product category.

- Research what market location has the best and worst profits to improve the sales strategy.

With this information, we can create subgroups if we consider that a group has large, scattered data.

Finding the optimal number of groups using the K-means elbow function

We use the elbow function as we did before, with the kmeanselbow R function. Set the parameters where the data source is. In this case, the profit for each product category is in the E column of the sheet. You can see how to set this range of values in *Figure 5.12*:

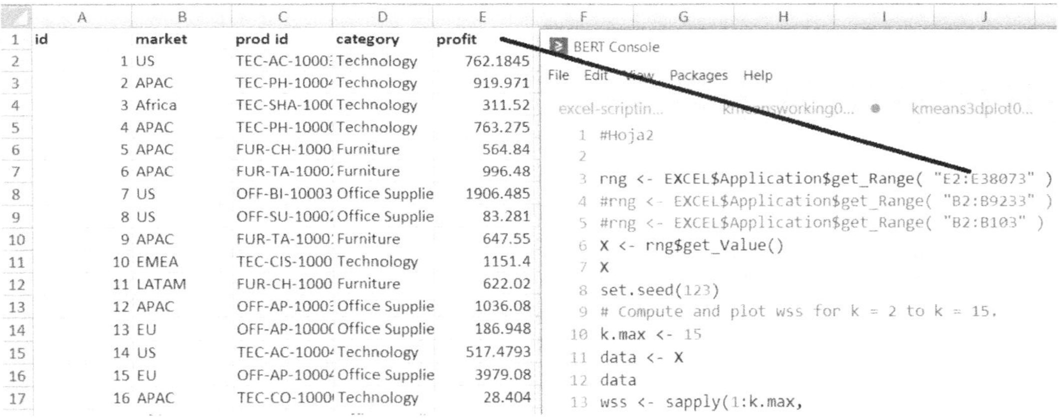

Figure 5.12 – Setting the parameter of data ranges for the elbow function

The next step is to execute the function by right-clicking and executing the entire buffer. The K-means elbow function returns a chart of the optimal number of groups. It will take some seconds because the dataset is large. Once we have the response, find the number where the curve starts to flatten. The result is shown in *Figure 5.13*. Write the range parameter in the function's sentence:

```
rng <- EXCEL$Application$get_Range( "E2:E38073" )
```

The `elbow` function returns the optimal number of groups for this data. Choose the value where the curve starts to flatten:

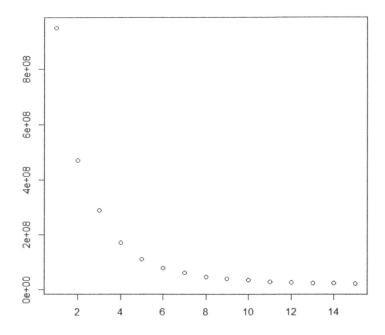

Figure 5.13 – Elbow results for profits of products

The elbow result of *Figure 5.13* shows that the curve flattens at a value of 5. Five is the optimal number of groups for the product's profit in *Figure 5.13*. Five will be the input of the number of groups for the K-means function we will execute in the next subsection.

Running the K-means function to do the group segmentation

We run the K-means function on the BERT Console passing the parameters of the number of groups to process, the range of the input data, and the range to store the group's assignment results. See *Figure 5.14* to remember how to write the parameters in the function sentences:

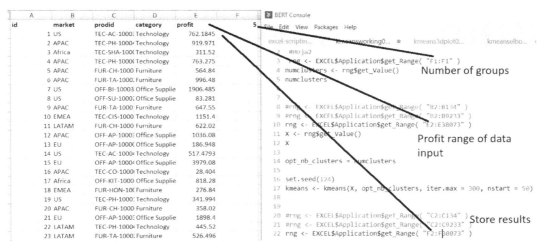

Figure 5.14 – Passing parameters to execute the K-means function

In *Figure 5.14*, we see the three parameters for the K-means function:

- Number of groups to process
- Range of data input (profit)
- Range to store the group assignment results

We write the number of groups to process ranges in the K-means sentence. This case is in cell F1:1:

```
rng <- EXCEL$Application$get_Range( "F1:F1" )
```

Then, write the range of the input data in E1:E38073 in the sentence:

```
rng <- EXCEL$Application$get_Range( "E2:E38073" )
```

Finally, write the range to store the group assignment for every value:

```
rng <- EXCEL$Application$get_Range( "F2:F38073" )
```

Execute the K-means function by right-clicking and executing the entire buffer. Remember that we are processing around 38,000 records in Excel, so it will take some time before it finishes, depending on the processor and memory of your computer.

After processing the K-means function, we get a group assignment as in *Figure 5.15*:

id	market	prodid	category	profit	cluster
1	US	TEC-AC-1000:	Technology	762.1845	4
2	APAC	TEC-PH-1000<	Technology	919.971	4
3	Africa	TEC-SHA-100(	Technology	311.52	2
4	APAC	TEC-PH-1000(	Technology	763.275	4
5	APAC	FUR-CH-1000	Furniture	564.84	4
6	APAC	FUR-TA-1000:	Furniture	996.48	4
7	US	OFF-BI-10003	Office Supplie	1906.485	5
8	US	OFF-SU-1000:	Office Supplie	83.281	3
9	APAC	FUR-TA-1000:	Furniture	647.55	4
10	EMEA	TEC-CIS-1000	Technology	1151.4	4
11	LATAM	FUR-CH-1000	Furniture	622.02	4
12	APAC	OFF-AP-1000:	Office Supplie	1036.08	4
13	EU	OFF-AP-1000(	Office Supplie	186.948	2
14	US	TEC-AC-1000<	Technology	517.4793	4
15	EU	OFF-AP-1000<	Office Supplie	3979.08	1
16	APAC	TEC-CO-1000(	Technology	28.404	3
17	Africa	OFF-KIT-1000	Office Supplie	818.28	4

Figure 5.15 – Group segmentation after running K-means

We are going to use the `market`, `category`, `profit`, and `cluster` or segment fields in the titles of *Figure 5.15* to do the pivot chart analysis.

Doing pivot analysis to get the group profit ranges

Use the maximum, minimum, and average profit in the square of the value of the pivot table to get the ranges for each group. Move the groups to the categories. See the results in *Figure 5.16*:

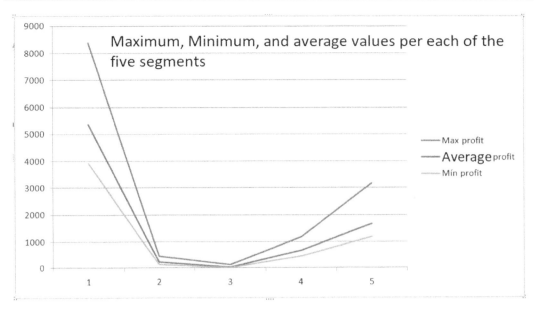

Figure 5.16 – Range of profit values for each group

In *Figure 5.16*, we see that group one has the highest profit. Group three has the lowest profit. Remember that the average is the centroid for each group. We can see that the elbow and K-means functions did good work of classifying the groups because the segments appear to be compact and close to the groups' centroids. Apparently, we don't have outliers inside the groups because the minimum and maximum values are relatively close to the centroid.

Now, we will research which market location and category has the highest and lowest profits to improve the sales strategy.

We will apply a filter for the bestselling group to the pivot table to display only group number one. Then, we'll add the product category and region fields to see what is most profitable inside group number one (see *Figure 5.17*):

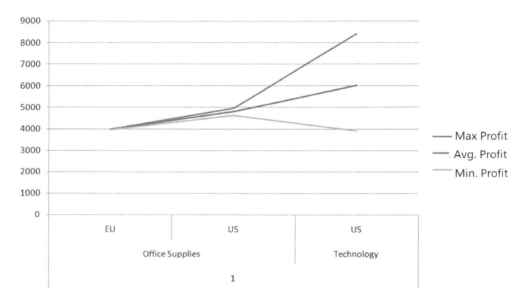

Figure 5.17 – Highest profit category and region in bestselling group number one

We see from *Figure 5.17* that the **Technology** category in the **US** region is the bestselling product of the business. We have to apply a special marketing strategy for this highly profitable segment.

Now, we are going to explore the region and category of the least profitable group of our business. This is group number three (see *Figure 5.18*):

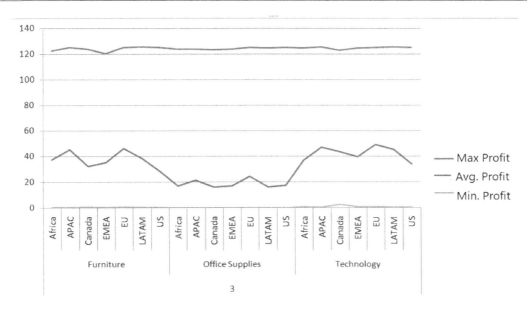

Figure 5.18 – Lowest profit category and regions

By analyzing the lowest market in *Figure 5.18*, we conclude that we need to do a segmentation of this group because the data is very scattered. See how the minimum for almost all the regions is 0. Also, the categories include almost the same regions. So, for this group, we need to again apply K-means because we don't have a clear conclusion. Doing this is left as an exercise to you because it is outside the scope of the book to run another analysis.

In this section, we used a practical example of segmentation by products, regions, and profits. We used a large dataset with almost 38,000 records to explore the K-means capability to find the optimal number of groups and classify them. We used one variable, profits, to do this segmentation. In the next chapter, we are going to expand this analysis to two or more variables using the K-means function.

Summary

In this chapter, we explained that we need the assistance of machine learning and the K-means algorithm to find the optimal number of groups and the segments of a dataset because a visual inspection is not accurate or quantitative. We learned how to install and execute R functions to find the optimal number of groups, as well as K-means execution. Once we had the grouping classification, we used pivot tables and charts to find the centroids for each group and the minimum and maximum ranges to get an idea of the distance between the values and the average or centroid. Remember that the best-case scenario is to have compact groups with a small standard deviation. If there were a large distance between values and the average, we'd probably have outliers that could affect the operation in the near future. Also, if a group has large, scattered datasets, we'd probably need to apply the K-means algorithm just for this group to create subsegments. That was the case with the lowest profit segment of the analysis of the products. With the knowledge gained from this chapter, you can apply the K-means add-in to create new segments of the data we used here and expand the analysis. In the next chapter, we are going to use two or more variables as input for the K-means algorithm.

Questions

The following are a few questions to assess your understanding of this chapter:

1. Can the number of segments be decided as an arbitrary number?

2. How do we decide the optimal number of groups from the elbow chart?

3. What are the parameters to execute the K-means function?

4. How do we determine whether a group is compact or not?

5. How do we interpret and process a group's scattered data?

Answers

Here are the answers to the preceding questions:

1. No. We need to do a visual inspection of the data to guess the possible number of groups for the data. Then, we run the K-means elbow function to get the optimal number of groups of the data.

2. We choose the number where the curve starts to flatten.

3. The following are the parameters to execute the K-means function:

    - Number of groups to process

    - The range of the input data

    - The range to put the results returned by the K-means function

4. Use a pivot table and chart analysis with the minimum, maximum, and centroid values for each group. If the maximum and minimum values have a large distance from the average (centroid), that means that the group has scattered values.

5. Scattered values with a large distance from the centroid are possible outliers that need further research. One approach could be to do another K-means process for this group to create subgroups to improve the data classification.

Further reading

To further understand the concepts of this chapter, refer to the following sources:

- Learn how to program the K-means algorithm using Python in this book: `https://subscription.packtpub.com/book/data/9781838552862/4/ch04lvl1sec30/K-means-clustering`.

- Read about the practical application of the K-means algorithm at this link: `https://www.datanovia.com/en/lessons/K-means-clustering-in-r-algorith-and-practical-examples/`.

6
Finding the Optimal Number of Multi-Variable Groups

In this chapter, we will expand the use of the Elbow and K-means functions for a multivariable analysis from two to four variables. We will use the Elbow function to find the optimal number of groups and then pass it as a parameter to the K-means function. The objective of the example is to find the highest revenue group that delivers smaller quantities of items to avoid logistics costs. The K-means function is useful for this multi-dimensional research in that it combines all these variables and returns the segments evaluating the variable's influence. We will explore the data scattered by exploring the distance between the data points of each group and its centroid.

The topics we will cover in this chapter are as follows:

- Calculating the optimal number of groups with two and three variables
- Determining the groups and average value (centroids) of two and three variables
- Using the Elbow and K-means functions with four variables

We are going to use the products with the best revenue and month of sale to use as input for a time series analysis to carry out a forecast of future sales in a further chapter.

Technical requirements

This list has the Excel file and the Excel add-in code to calculate the optimal number of groups and the K-means function to get the groups' segments.

- Download the Excel file for this chapter here:

  ```
  https://github.com/PacktPublishing/Data-Forecasting-and-
  Segmentation-Using-Microsoft-Excel/blob/main/Chapter06/
  kmeansClustersChapter4_5_6_7.xlsm
  ```

- To create and include the function to calculate the optimal number of groups, download the Excel add-in function from here:

  ```
  https://github.com/PacktPublishing/Data-Forecasting-and-
  Segmentation-Using-Microsoft-Excel/blob/main/Chapter06/
  kmeanselbow.r
  ```

- Download the K-means function to group the data into segments from here:

  ```
  https://github.com/PacktPublishing/Data-Forecasting-and-
  Segmentation-Using-Microsoft-Excel/blob/main/Chapter06/
  kmeansworking01.r
  ```

- Download the K-means function to plot 3D charts from here:

  ```
  https://github.com/PacktPublishing/Data-Forecasting-and-
  Segmentation-Using-Microsoft-Excel/blob/main/Chapter06/
  kmeans3dplot01.r
  ```

- The data source from the Excel example workbook is Kaggle and is found in this link:

  ```
  https://www.kaggle.com/tanmaygangurde/global-
  superstore-ml/notebook
  ```

Calculating the optimal number of groups for two and three variables

In this section, we will explore the groups of products and sales results for two and three variables. In the previous chapter, we analyzed the groups using the single variable of revenue. Now, we will perform a multivariable grouping calculation by performing the following activities:

- Finding the optimal number of segments for two variables:

  - Revenue

  - Quantity

- Using the `elbow` function to get the number of groups for three variables:

  - Revenue

  - Quantity

  - Month of sale

Computing the optimal number of segments for two and three variables is more complex than the simple example of the last chapter. We will do a chart of the variables before we use the Elbow function to get an idea of the data dispersion. For the three variables, we will use the R function included in this book to execute a 3D chart.

Finding the optimal number of segments for two variables – revenue and quantity

An analysis involving revenue and quantity will give an idea of the products that achieve the best earnings while selling the lowest quantities. Remember that our best-case scenario is products that achieve the highest revenue with the lowest sales quantities because we don't incur logistics costs and complexity. The steps involved in this analysis use the `ProductsTwoVars` sheet of the `KmeansChapters_5_5_6_7.xlsm` Excel file:

- Charting two variables (revenue and quantity) to explore the possible number of data groups

- Running the Elbow algorithm

- Using the `ProductsTwoVars` sheet

Since the revenue and quantity do not have the same units of measure (money and quantity), we chart each variable separately in a combination chart. As a result, in *Figure 6.1*, you can see that it is very difficult to visualize how to group this data, which involves a large number of products and two variables:

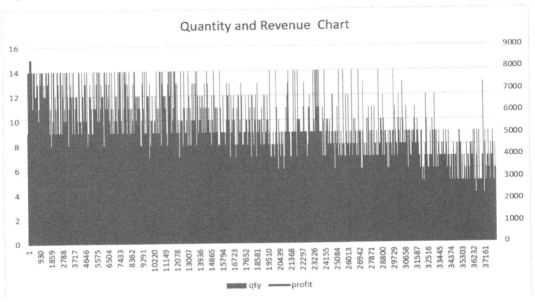

Figure 6.1 – Chart for two variables, quantity and revenue, to visualize groups

As you can see in *Figure 6.1*, it is complicated to try to determine the possible number of data groups using the two variables, quantity and revenue.

We are going to run the Elbow function to use the K-means algorithm and ascertain the optimal number of groups for this data. *Figure 6.2* includes the steps to pass the parameters necessary for the Elbow function:

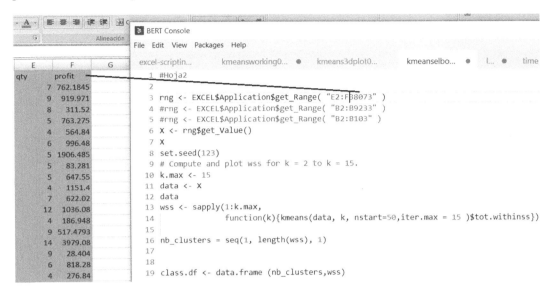

Figure 6.2 – K-Means and Elbow function data parameter range

From *Figure 6.2*, we pass the parameters of the range of data we want to process. The range is the two variables, quantity and profit, located in Excel sheet cell E2:F38073. Write this value in the function sentence:

```
rng <- EXCEL$Application$get_Range( "E2:F38073" )
```

Then, we execute the function by right-clicking and choosing to execute the entire buffer. It will take some minutes to finish because a large amount of data is involved. We get the chart in *Figure 6.3* that represents the optimal number of groups:

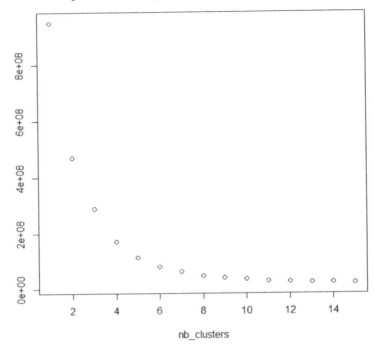

Figure 6.3 – K-Means Elbow chart for two variables – quantity and revenue

From *Figure 6.3*, we conclude that seven is the optimal number of groups because it is the value where the curve starts to flatten. This number will be the input to the K-means function we are going to execute in the next section. When we executed the K-means function with one variable (profit) in the last chapter, the optimal number of groups was five. So, the other variable adds two more groups to the analysis.

In this section, we found the optimal number of groups for the profit and quantity variables using the Elbow function. These two variables represent seven groups of data. In the next section, we are going to add the variable month to the analysis. With this information, we will visualize the months with greater revenue and increased demand.

Using the elbow function to get the number of groups for three variables – revenue, quantity, and month of sale

The month of sale in the three variables' analysis – revenue, quantity, and month of sale – provides information about which season has the greatest revenue, as well as which months involve a greater quantity of products being moved, to prepare our logistical infrastructure. In the four-variables analysis, we will include shipping costs.

Excel is not able to do a 3D chart. We are going to add a function to the BERT console. Add a new file and name it `kmeans3dplot01.r`. Copy and paste the code from the GitHub site of the book here:

```
https://github.com/PacktPublishing/Data-Forecasting-and-
Segmentation-Using-Microsoft-Excel/blob/main/Chapter06/
kmeans3dplot01.r
```

In *Figure 6.4*, we pass the range parameter to the 3D function to plot the data. We are going to plot quantity, profit, and month:

	A	B	C	D	E	F	G
1	id	market	prodid	category	qty	profit	month
2	1	US	TEC-AC-10	Technolo	7	762.1845	7
3	2	APAC	TEC-PH-10	Technolo	9	919.971	10
4	3	Africa	TEC-SHA-1	Technolo	8	311.52	11
5	4	APAC	TEC-PH-10	Technolo	5	763.275	6
6	5	APAC	FUR-CH-1	Furniture	4	564.84	11
7	6	APAC	FUR-TA-1	Furniture	6	996.48	4
8	7	US	OFF-BI-10	Office Sup	5	1906.485	10
9	8	US	OFF-SU-10	Office Sup	5	83.281	4
10	9	APAC	FUR-TA-1	Furniture	5	647.55	4
11	10	EMEA	TEC-CIS-1	Technolo	4	1151.4	12
12	11	LATAM	FUR-CH-1	Furniture	7	622.02	11
13	12	APAC	OFF-AP-10	Office Sup	12	1036.08	6
14	13	EU	OFF-AP-10	Office Sup	4	186.948	7
15	14	US	TEC-AC-10	Technolo	9	517.4793	11
16	15	EU	OFF-AP-10	Office Sup	14	3979.08	9
17	16	APAC	TEC-CO-1	Technolo	9	28.404	1
18	17	Africa	OFF-KIT-1	Office Sup	6	818.28	12
19	18	EMEA	FUR-HON-	Furniture	4	276.84	8
20	19	US	TEC-PH-10	Technolo	6	341.994	10

```
3
4
5  #install.packages("scatterplot3d")
6  library("scatterplot3d")
7
8  rng <- EXCEL$Application$get_Range( "E2:G38073" )
9  X <- rng$get_Value()
10
11
12 scatterplot3d(x=X[,1],y=X[,2],z=X[,3])
13
```

Figure 6.4 – Parameter range for the 3D plot chart function E2:G38073

In *Figure 6.4*, we pass the range parameters of the data we want to chart. Plot three variables – quantity, profit, and month. Write this range in the sentence:

```
rng <- EXCEL$Application$get_Range( "E2:G38073" )
```

Then, follow these steps to execute the 3D chart function:

1. Right-click the function and choose the entire buffer.

2. Generate the chart in *Figure 6.5*.

3. Visualize the three variables, quantity, revenue, and month, from the 3D chart.

Remember that there is a large amount of data to process, so the function may require a few minutes to generate the 3D chart.

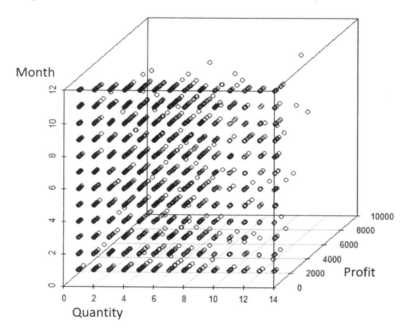

Figure 6.5 – 3D plot chart for profit, quantity, and month

From *Figure 6.5*, we can see the difficult task of visualizing the optimal number of groups for the data pertaining to revenue, quantity, and month. To get a quantitative number, we will run the Elbow function for these variables. *Figure 6.6* includes the parameters of the function to execute. Remember that it could take several minutes to complete the execution.

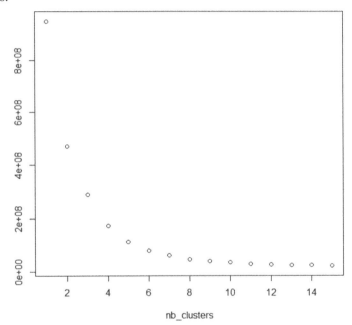

Figure 6.6 – Parameters of quantity, profit, and the month range for the Elbow function

Execute the function by right-clicking and choosing to execute the entire buffer. We are going to get the Elbow chart of the optimal number of groups for the profit, quantity, and month variables. The chart results can be seen in *Figure 6.6*. The execution could last several minutes.

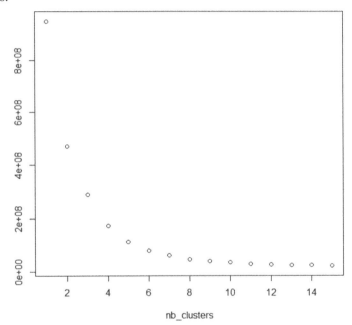

Figure 6.7 – Elbow chart for the optimal number of groups for revenue, quantity, and month

From *Figure 6.7*, we can see that, similar to the analysis involving two variables, seven is the optimal number of groups for the three variables. This number will be the input for the K-means function.

In these sections, we established the optimal number of groups for two and three variables. We can see that the Elbow charts for two and three variables are similar, and we identified seven as the best number of groups in both cases. We used the included Elbow function to perform these calculations. The number of groups is an input parameter for the K-means function to get the groups of two and three variables we will execute in the next section.

Determining the groups and average value (centroids) of two and three variables

Now that we know the optimal number of groups for two and three variables (revenue, quantity, and month) by running the Elbow function, we will perform these activities:

- Getting the groups with the K-means algorithm for two and three variables
- Visualizing centroids or the average value of each group for two and three variables
- Charting the product value range of each group for revenue, quantity, and month

For the revenue and quantity variables, we can visualize the minimum and maximum values of quantity for the best revenue group.

Also using three variables (revenue, quantity, and month of sale), we can explore which months of the year demand a higher quantity of products and what are the revenue ranges to see whether it is worth moving this large logistic operation to get the revenue.

Getting the groups with the K-means algorithm for two and three variables

We are going to calculate the range values of the seven groups for quantity and revenue. Use the kmeansworking01.r function included in the book to run the algorithm and pass the parameters, as in *Figure 6.8*. We are going to pass the number of groups to process (seven), the range of the input data, and the range where we want to save the results.

Figure 6.8 – Passing parameters to the K-means function

To execute the K-means function, follow these steps:

1. Pass the number of groups in cell G1 : G1. Write in this sentence:

```
rng <- EXCEL$Application$get_Range( "G1:G1" )
```

2. The input data of quantity and revenue range is in the range E2 : F38073. Write in this sentence:

```
rng <- EXCEL$Application$get_Range( "E2:F38073" )
```

3. The range to save the results of the K-means function is G2 : G38073. Write in this sentence:

```
rng <- EXCEL$Application$get_Range( "G2:G38073" )
```

Execute the function by right-clicking and choosing **Execute entire buffer**. It will take several minutes to finish.

Write the title GROUPS on the G1:G1 column to build the pivot table. The groups' chart can be seen in *Figure 6.9*. With this chart, we can have an idea of the value ranges for each of the seven groups.

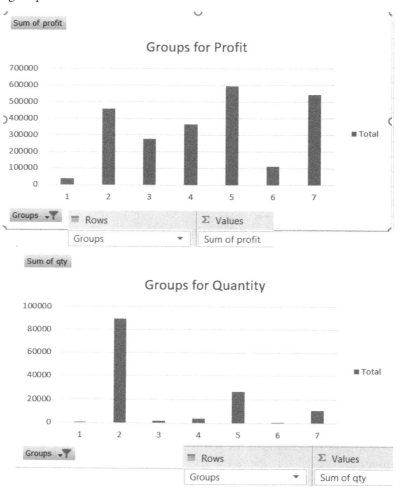

Figure 6.9 – Group values for revenue and quantity

From *Figure 6.9*, we move the sum of quantity and revenue for each chart because they have different measures and numeric scales. Remember that we are looking for the product group that generates more revenue with a smaller quantity because it has fewer logistical complications. In this case, the best profit group is number five and it occupies second place in terms of quantity group, meaning our most profitable group of products does not have a higher quantity of products. The most demanding quantity of products is group two. This group's profit requires more work for our company in terms of logistics.

We are going to explore what the products are for each group and the range of values in the next section.

Now, we will calculate the groups for three variables – quantity, revenue, and month. The optimal number of groups for three variables is also seven. We pass the parameters for the K-means function using *Figure 6.10* as a reference. With this information, we are going to identify which are the most profitable month groups.

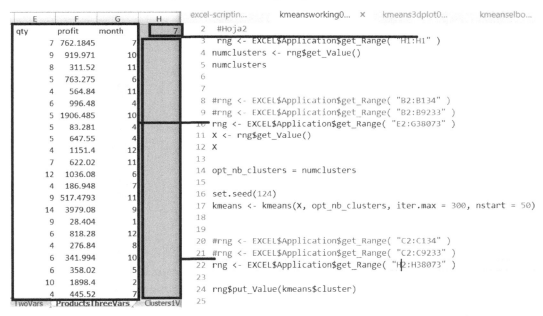

Figure 6.10 – Passing the parameters of month, revenue, and quantity to a K-means function

To execute the K-means function, follow these steps:

1. Pass the number of groups in cell G1:G1. Write in this sentence:

    ```
    rng <- EXCEL$Application$get_Range( "H1:H1" )
    ```

2. The input data of the quantity and revenue range is in the range E2:G38073. Write in this sentence:

    ```
    rng <- EXCEL$Application$get_Range( "E2:G38073" )
    ```

3. The range to save the results of the K-means function is H2:H38073. Write in this sentence:

    ```
    rng <- EXCEL$Application$get_Range( "H2:H38073" )
    ```

Execute the function by right-clicking and choosing **Execute entire buffer** in the options list. This will take some minutes to complete.

Once we have the results, write `Groups` in cell `H1:H1` to build the pivot table. The results can be seen in *Figure 6.11*. We are going to do a different chart for each variable due to different numeric scales. From these charts, we will identify the groups of interest to research how they relate to one another. In *Figure 6.11*, we have the groups for the quantity variable:

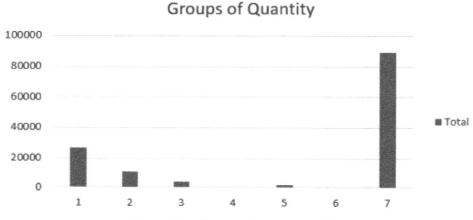

Figure 6.11 – Groups of quantity variables

From *Figure 6.11*, we can see that group number seven has the greatest quantity value of products delivered, followed by group one. The profit per month groups can be seen in *Figure 6.12*:

Figure 6.12 – Groups of profit variables

In *Figure 6.13*, we have the groups for the highest profit months of December, November, and September:

Figure 6.13 – Profit per month; groups for December, November, and September, along with groups for quantity

An analysis of three variables is more complex because we have to combine the results to get the groups with more revenue. Refer to the profit per month chart (second chart) of *Figure 6.12* and visualize that the most profitable months are December, November, and September. With these months, build a filter in the pivot table, and the third chart (*Figure 6.13*) shows that groups one, two, and seven are the most profitable for these months. From the chart of quantity groups (*Figure 6.11*), we see that one and two are not the groups with the greatest demands in terms of product quantities. We conclude that for the most profitable months (December, November, and September), we do not use all the available logistical resources, meaning that we are getting high profits without complex deliveries.

In this section, we explored the groups for two and three variables. We looked at the best-case scenario of maximum profit for the smallest quantity of products delivered and which months afforded the best revenue. In the next section, we are going to continue using pivot analysis to identify the products that comply with these conditions and what the profit and quantity value ranges are for these groups. At this point, you should realize that business intelligence analysis alone is not enough to obtain this information. It is necessary to apply machine learning with K-means to group our data and use several analysis variables.

Visualizing centroids or the average value of each group for two and three variables

Charting the centroids for each group and variable is important in identifying whether the data could have outliers or points that exhibit very different behavior from the rest of the information, which could lead to suspicious activity or the creation of subgroups to improve the segmentation. We will have to do a different centroid chart for each variable because of the different numeric scales. In *Figure 6.14*, we have the charts for two variables – profits and quantity. Check which groups could have outliers because the data has a large degree of separation in relation to its centroid:

Row Labels	Max of profit2	Average of profit	Min of profit2
1	8399.976	5376.550957	3919.9888
2	56.2032	16.02924808	0.036
3	1371.9804	901.9504238	698.4
4	694.5015	488.1729959	366.282
5	170.1	96.3464085	56.16
6	3177.475	1850.891361	1379.977
7	365.64	244.0722227	170.235

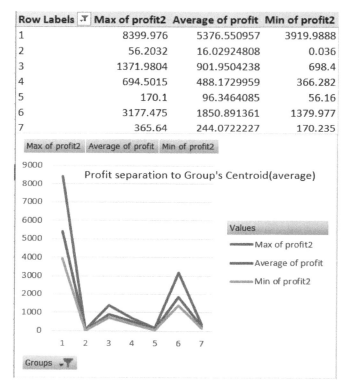

Figure 6.14 – Profit separation to the group's centroid or average

From *Figure 6.14*, we see that group number one has the highest profit level. It is not the same group as quantity. In terms of quantity, the largest value group is number seven (see *Figure 6.15*):

Row Labels ▼	Max of qty2	Average of qty	Min of qty3
1	14	6.857142857	3
2	14	3.123471925	1
3	14	6.202614379	2
4	14	5.476697736	1
5	14	4.325942709	1
6	14	7.704918033	2
7	14	4.75168995	1
Grand Total	**14**	**3.492724312**	**1**

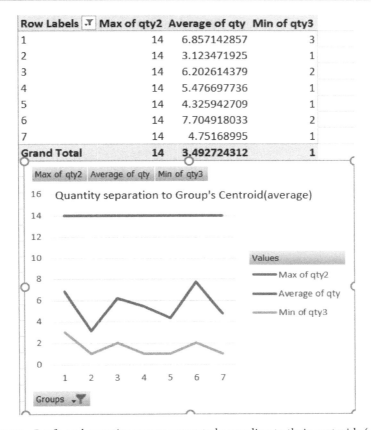

Figure 6.15 – Profit and quantity groups separated according to their centroids (average)

From *Figure 6.15*, we see the group's data separation into their centroids (average) of profit and quantity. The first chart, profit, shows that groups one, three, and six have greater separation from their centroids. The second chart, quantity, provides evidence that groups two, five, and seven have the most scattered data. As regards quantity, the upper value is 14 for all groups. The difference is the lowest value, which varies in all the groups. We don't have the same groups with scattered data for the two variables. One approach to this is to choose the profit's bigger separation group, number one (see *Figure 6.14*), and create subgroups for it. With this operation, we will better classify this group, which has large amounts of scattered data. To create a subgroup of group one, select the data for just this group. Then, apply the same procedure we have used. Find the optimal number of groups and then run the K-means function. The subgroup results are just for group number one. Each subgroup will have a smaller separation from its centroids because we are processing fewer data values.

Next, we will create the charts of centroids and the data separation for the groups of three variables – profits, quantity, and month (see *Figure 6.13*). Combine the profits, group, and month to get the most profitable season and the groups with less separation to the centroid. Then, we will use the quantity variable to see the months and groups that demand more of our logistical operation and also have less separation from the centroids.

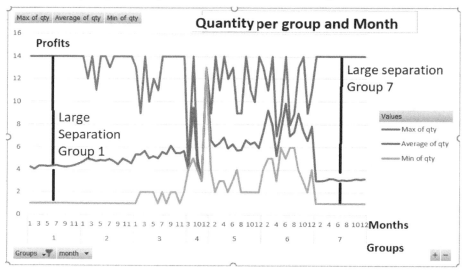

Figure 6.16 – Profits and quantity per month and groups

The first profits, groups, and months chart of *Figure 6.16* shows that groups four, five, and six have greater separation from the centroids. Look at the distance from the maximum and minimum range to the average. Also, groups four, five, and six are the groups with the highest profits. In the next section, we will explore what the products are with these higher profits that belong to these groups. In the second chart of *Figure 6.16*, covering quantity, month, and profits, we see that groups one and seven have a larger distance between the minimum and maximum ranges of the centroids. So, these groups will likely need a process to create subgroups to focus just on this data.

In this section, we examined the distance between the maximum and minimum ranges of two and three variables to the centroids of each group to ascertain whether the group is a possible anomaly/outlier or whether these groups need another process to create subgroups and close the distance to the scattered data. In the next section, we are going to explore the products that are generating higher profits and quantities that demand more of the logistical infrastructure. So far, we can conclude that the most profitable groups are not delivering the largest quantity of products. This is a good scenario because we want to generate profits using a less complex logistical infrastructure.

Charting the product value range of each group for revenue, quantity, and month

Now, we are going to research what products are behind the groups with higher profits and that require the delivery of greater quantities, and those months in the season where we see our logistics and profits grow. It is important to write that we are going to keep an eye on those products with higher profits because we will perform a time series analysis in a future chapter to explore whether we can do a machine learning forecast for these sales.

The first task is to look at which groups have higher profits. Then, we are going to explore the months for these groups and identify the most profitable season. From here, we are going to display which products generate higher revenue during peak season. See *Figure 6.17* to identify the groups with the highest revenue:

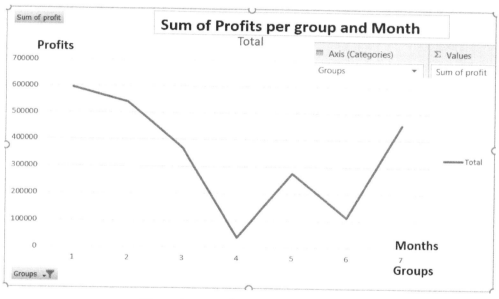

Figure 6.17 – Profits per group and month

From *Figure 6.17*, we can see that groups one and two are the highest profit groups. Within these two groups, we are going to display the months that exhibit the best profit performance. This analysis can be seen in *Figure 6.18*. These months are the best-selling season for our business:

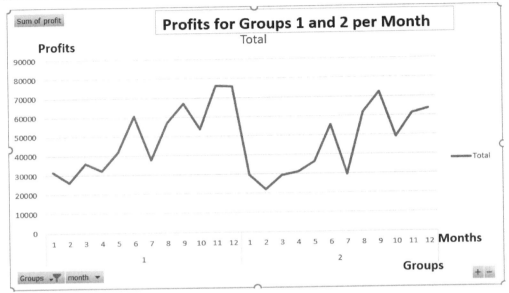

Figure 6.18 – Profits for groups 1 and 2 per month

This analysis of the higher profit groups one and two per month displays the following:

- **Group number one**: The most profitable months are November and December.
- **Group number two**: The most profitable months are September and December.

With this information for each group and month, we are ready to see which products in each group are our company's best-sellers (see *Figure 6.19*):

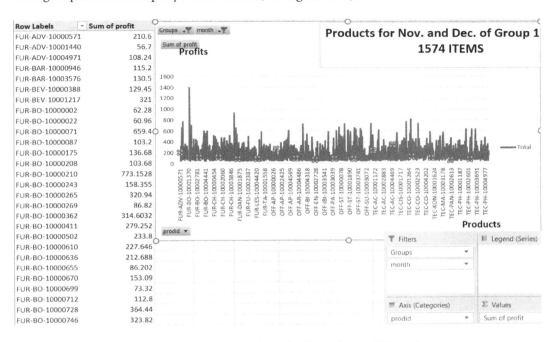

Row Labels	Sum of profit
FUR-ADV-10000571	210.6
FUR-ADV-10001440	56.7
FUR-ADV-10004971	108.24
FUR-BAR-10000946	115.2
FUR-BAR-10003576	130.5
FUR-BEV-10000388	129.45
FUR-BEV-10001217	321
FUR-BO-10000002	62.28
FUR-BO-10000022	60.96
FUR-BO-10000071	659.40
FUR-BO-10000087	103.2
FUR-BO-10000175	136.68
FUR-BO-10000208	103.68
FUR-BO-10000210	773.1528
FUR-BO-10000243	158.355
FUR-BO-10000265	320.94
FUR-BO-10000269	86.82
FUR-BO-10000362	314.6032
FUR-BO-10000411	279.252
FUR-BO-10000502	233.8
FUR-BO-10000610	227.646
FUR-BO-10000636	212.688
FUR-BO-10000655	86.202
FUR-BO-10000670	153.09
FUR-BO-10000699	73.32
FUR-BO-10000712	112.8
FUR-BO-10000728	364.44
FUR-BO-10000746	323.82

Figure 6.19 – Group 1 products for November and December

For group one and the higher profit months of November and December, we identify 1,574 products in *Figure 6.19*. We can continue creating subgroups inside this information until we get whatever details we want. The important concept here is that the K-means function helps to segment the big data of our company. For group two, we can see *Figure 6.20*:

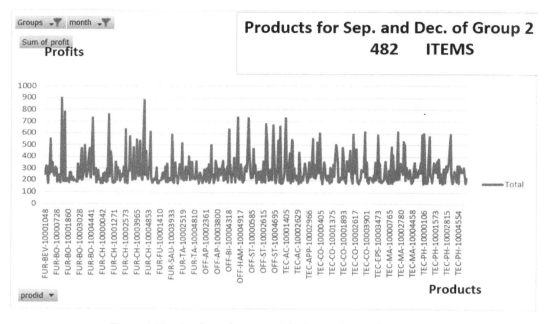

Figure 6.20 – Products for group 2 for September and December

Figure 6.20 shows that for group two for the months of September and December, there are 482 highest revenue items.

In conclusion, we have the highest groups, for the highest season (September, November, and December), and the products that belong to this segment. With this information, we can prepare a better marketing strategy of continuing a more detailed segmentation analysis using K-means.

We are going to remember the products in the highest revenue group, group one, because we are going to apply this information as input to a time series analysis and see whether we can forecast the revenue for future years.

We can apply the same approach to find the groups that demand higher quantities of products and the months when this is the case. Then, we can extract the data of the products that are sold in greater quantities and that use more logistical resources. See *Figure 6.21* for the quantity per group. Remember that we have identified that the most profitable products are *not* those that are sold in greater quantities.

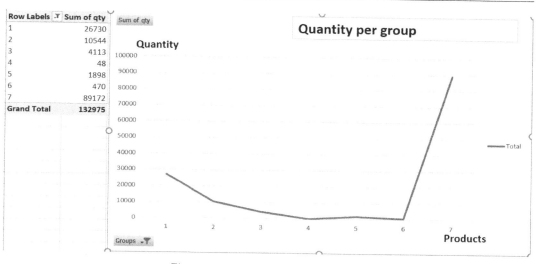

Figure 6.21 – Quantity sold per group

Figure 6.21 states that group seven is by far the group that sells the most products. Look at *Figure 6.17* and visualize that group seven occupies third place in terms of revenue. This means that we have higher profits but with smaller quantities of products sold, as you can see from the group one data in *Figure 6.18*.

Now, we are going to visualize which months are the most demanding for group seven in terms of having an idea of the seasons of the year when we have to be ready with logistics to deliver the items. This information is available in *Figure 6.22*:

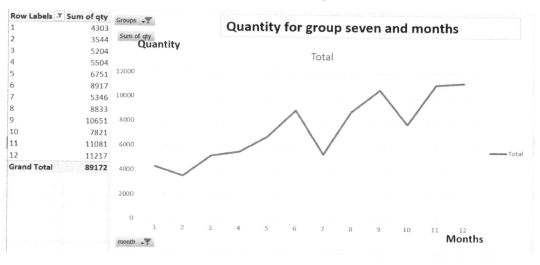

Figure 6.22 – Quantity for group seven per month

In *Figure 6.22*, for the sales months of group seven, we see that November and December are the months with the most demanding logistical structures. Next, in *Figure 6.23*, we will explore which products we are delivering during these months for group number seven:

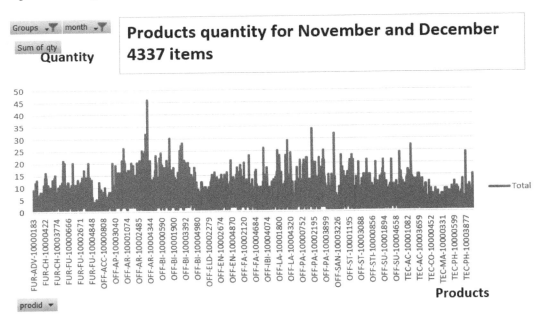

Figure 6.23 – Products of group seven quantities delivered for November and December

For the group seven products for November and December, we can see that we deliver a total of 4,337 items, which demands logistical resources for these months. Remember *Figure 6.19*, where the group with the highest profit, group one, delivers 1,574 items, a much smaller quantity than group seven for these months. This means that our best revenue group does not demand a large effort from the point of view of logistics. This information indicates that we must improve group number seven to generate delivery savings for these demanding months.

In this chapter, we explore the groups that generate more revenue and the group that demands more logistic effort although that does not mean it generates enough profit. This is the case of group number one, which has the highest profit but does not require the largest logistic infrastructure because it delivers 1,574 items, compared with group number seven for November and December, which delivers 4,337 items. This type of information is thanks to the three-variable K-means analysis with revenue, quantity, and month. In the next section, we will include a fourth variable in the K-means. We will use the shipping cost. With this variable, we will compare how logistics influence the profits of our business.

Using the Elbow and K-means functions with four variables

Now, we are going to add a fourth variable, the shipping cost, to the analysis. With this information, we will explore the influence of the logistics demanding infrastructure on the profits of the company. Remember that we pursue to get more revenue without investing more in fixed costs such as delivery operations. We will apply our knowledge of the Elbow and K-means functions to get the optimal number of groups, and then get the segmentation with K-means. See *Figure 6.24* where the elbow function returns the number of groups. There is no chance to plot a chart of four variables, so we will have to trust in our expertise and judgment to interpret the groups that K-means will return.

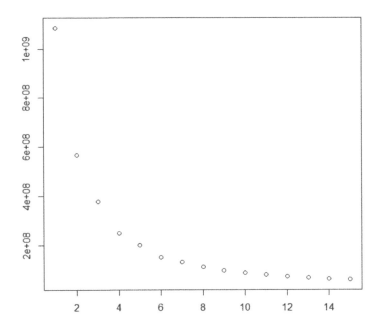

Figure 6.24 – Elbow chart for four variables

In *Figure 6.24*, we can see that the optimal number of groups for the four variables (revenue, month, quantity, and shipping costs) is eight because this is when the curve starts to flatten. It is one group more compared with the analysis involving two and three variables in the previous sections.

Figure 6.25 shows the shipping costs for every group. We have to know whether the shipping costs affect the most profitable group or the group that delivers the greatest number of items.

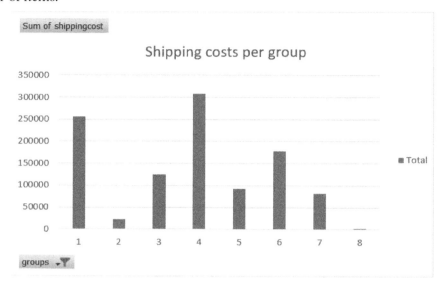

Figure 6.25 – Shipping cost per group

Figure 6.25 shows that the most expensive group in terms of logistics costs is group number four. The highest revenue group (one) is not the most expensive from the point of view of logistics costs, and group seven, which delivers the highest quantity of items, is not the most expensive in terms of shipping either.

Then, we explore which months are more expensive as regards shipping within group number four to prepare the cash flow (see *Figure 6.26*):

Figure 6.26 – Shipping costs per month

Group number four demands a higher cash flow to pay for shipping costs in November and December. We have to explore the product's dimensions and weight and the destination because the group that delivers the greater number of items is group number seven, but it is not the most expensive in terms of logistics costs. The products for group number four in November and December can be seen in *Figure 6.27*:

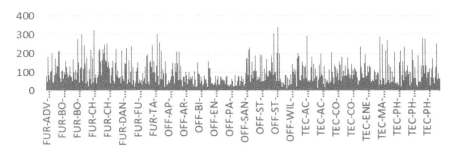

Figure 6.27 – Shipping costs for group four and the number of items delivered

We see from *Figure 6.27* that group number four delivers 1,296 items and is the most expensive group in terms of shipping costs. Compare this with group seven, which delivers 4,337 items, and is not the most expensive group. We conclude that group four is not the product with the highest revenue, nor does it deliver the greatest quantity of items, but it is the most expensive. We should review the dimensions and weight and the origin-destination of these products to see whether we can lower these high shipping costs.

In this section, we did a four-variable grouping analysis. This is a complex approach because there is no opportunity to chart the data; we have to trust our experience to see whether the K-means function is returning the correct information. The fourth variable breaks much of what we concluded previously about the revenue and quantity because the most expensive group in terms of logistics costs is a group that delivers fewer items than group seven, which has the highest number. We have to apply our experience to find the correct answers once we do the business intelligence analysis involving a pivot table and charts. Because we have to combine four variables and get a sense of the results, it is not possible to find the answers with just one chart. We are going to keep these results of products, revenue, and month of sale because we will apply a time series analysis to see whether we can forecast sales in the future. In the next chapter, we will use K-means to establish outliers and apply this to anomaly detection and fraud.

Summary

In this chapter, we applied the Elbow and K-means functions to find the optimal number of groups and segments for two and three variables. Once we obtained the results, we did a business intelligence analysis using pivot tables and charts. In the product sales example developed in this chapter, we used segmentation to find the groups that generated higher revenues and what quantity of items were delivered. Grouping helps to achieve the target of selling smaller quantities of products to avoid logistics costs. The four variables segmentation analysis showed that the group with the highest revenue was not the group delivering more items, nor was it the most expensive in terms of shipping costs. Multivariable K-means segmentation helps to do this complex analysis, which would be impossible with just business intelligence and pivot tables and charts. In this chapter, you learned to combine different variables with different units, such as quantity and profit, to research which groups require more logistical resources and represent more profit for the company. It is not possible to have all this information in just one chart. You could see that the multivariable grouping analysis required the combination of several pivot analyses of business intelligence. In the next chapter, we will use K-means in another way to locate anomalies and detect fraud.

Questions and answers

Test your knowledge by reviewing these questions and answers by remembering the importance of a smart build of pivot tables for business intelligence in group segmentation:

1. Can we include two different variable group analyses in a single pivot chart?
2. What is the best-case scenario for product revenue within a company?
3. What information can we derive from revenue and the month of sales once we find the segments?
4. What is the advantage of segmentation in sales quantities?
5. What could be the reason why a group has the highest shipping costs but does not deliver the highest quantity of items?

Answers

Here are the answers to the preceding questions:

1. No. The variables would be of different numeric dimensions.

2. To achieve higher revenue by selling smaller quantities of items to avoid logistics costs.

3. We can use time series to build a forecast of sales in subsequent years.

4. We can optimize inventory management by understanding which groups have a higher product rotation and at what time of the year.

5. Reasons could include the product's dimension and weight and the origin and destination. A group with these characteristics could affect the profits of the company if it does not adopt the correct approach.

Further reading

To further understand the concepts of this chapter, refer to the following sources:

*   Applied unsupervised learning with R:

    ```
    https://www.packtpub.com/product/applied-unsupervised-
    learning-with-r/9781789956399
    ```

*   Advanced machine learning with Python:

    ```
    https://subscription.packtpub.com/book/big_data_and_
    business_intelligence/9781784398637/1/ch01lvl1sec11/
    introducing-k-means-clustering
    ```

*   Customer segmentation using K-means clustering:

    ```
    https://towardsdatascience.com/customer-segmentation-
    using-k-means-clustering-d33964f238c3
    ```

7
Analyzing Outliers for Data Anomalies

In this chapter, we are going to use the K-means grouping function to find the outliers of three of the most used datasets in Kaggle: credit card fraud detection, suspicious logins, and insurance money amount complaints.

2D and 3D charts help us to understand the possible outliers that could lead to fraud in credit card transactions, possible security breaches in login attempts, and the special cases that demand more money from insurance companies.

The methodology of this chapter is to visualize the outliers in charting 2D and 3D variables to get familiar with the data and find possible out-of-the-ordinary behavior and the possible number of groups. Then, we'll use pivot chart business intelligence to classify the ranges of the groups and identify the groups and variables that lead to outliers.

With these practical datasets, we will get experience in applying the K-means function add-in of Excel to other real data. This chapter demands knowledge of how to use the K-means function add-in process in Excel included in the book.

This chapter will cover the following topics:

- Representing the data in a 3D chart
- K-means data grouping
- Pivot analysis of the outliers

Let's begin by looking at the prerequisites of this chapter in the next section.

Technical requirements

Download the Excel files for this chapter using the following links:

- For credit card transactions, go to the following:

  ```
  https://github.com/PacktPublishing/Data-Forecasting-and-
  Segmentation-Using-Microsoft-Excel/blob/main/Chapter07/
  creditcard01.xlsx
  ```

- For insurance money complaints, go to the following:

  ```
  https://github.com/PacktPublishing/Data-Forecasting-and-
  Segmentation-Using-Microsoft-Excel/blob/main/Chapter07/
  insurance.xlsx
  ```

- For suspicious logins, go to the following:

  ```
  https://github.com/PacktPublishing/Data-Forecasting-and-
  Segmentation-Using-Microsoft-Excel/blob/main/Chapter07/
  suspiciuslogins.xlsx
  ```

Representing the data in a 3D chart

The first example is to apply our knowledge of grouping to find the outliers as possible candidates for research on fraud. For example, we could identify outliers with small amounts of spending and very early transaction hours across 6 consecutive days. This behavior will probably not correspond to the average amount of and typical working hours of transactions.

Kaggle credit card fraud dataset

The credit card fraud data has several columns:

- The number of seconds since the first transaction was recorded in the dataset.

- The amount expended by the cardholder.
- The V1 to V12 columns represent encrypted data to protect the original information. These are numerical fields, and the K-means algorithm can classify these values into groups.

The only true values of the data are seconds and amount. The V1 to V2 fields have data alteration with encryption techniques for privacy measures.

We are going to perform statistical grouping into three fields:

- The amount expended by the cardholder
- The V1 field with numerical encrypted data
- The number of seconds since the first transaction in records to find the outliers of the data and provide a clue that could indicate possible fraud

The steps to perform the statistical grouping of the credit card fraud data are as follows:

1. Explore the possible grouping using a 3D chart of the Amount, V1, and Time (in seconds) since the first transaction fields.
2. Run the elbow K-means algorithm add-in for Excel to get the optimal number of groups of the data.
3. Run the K-means algorithm with the number of optimal groups to assign the clusters to every row of data.
4. Chart the maximum, average (centroid), and minimum values of the Amount and V1 fields. The number of seconds since the first transaction is not relevant for the analysis.

With this information, we can find the possible outlier group of the amount expended and V1. Look for groups with high-value separation between the minimum and maximum values and the group centroid. Remember that the best-case scenario for grouping is to have compact clusters. In the next section, we are going to visualize the Amount and Time fields with the V1 data field in a 3D chart to understand what the possible groups and outliers of the dataset are.

Creating a 3D chart of amount, V1, and time (number of seconds)

The following 3D chart indicates that the possible outliers of the Amount field are the small values. The majority of amount records have high values at the top of the amount axis. We can identify four different groups in the Amount field:

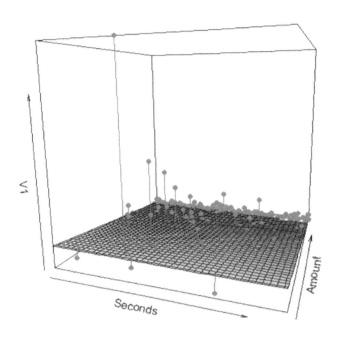

Figure 7.1 – 3D chart of V1, seconds, and amount of credit card transactions

In *Figure 7.1*, we can identify a uniquely large value for the V1 field, which could indicate an anomaly. The V1 field is a numerical datatype. Then, some small values are below the regression line. The majority of points of V1 have small values on the V1 axis, combined with high values on the Amount axis. There is another group of medium values of V1. Based on these descriptions of the 3D chart explained before, there are four possible groups for the V1 field.

Kaggle suspicious logins

We will try to identify the outliers of this dataset with the number of packets and the duration of each one for every login attempt.

We will follow the same methodology we used with the credit card dataset:

1. Chart the packets and duration variables.
2. Calculate the optimal number of groups using the elbow function.
3. Run the K-means add-in for Excel to assign the group to each record.
4. Perform the `PivotTable` analysis for each group for the number of packets and duration variables.

The 2D chart of the number of packets and duration is shown in *Figure 7.2*. Identify the groups and the possible outliers that could lead to a suspicious login attempt and a breach in the system security:

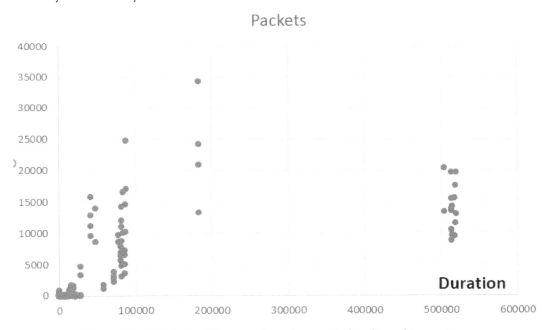

Figure 7.2 – 3D chart of V1, seconds, and amount of credit card transactions

The chart shows clear outliers with a high duration value. Also, there are a high number of packets with a middle duration value. From *Figure 7.2*, we can see that the data splits into three groups. The group that appears to be the outlier has a high time duration login attempt.

Kaggle insurance money amount complaints

We will analyze the incidence of age and **body mass index** (**BMI**) in insurance money complaints. Using this dataset, we will find out which value ranges of BMI and age create outliers in insurance requests.

The 3D chart in *Figure 7.3* shows that the largest money demands happen with a high BMI, no matter the age range:

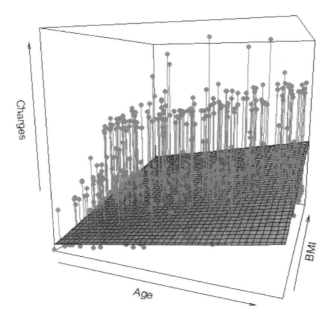

Figure 7.3 – Insurance charges by age and BMI

We can identify five groups to classify. We will confirm this number with the elbow function in the next section before we run the K-means algorithm.

In this section, we learned how 3D and 2D charts help to identify the potential outliers and the number of groups, which we will confirm with the elbow function. We have to indicate to the K-means algorithm how many groups we need to classify. For that, use the elbow function, which returns the curve line of the number of groups for the data. The best number is where the curve starts to flatten. In the case of *Figure 7.5*, for example, the number is five. In the next section, we will run the K-means algorithm, but first, we will use the elbow process to get the optimal number of groups.

K-means data grouping

Before running the K-means function, we need to calculate the parameter of the optimal number of groups. In the last section, we saw that the first approach is to visualize the 2D and 3D charts. However, the best way to get the number of groups is by calculating the elbow function and choosing the number of groups when the curve of the elbow starts to flatten.

Running the elbow algorithm

Now that we have an idea of the number of groups for the credit card fraud dataset, we are ready to use the elbow K-means algorithm to get a statistical value of the optimal number of groups.

Kaggle credit card fraud dataset

Before we run the K-means function, we have to calculate the optimal number of groups for the `V1`, `Time` (seconds), and `Amount` fields of the credit card transactions.

We run the elbow algorithm, changing the range of data in line 3 of the `kmeanselbow.r` add-in, as you can see in *Figure 7.4*. Use the `credicard01.xlsx` file included in this chapter's GitHub repository:

	A	B	C	D
284787	172768	0.032887	1.79	0
284788	172768	-2.07617	8.95	0
284789	172769	-1.02972	9.99	0
284790	172770	2.007418	3.99	0
284791	172770	-0.44695	60.5	0
284792	172771	-0.51551	9.81	0
284793	172774	-0.86351	20.32	0
284794	172774	-0.72412	3.99	0
284795	172775	1.971002	4.99	0
284796	172777	-1.26658	0.89	0
284797	172778	-12.5167	9.87	0
284798	172780	1.884849	60	0
284799	172782	-0.24192	5.49	0
284800	172782	0.219529	24.05	0
284801	172783	-1.77513	79.99	0
284802	172784	2.03956	2.68	0
284803	172785	0.120316	2.69	0
284804	172786	-11.8811	0.77	0
284805	172787	-0.73279	24.79	0
284806	172788	1.919565	67.88	0
284807	172788	-0.24044	10	0
284808	172792	-0.53341	217	0

```
BERT Console
File  Edit  View  Packages  Help
excel-script...     kmeansworkin...     kmeans3dplo...     kmea
1  #Hoja2
2
3  rng <- EXCEL$Application$get_Range( "A2:C284808" )
4  #rng <- EXCEL$Application$get_Range( "B2:B9233" )
5  #rng <- EXCEL$Application$get_Range( "B2:B103" )
6  X <- rng$get_Value()
7  X
8  set.seed(123)
```

Figure 7.4 – Running the elbow function add-in for Excel

The function with data from *Figure 7.4* returns the optimal number of groups. We choose the value where the curve starts to flatten, shown in *Figure 7.5*:

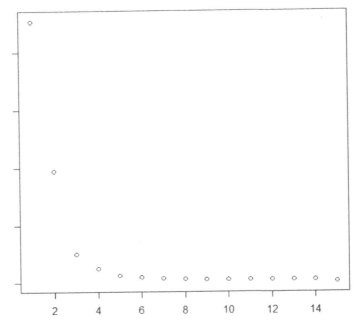

Figure 7.5 – Elbow chart for V1, seconds, and amount of data of credit card

The elbow says that the optimal number of groups is five. It is one more than we predicted from the 3D chart for the Amount and V1 fields.

In this subsection, we ran the elbow function to get the optimal number of groups of credit card transactions. We'll use this number as an input value to the K-means function that we will run in the next step. K-means assigns the groups to every record of the dataset. The elbow function in *Figure 7.5* shows that the optimal number of groups is three, the same as we predicted in the 2D chart previously, in *Figure 7.2*.

Kaggle suspicious logins

We can see that the elbow function for the suspicious login dataset in *Figure 7.6* gets flattened very fast, starting at three. That gives more evidence that the optimal number of groups for this data is three:

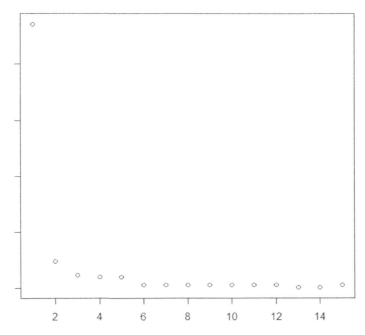

Figure 7.6 – Elbow chart for suspicious login dataset

The majority of packet numbers have a number between 0 and 15,000 and a duration of fewer than 100,000 milliseconds. Then, we have a group with a duration of 200,000 milliseconds. The outlier is a duration of above 500,000 milliseconds. These are the three groups detected by the elbow function in *Figure 7.6*.

Kaggle insurance money amount complaints

The elbow chart in *Figure 7.7* indicates five as the optimal number of groups:

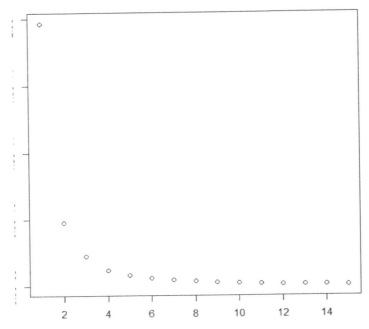

Figure 7.7 – Elbow chart for Kaggle insurance money amount complaints

This is a case where it is better to use the elbow function to get the optimal number of groups because, in the case of the 3D chart (*Figure 7.3*) with the Charges, Age, and BMI variables, it is difficult to visualize the number of groups for all this data.

Running the K-means function

Once we have the optimal number of groups for the credit card fraud dataset, we are ready to run the K-means algorithm for the three fields, using Amount, Time (seconds), and V1 as input to classify the data.

Kaggle credit card fraud dataset

The K-means function assigns a group to every transaction of the credit card dataset. We then analyze the V1 and Amount records to find the outliers of the transactions. We run the K-means function, writing the number of groups to assign on cell E1:E1 of the Excel sheet. Then, we change line 3 of the K-means function to E1:E1. You can see the input parameters in *Figure 7.8* with the K-means function code:

	A	B	C	D	E
1	Time	V1	Amount	Class	5
2	0	-1.35981	149.62	0	5
3	0	1.191857	2.69	0	1
4	1	-1.35835	378.66	0	3
5	1	-0.96627	123.5	0	5
6	2	-1.15823	69.99	0	1
7	2	-0.42597	3.67	0	1
8	4	1.229658	4.99	0	1
9	7	-0.64427	40.8	0	1
10	7	-0.89429	93.2	0	5
11	9	-0.33826	3.68	0	1
12	10	1.449044	7.8	0	1
13	10	0.384978	9.99	0	1
14	10	1.249999	121.5	0	5
15	11	1.069374	27.5	0	1
16	12	-2.79185	58.8	0	1
17	12	-0.75242	15.99	0	1
18	12	1.103215	12.99	0	1
19	13	-0.43691	0.89	0	1
20	14	-5.40126	46.8	0	1
21	15	1.492936	5	0	1
22	16	0.694885	231.71	0	5
23	17	0.962496	34.09	0	1

```
excel-script...        kmeansworkin...  ●      kmeans3dplo...         kmeanselb...  ●   ...  ●
 1
 2  . #Hoja2
 3  rng <- EXCEL$Application$get_Range( "E1:E1" )
 4  numclusters <- rng$get_Value()
 5  numclusters
 6   |
 7
 8  #rng <- EXCEL$Application$get_Range( "B2:B134" )
 9  #rng <- EXCEL$Application$get_Range( "B2:B9233" )
10  rng <- EXCEL$Application$get_Range( "A2:C284808" )
11  X <- rng$get_Value()
12  X
13
14  opt_nb_clusters = numclusters
15
16  set.seed(124)
17  kmeans <- kmeans(X, opt_nb_clusters, iter.max = 300, nstart = 50)
18
19
20  #rng <- EXCEL$Application$get_Range( "C2:C134" )
21  #rng <- EXCEL$Application$get_Range( "C2:C9233" )
22  rng <- EXCEL$Application$get_Range( "E2:E284808" )
23
```

Figure 7.8 – Running the K-means function add-in for Excel

Look at *Figure 7.8* and how the number of groups input parameter in line 3 is set to the cell E1:E1. On line 10, we set the range of the dataset to A2:C284808. The groups are stored in the range E2:E284808 set in line 22.

So far in this chapter, we ran the elbow function to find the optimal number of groups. Then, we used this number to run the K-means function. This function saved the groups for every record in column E (see *Figure 7.8*). With this information, we can do a pivot analysis of the outliers in the next section.

For the suspicious logins and insurance amount claims, we run the K-means function using the same procedure that we applied to the credit card dataset.

In this section, we learned how to calculate the elbow function to get the optimal number of groups and the K-means function to assign the groups to each record for the following:

- Credit card transactions
- Suspicious logins
- Insurance money amount claims

In the next section, we will see how to do pivot analysis with business intelligence to find out what the possible group outliers of the data are.

Pivot analysis of the outliers

We can apply the business intelligence pivot tables to explore the ranges of the groups for every variable of the dataset. Using this method, we can visualize the groups that appear to be outliers.

Kaggle credit card fraud dataset

With the information of the group assignment with K-means clustering, we can explore the outliers for each dataset. From the amount chart of credit card transactions in *Figure 7.9*, we see that groups three and four have compact and similar values with a combined range between 355 and 1402:

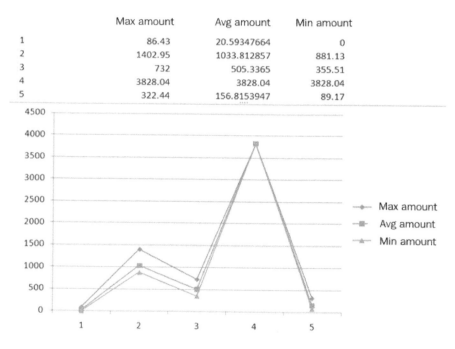

	Max amount	Avg amount	Min amount
1	86.43	20.59347664	0
2	1402.95	1033.812857	881.13
3	732	505.3365	355.51
4	3828.04	3828.04	3828.04
5	322.44	156.8153947	89.17

Figure 7.9 – Credit card amount field groups

From *Figure 7.9*, we could conclude that the possible outliers are as follows:

- Group 1 (ranges between 0 and 86)
- Group 5 (ranges between 89 and 322)
- Group 4 (has just one record with a big value of 3828, which indicates an anomaly)

Combining the analysis with the V1 field groups, in *Figure 7.10*, we can examine whether we can confirm the outliers by the Amount groups or V1:

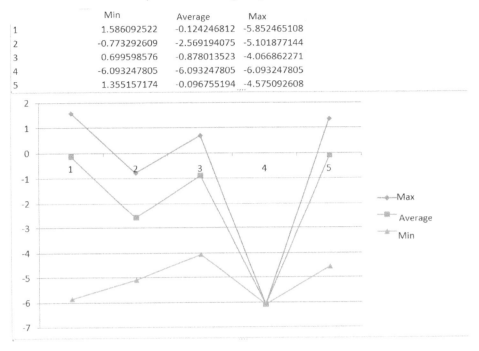

	Min	Average	Max
1	1.586092522	-0.124246812	-5.852465108
2	-0.773292609	-2.569194075	-5.101877144
3	0.699598576	-0.878013523	-4.066862271
4	-6.093247805	-6.093247805	-6.093247805
5	1.355157174	-0.096755194	-4.575092608

Figure 7.10 – Credit card V1 field groups

The groups with similar characteristics in the amount field are two and three. In the case of V1, we see that the average or centroids have similar values but both groups have large distances of minimum and maximum values from the average, concluding that these clusters are not compact and do not have similar behavior compared with the Amount value. The Amount outlier groups one and five have a large value separation for the V1 field. In this case, V1 could support the evidence that groups one and five are outliers.

Group four has a single big value for Amount and a small value for V1. For sure, it is a transaction with anomalies. Group four has a small V1 value of -6.04.

In this section, we review the results of the credit card transactions dataset. The Amount values in groups indicate that groups one and five are outliers. The V1 values for groups one and five show a large separation and could confirm that they are outliers. For sure, group number four, with just one big value for Amount and a low value for V1, is an outlier. In the next section, we will review the suspicious logins groups dataset.

Kaggle suspicious logins

After running the K-means function, we plot the groups for the following with pivot tables:

- Number of packets
- Duration of packets of each login attempt

In the time duration groups chart in *Figure 7.11* (groupsduration.png), we identify that group number one has the highest value, as we visualized in the 2D chart:

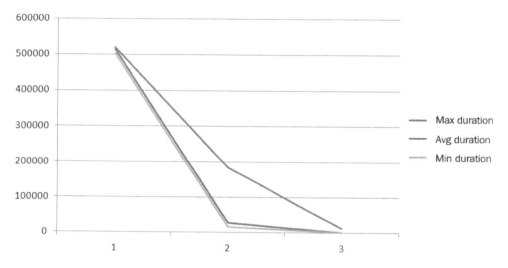

Figure 7.11 – Duration groups for suspicious login

This group, in *Figure 7.11*, is compact with the maximum and minimum close to the average or centroid value. Having a high time duration compared to groups two and three presents this group as an outlier. This prompts us to research whether these login attempts represent suspicious events.

Combining the information with the number of packet groups in *Figure 7.12*, again, group one gives evidence of outlier behavior:

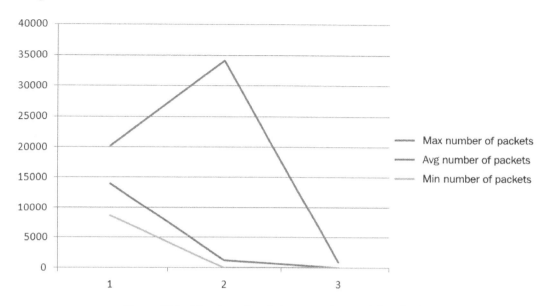

Figure 7.12 – Number of packets groups for suspicious login

The average number of packets is higher in group one than in groups two and three. Also, group one's number of packets is not compact because the maximum and minimum values are far off from the group centroid.

With this evidence, we conclude that group one's time duration and the number of packets of logins make it an outlier. The stronger fact for this conclusion is the high value of time duration compared with groups two and three.

In this section, we analyzed the outliers of suspicious logins, concluding that group one is an outlier because it has a high number of packets and duration. In the next section, we will do the pivot analysis of the insurance money amount complaints.

Kaggle insurance money amount complaints

The insurance group charges in *Figure 7.13* indicate group five has the highest money claims:

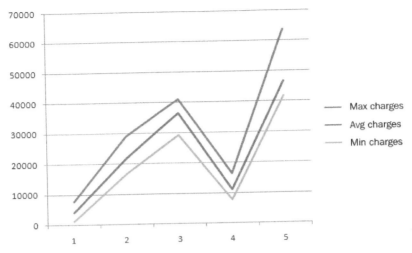

Figure 7.13 – Charges insurance groups

Using this information, we are going to research what the behavior of group five with the other variables, age and BMI, is.

With the BMI insurance groups chart in *Figure 7.14*, we confirm that group five has the highest range value of BMI:

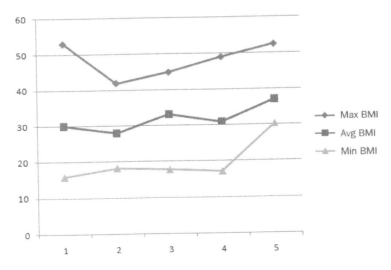

Figure 7.14 – BMI insurance groups

In *Figure 7.14*, we see the maximum and minimum BMI values of group five have a large distance from its centroid, so it is not a compact group, but all the groups have a higher BMI value with a range between 30 and 50.

The age insurance group chart in *Figure 7.15* confirms that group five has a large distance between the maximum and minimum values and the average or centroid of the group:

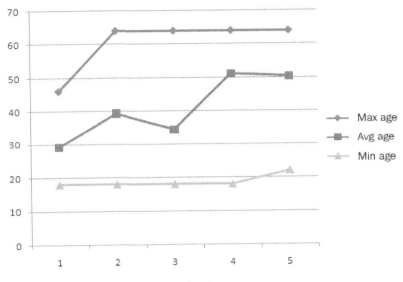

Figure 7.15 – Age insurance groups

This confirms our first impression that insurance complaints depend more on the BMI than on the age of the clients. The age range for group five is between 20 and 65 years old, according to *Figure 7.15*.

In this section, we analyzed the ranges that are out of the *normal* behavior of data and could indicate they are outliers. In the examples we worked on, the outliers could be as follows:

- Credit card fraud
- Security breach in the login attempts
- The group with more money complaints to the insurance companies

In the next chapter, we are going to learn how to determine whether two variables have a relationship to build a predictive model with their data.

Summary

In this chapter, we applied our knowledge of grouping statistics to three of the most used Kaggle datasets. We learned that credit card transaction fraud could be analyzed by amounts that are out of the scope of regular transaction money payments. The K-means grouping algorithm can be applied to find out what the quantity and duration of the packets in login attempts are to find out whether there is suspicious login activity or not. Finally, the K-means function can help to conclude that age is not an important factor for money complaints. It is more important to keep the BMI under low-risk levels than the age of an insurance company's clients.

In the next chapter, we are going to build a prediction model based on the possible relationship between two variables.

Questions

Here are a few questions and their answers to revisit what we have learned in this chapter:

1. Why is it a good idea to plot a 2D or 3D chart before the elbow calculation?
2. What was the suspicious behavior of the login attempts developed in this chapter?
3. Describe a possible heuristic process to identify an outlier.
4. Is age a risk factor for the insurance data explored here?
5. What was the variable used in the credit card dataset to explore the outliers?

Answers

Here are the answers to the preceding questions:

1. Because we can visualize the possible outliers and the value range that is outside of the normal behavior of the data.
2. Identify the group with different behavior in one of the variables of the dataset using pivot tables. Explore whether this same group has suspicious behavior compared to the rest of the variables analyzed.
3. No, the most important factor is BMI. Age is not relevant for the number of complaints to the insurance company.
4. High duration of a medium number of packets.
5. The variable used was the money expended. The outlier was confirmed by the V1 variable.

Further reading

To further understand the concepts of this chapter, you can refer to the following sources:

- *Credit Card Fraud Detection using K-Means and KNN*:

  https://www.kaggle.com/isaikumar/credit-card-fraud-detection-using-k-means-and-knn

- *Network Security Based on K-Means Clustering Algorithm in Data Mining Research*:

  https://www.atlantis-press.com/proceedings/snce-18/25895315

Part 3 – Simple and Multiple Linear Regression Analysis

Linear regression involves the relationship of two or more variables that can create a model that predicts future values. Residuals represent a linear function separation of real data and are useful to test the accuracy of a model. Once the model is validated with t-statistics and r-squared tests, it can be used to make predictions. Train the model with 80% of the data sample and test it with the remaining 20% .

This part includes the following chapters:

- *Chapter 8, Finding the Relationship between Variables*
- *Chapter 9, Building, Training, and Validating a Linear Model*
- *Chapter 10, Building, Training, and Validating a Multiple Regression Model*

8

Finding the Relationship between Variables

The linear regression algorithm is a supervised machine learning algorithm. We need to train and adjust the linear model before making predictions. We have to understand the data before applying linear regression to be sure that it will be useful for predictions.

You need a certain level of confidence that the variable you want to predict has a relationship with the variables that influence it. If you don't test the extent of this relationship, the predicted values will be errors, and the results will be garbage.

In this chapter, we will learn two methods to test the dependence of the variables to ensure our model's accuracy. We will measure the difference between the expected values from the training dataset and the model's results, and use statistical methods to examine the significance of the relationships between the variables to see whether they are useful for predicting values.

The goal of measuring how close the model's results are to the expected values from the training data and using statistical methods to measure the relationships between the variables is to find out whether the data can be used with linear regression to predict values. This is important and a key prerequisite for all linear regression with one or more variables. We always have to be sure that the prediction variables affect the result; otherwise, there is no way we can predict results with new predictor values.

By the end of the chapter, we will have learned that a linear model gives prediction scenarios that are useful for predictions within a range of values. This range depends on the relationship quality of the variables.

This chapter covers the following main topics:

- Charting the predictive model's regression variables

- Linear model confidence

- The coefficient of determination

- The correlation coefficient

- Statistical significance of the slope

- The regression model's predicted value ranges

Technical requirements

The technical requirements for this chapter are as follows:

- The `chaptereightRelationshipbetweenvariables.xlsx` Excel file included with the book. Download it from here: `https://github.com/PacktPublishing/Data-Forecasting-and-Segmentation-Using-Microsoft-Excel/blob/main/Chapter08/chaptereightRelationshipbetweenvariables.xlsx`.

- The statistical table at this link: `https://www.medcalc.org/manual/t-distribution-table.php`.

Charting the predictive model's regression variables

Regression is a supervised learning algorithm. It needs five steps to be functional:

1. Build the regression model.

2. Check whether the cause variables have an effect on the dependent variable with statistical tests.

3. Train the model with a percentage of the dataset.

4. Test the model with the remainder of the dataset. See whether the results from the model fit the expected values of the dataset.

5. Finally, predict the values using the model.

The main target of a **machine learning regression analysis** is to build a model that predicts the value of interest (for example, sales of a product or plant growth in biology) based on a predictor variable (for example, marketing expenditure in the case of sales, or soil moisture in the plant growth scenario).

We need to find out whether the factor we want to predict has enough of a relationship with the variable we assume affects it. We have to prove that if we spend more money on marketing, it will have a direct effect on the sales of the product. Another scenario we can examine with regression analysis is whether plant growth has a relationship with soil moisture levels. We measure the soil's moisture and the amount of plant growth for a period of time and experiment to see whether they have a relationship via statistical analysis.

If we are confident in the hypothesis that one variable (soil moisture) affects the other (plant growth), we can use this data to predict plant growth using hypothetical soil moisture measures.

The process of analyzing whether two variables have a relationship and could be useful to predict future values is as follows:

1. Plot the variables to visualize the possible relationship.

2. Test the dataset with statistical coefficients, such as the t-statistic and the p-value.

3. Examine the model with known values to see whether the linear regression fits the expected values and makes sense.

4. Use the model to predict new values. Be sure the results make sense with your experience.

Plotting the variables to analyze the possible relationship

We mentioned the example of the possible relationship between sales volume and investment in marketing. We will now plot the relationship between investment in TV marketing and sales quantity to find the following:

- Visual identification of the possible impact of investment in TV marketing and sales

- The linear regression that represents this relationship

Once we have identified in a chart that the link between the variables can be used to predict future values, we write the regression formula. The regression formula is the straight line that best fits the relationship among the variables. We will learn how to write this later in the chapter. Then, we do statistical tests to confirm the significance of the relationship between the variables.

The machine learning linear regression process has the following steps:

1. Generate the linear regression model. Write a formula for the slope (positive or negative) of the model.

2. Train the model with a part of the dataset. Conduct the statistical analysis of the variable relationship with 80% of the known data to train the model.

3. Test the model with the rest of the dataset. Use the remaining 20% of the data to test whether the model fits the known data and the percentage of error. This percentage of error indicates the accuracy of the model in making predictions, since we already know the correct values. We can check the model confidence with this known data.

4. Predict new values with the model. Enter new values into the model and see whether the results make sense.

Visualizing investment in TV marketing versus the impact on sales

Before doing any statistical analysis and measuring the difference between the expected values and the model's results, we have to do a visual inspection with a chart. This will give us a first impression of whether the variables have a relationship and whether it makes sense to use this model for predictive purposes. Take a look at *Figure 8.1*. We can see a possible relationship inside the rectangles. Also, there are values that fall outside that possible relationship, in the triangle:

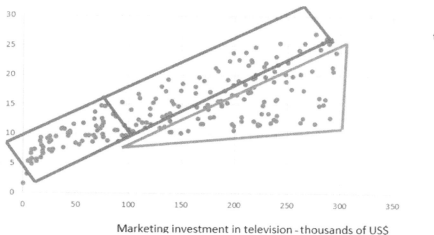

Marketing investment in television - thousands of US$

Figure 8.1 – Investment in TV marketing versus sales

In the chart, we can identify the following:

- The rectangles show evidence that sales increase with marketing investment. We can see the group of sales between 3,000 and 10,000 units corresponds to investments of 5,000 to 50,000 US dollars. This is the lowest investment in TV marketing. That means that even with a low budget, we can increase sales. Investments over 50,000 US dollars lead to more scattered points, meaning that we have to find a balance between marketing and sales. A large investment in marketing does not mean an exponential growth in sales.

- The green triangle shows that even with the investment increasing from 150,000 to 300,000 US dollars, there is not much of an increase in sales in this group. This could affect the relationship between marketing investment and sales. We are probably losing money in marketing and getting no good results in sales.

Representing the relationship with linear regression

Design a formula that fits the trend of the plot of sales and marketing in *Figure 8.1*. This linear model formula could predict future values if we find that the relationship between the variables is statistically significant.

Now, we will plot the regression model that represents the relationship between marketing and sales. We need several statistical tests to prove that the relationship between the variables is enough to build a predictive regression. The plot gives us a visual indication of the possible link between variables:

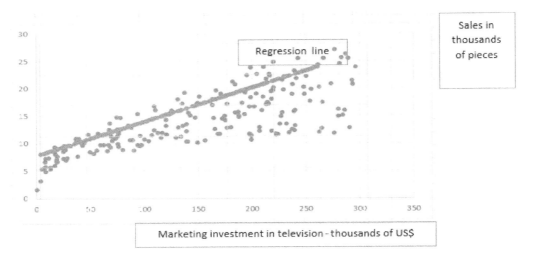

Figure 8.2 – Regression line of the impact of investment in TV marketing on sales

The line representing the regression gives us an idea of the trend of the data. It could represent a positive relationship – that is, that more investment in marketing means better sales. However, we need to run several tests to confirm this.

In the following plot, predictive values for sales represent the target of the linear regression model. The red box represents the model's prediction of the sales when more is spent on marketing.

Figure 8.3 predicts the possible sales when between 300,000 and 350,000 US dollars is invested in marketing:

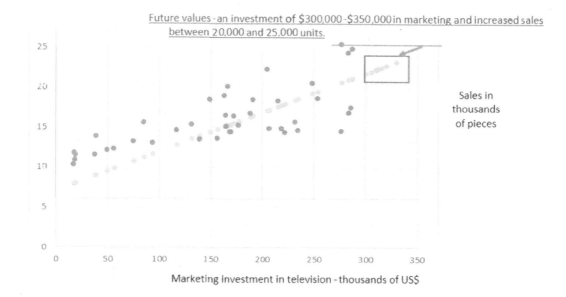

Figure 8.3 – Prediction of future values

The rectangle encloses the values predicted by the model. We can calculate how accurate these values are because there are sales that do not increase, even as marketing investment increases.

The linear regression model also gives us a confidence range for predicted values. This makes sense for predictive models, since the values have a level of uncertainty, depending on the relationship between the variables.

The predictive values scenario uses the confidence range to display three possible values:

- A predictive scenario without the level of confidence
- An upper value of confidence
- A lower value of confidence

It is important to show the upper and lower thresholds of the regression model because it does not exactly fit the values of the variables. This range tells us the prediction's range and whether we can accept this level of uncertainty.

Figure 8.4 represents the range values of the model. The upper and lower thresholds are statistically calculated using the slope and the *t*-statistic:

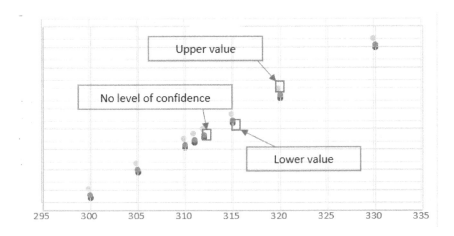

Figure 8.4 – The model confidence ranges

This chart represents the confidence level of the predictions. The marketing investment and sales variables have a good relationship because the confidence values (both upper and lower) have a short distance between them.

Generating the linear regression model and testing the accuracy:

Linear regression is a supervised machine learning algorithm. It uses a dataset to generate a model (the line that fits the dataset). Then, the algorithm uses this model to predict new values. The **K-means** algorithm is an unsupervised algorithm. It searches for patterns in the data until it finds the best classification. Unsupervised algorithms do not need a dataset for training.

We are going to use 80% of the dataset to train our linear model. Then, we will use the remaining 20% to see whether the model can accurately predict the results we already have. *Figure 8.5* shows how accurate our model is. Finally, we will try our model with new values.

This is the linear model for **80%** of the marketing and sales dataset:

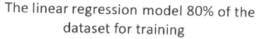

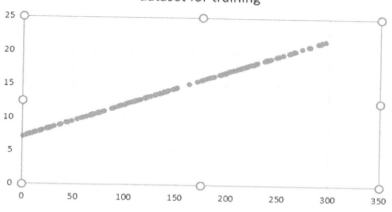

Figure 8.5 – Training linear regression

We test the remaining 20% of the dataset, and we get this chart. The model is the straight line joining the dots. The 20% of data points for testing are inside the black lines. The distance between the straight line and the test points gives the accuracy of the regression:

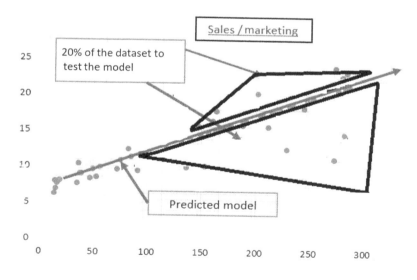

Figure 8.6 – Testing the model with 20% of the dataset

You can see that some points are far from the predicted model within the black lines. This is the tolerance level.

In *Figure 8.7*, we plot the difference between the expected values and the regression line in *Figure 8.6*. We can see from the blue dots in *Figure 8.7* that this differences ranges between -6 and 9. The ideal scenario is that the blue dots are close to zero. This determines how accurate the model is. We will analyze this accuracy with statistical methods:

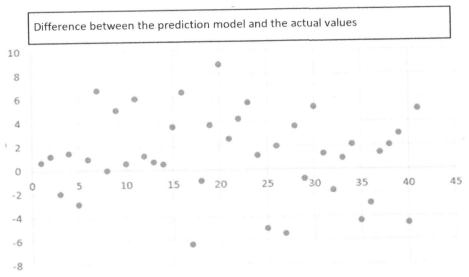

Figure 8.7 – The difference between the actual values of sales and the prediction by the model

The mean difference value is 1.19. The standard deviation is 3.51, which can explain how accurate the model is. The ideal case is to have a small standard deviation of the differences. This means that the expected values are close to the regression line.

In this section, we learned that we have to visualize and use our experience to evaluate the relationship between the variables, using a chart before using statistical and numerical methods. This is the first step to verifying whether the data is useful to design a predictor model. The statistical methods will give us an idea of whether the relationship between the variables is significant to build a useful regression model. We can use 80% of the dataset to train the model and examine the link between the variables, and use the remaining 20% of the dataset to test how the model fits. Finally, we use the model to predict new values. In the next section, we will learn how to calculate the confidence of the relationship of the variables using numerical and statistical methods.

Calculating the linear model confidence percentage

The regression line represents the relationship between the variables. The best case is that the difference between the expected values and the model line is minimal, with a low mean and standard deviation. The difference is on the red line in *Figure 8.8*.

This line follows the formula $Y = B0 + B1X$:

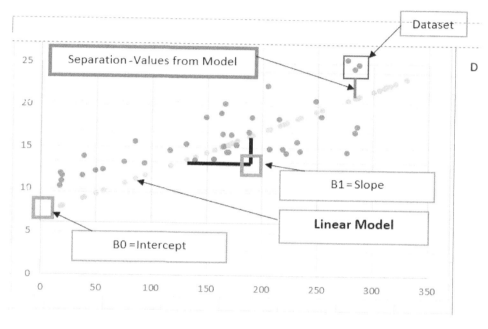

Figure 8.8 – The difference between the linear model and the dataset

B1 is the slope of the regression line, the change in the Y value (sales – an increase or decrease) for every unit of change in the X value (marketing investment). The formula for **B1** is as follows:

$$B1 = \frac{\Sigma(X_i - \overleftrightarrow{X})(Y_i - \overleftrightarrow{Y})}{\Sigma(X_i - \overleftrightarrow{X})^2}$$

Let's look at this formula in more detail:

- Subtract the mean of all the X values from each X_i value.
- Subtract the mean of all the Y values from each Y_i value.
- Subtract the mean of all the X values from each X_i value and then square it.

For this example, the **B1** slope is *0.0489*.

B0 is the intercept of the line to the Y axis. In practice, this is the value of Y when the X value is zero. For example, what is the sales value when the marketing investment is zero?

The formula for the **B0** intercept is $B0 = \bar{Y} - B1 * \bar{X}$. Let's look at this formula in more detail:

- $\overleftarrow{Y}$ is the average of Y values.
- The slope is *B1*.
- $\overleftarrow{X}$ is the average of X values.

For this example, the **B0** intercept is *7.0734*.

We will use charts to explain two indicators of the model confidence:

- The **coefficient of determination** indicates how well the regression line fits the data.
- The **correlation coefficient** measures the strength of association between X and Y.

The following chart shows the elements used to calculate these coefficients. It is critical to understand these elements to have a full understanding of a linear regression model:

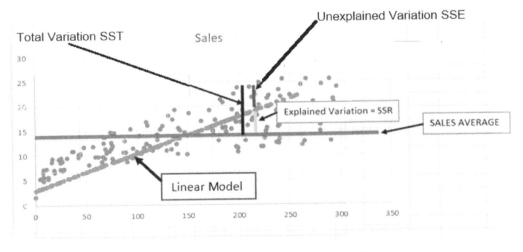

Figure 8.9 – Elements used to calculate the model confidence percentage

Each coefficient field indicated in the chart is explained as follows:

- **Sales and marketing values**: The plot of the Y (sales) and X (marketing investment) relationship.

- **Sales average** (the red line): The mean of the variable we want to predict if X has an effect on it.

- **Linear model** (orange line): Calculated from the following formula:

$$Y^{\wedge} = B0 + B1 * X \ (value)$$

- **Total variation sum of squares total (SST)**: The difference between the Y (sales) and X (marketing) values in the original dataset and the mean Y (sales). Remove the negative symbols by squaring the difference. The formula to calculate this is as follows:

$$\left(Yi - average(Y)\right)^2$$

Subtract the average of the sales from each sales value. Then, square the result to remove all the negative symbols.

- **Unexplained variation – the Sum of Squared Errors (SSE)**: The difference between the Y (sales) and the X (marketing) values in the original dataset and the line regression model. This is a way to measure the error of the model to fit the values of the dataset that are supposed to have a relationship. The SSE is the distance between the data and the straight line of the model that represents the relationship. The best-case model scenario is a short distance between the data and the regression line. Remove the negative symbols by squaring the difference. The formula to calculate this is as follows:

$$(Yi - \ Linear \ Prediction \ model \ (Y'))^2$$

Each blue dot subtracts the linear model value, Y', represented by the orange line.

- **Explained variation – the Sum of Squared Regression (SSR)**: The difference between the linear regression model and the average of Y (sales). This is another measure of how the model fits the variable that we are trying to predict. Remove the negative symbols by squaring the difference. The formula to calculate this is as follows:

$$\left((Linear \ Prediction \ model \ (Y') - average(Y)\right)^2$$

Subtract the average of Y (sales) of the original dataset from the linear prediction values in the regression line.

The variations are the differences between the expected values from the training data and the linear regression model results. They give numerical information about how accurate the model is and whether it can be used for prediction. The variations are the input data for the coefficients of correlation and determination, which measure the statistical significance of the link between variables. In the next sections, we will explain how to calculate these coefficients.

Coefficient of determination

This is a factor of the SSR with respect to the SST. Refer to *Figure 8.10* to see the relationship between these two terms. The SSR is the difference between the regression line and the average of the sales. The SST is the difference between the expected value (represented in dots figures) and the average of the sales.

The formula to calculate the coefficient of determination, r^2, is the SSR divided by the SST.

Figure 8.10 explains how the coefficient of determination gives us the percentage of accuracy of the linear model. The ideal case is that the SSR divided by the SST is close to 1. This means there is a close to 100% percent relationship between the expected values and the regression line:

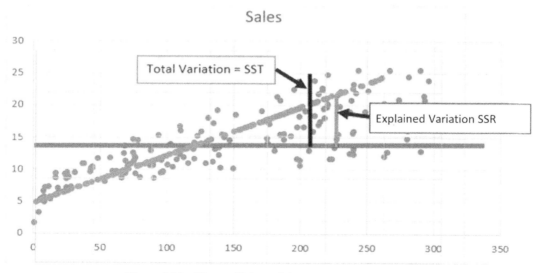

Figure 8.10 – The coefficient of determination = SSR/SST

The best-case scenario is to have a coefficient of determination that's close to 1, which indicates a close relationship between the variables.

> **Important Note**
>
> r^2 is the percentage of the change in Y (the dependent variable – sales) that is influenced by X (the independent variable – TV marketing investment).

For this example, we have an SSR of 2,794.65 from the formula explained previously:

$$\left(Linear\ Prediction\ model\ (Y') - average(Y)\right)^2$$

Subtract the average of Y (sales) of the original dataset from the linear prediction values represented by the orange line.

The SST is represented by the black line. For this example, it is 4,346.22, which is calculated with the following formula:

$$\left(Yi - average(Y)\right)^2$$

Each dot value is divided by the average of all the dots. The dots are the sales values.

The coefficient of determination is calculated as follows:

```
r2= SSR / SST = 2794.65 / 4346.22 = 0.643
```

> **Important Note**
>
> The r^2 value says that the model has 64% confidence in the influence of marketing investment on sales performance. This is important information for making better decisions about marketing investment.

The coefficient of determination is the level of confidence in the model's ability to determine the value of Y based on the value of X.

Now, we need to know whether the relationship between the X and Y variables is directly or inversely proportional. *Directly* means that if X grows or decreases, Y grows or decreases too, whereas *inversely* means that if X grows or decreases, Y does the opposite.

The direct or inverse proportionality of the relationship depends on the slope of the formula.

Correlation coefficient

The correlation coefficient measures the statistical importance of the link between the two variables. The prediction accuracy depends on a strong link between marketing investment and sales. Also, the correlation coefficient uses the sign of the slope to indicate the type of relationship. Positive is directly proportional and negative is an inverse relationship.

Now, let's take a look at the types of slopes in linear models. If we plot the relationship between sales (Y) and marketing (X), we can check whether the slope is zero and whether it is positive or negative. If the slope equals zero, it means that there is no relationship between the variables. The t-statistic confirms or rejects whether the slope equals zero. *Figure 8.11* shows the types of slope, based on whether the relationship is direct (positive) or indirectly proportional (negative), or there is no relationship at all (the slope equals zero). It gives you an idea of whether the variables are linked or not:

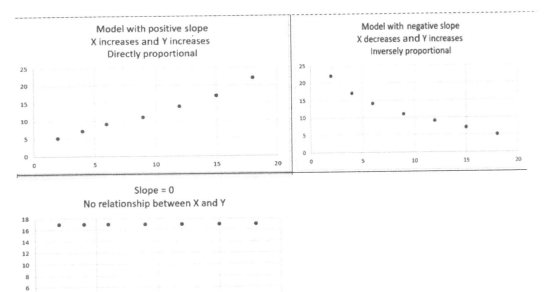

Figure 8.11 – Types of slope

The first plot in *Figure 8.12* has a positive slope, which indicates a direct relationship between the variables. If the X variable grows, so does the Y variable. The second chart is the opposite case. It has a negative slope; when X grows, Y decreases. This is an inverse relationship. The third chart shows the case when no predictor model is possible with this data. The slope equals zero, which means that there is no relationship between the variables. The X variable cannot be used to predict the value of Y.

The values of the correlation coefficient are between 1 and -1:

- $r = +1$ means a perfect linear relationship between the X and Y variables.

- $r = -1$ means a perfect negative linear relationship.

- $r = 0$ means there is no linear relationship. The slope is equal to zero.

The formula for the correlation coefficient is as follows:

$$r_{xy} = sign\ of\ b1\ \sqrt{Coefficient\ of\ determination} = sign\ of\ b1\sqrt{r^2}$$

The sign of $b1$ is the sign of the slope of the linear model.

For this example, the $b1$ slope = $+0.04$. The coefficient of determination = 0.643.

The correlation coefficient is $= +\sqrt{r^2} = \sqrt{0.643}$.

---

r_{xy} **Sales and Marketing**

r_{xy} with a value of 0.80 means that there is a strong relationship between the X predictor variable and the Y result variable. With the positive value of the slope, we have enough *evidence* that sales increase when we invest more in TV marketing.

Now that we have learned about all these elements, it should be easy for us to understand the functions of linear regression in Excel, R, and Python. *Figure 8.13* shows the results after executing the linear function. It gives the intercept and the slope to build the regression formula and the coefficients to know the model's accuracy:

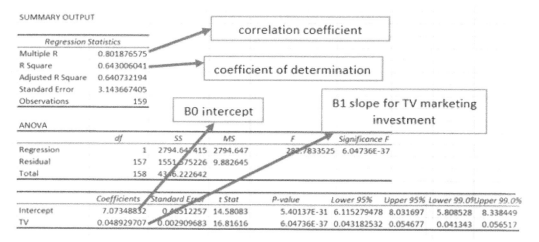

Figure 8.12 – Response output for linear regression

The coefficient of determination, r^2, has a value of 0.643. The coefficient of correlation, r_{xy}, has a value of 0.8. With these values, we can be confident that the X and Y variables have a relationship that could lead to a useful predictive model. We are on track to have a model to prove that we will improve sales performance by investing in TV marketing. But we still have to test the statistical relevance of the sales and marketing investment variables by analyzing the slope, which is the next step in our analysis.

Statistical significance of the slope

Remember that the slope determines the relationship between the X and Y variables.

To check the significance of the slope of the variables' relationship and the viability to build a predictive model, we are going to use the **t-test**. The *t*-test requires two hypotheses:

- **H0 – null hypothesis**: The slope equals zero. This means that there is no relationship between the variables.

- **HA – alternative hypothesis**: The slope is *NOT* equal to zero. This means that the variables have a relationship.

The *t*-test calculation steps are as follows:

1. Calculate the *s* value by dividing the SSE by the number of data elements minus two. In this example, the number of elements of data is 159.
2. Divide the slope by the *s* value.
3. Check whether the *t*-test is greater than the critical value given by the *t*-test table (`https://www.sjsu.edu/faculty/gerstman/StatPrimer/t-table.pdf`). If the value is greater than the critical value, it means that we can reject the `null` hypothesis and accept the alternative hypothesis that there is a relationship between the variables.

The formula for the *t*-test is as follows:

$$Test\ Statistic = \frac{Slope\ B1}{S_{B_1}}$$

Where:

$$S_{B_1} = \frac{s}{\sqrt{\Sigma(X_i - \overleftrightarrow{X})^2}}$$

Subtract the average of all the X_i values from each X value and then square the result.

The formula for *s* is as follows:

$$s = \sqrt{\frac{Unexplained\ variation\ SSE}{Number\ of\ elements - 2}}$$

Remember that the SSE is the difference between the expected values and the linear regression model values in the straight line (see *Figure 8.10*).

For this example, the value of the SSE is *1551.5752*.

The number of elements is *159*.

The *s* value is calculated as follows:

$$s = \sqrt{\frac{1551.5752}{159 - 2}}$$

Therefore, the value of *s* is *3.1436*.

Let's now calculate the value of S_{B_1}:

$$S_{B_1} = 0.002909683$$

The test statistic value is now calculated by the following formula:

$$Test\ Statistic = \frac{Slope\ B1}{S_{B_1}}$$

$$Test\ Statistic = \frac{0.0489}{0.002909683}$$

$$Test\ Statistic = 16.81616343$$

Now, we are ready to use the test statistic to see whether we keep the null hypothesis (*slope = 0* – no relationship between the variables), or whether we reject it and accept the alternative hypothesis with a slope not equal to zero (which means there is a relationship between the variables).

We are going to compare the *t*-test value with a *critical value* given by the *p-value* that will indicate whether the *t*-test has evidence to reject the null hypothesis.

Before comparing the *t*-test with the *p*-value, we set the critical value to the confidence value we want to reject the null hypothesis. We want *99.99%* confidence to accept the alternative hypothesis. The letter *alpha* is the value we will look at in a statistical table to find the critical value to accept the alternative hypothesis. The value of *alpha* is *0.01(subtract 100 – 99.99%).*

Since the bell curve has two tails, that means we divide *alpha* by two. So, *alpha* equals *0.005*:

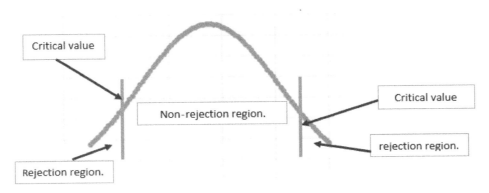

Figure 8.13 – A bell curve rejection region for the hypothesis

The number of points for this example is *159*. They are the number of degrees of freedom for the effects of the calculation formula:

Number of points (number of degrees of freedom) = number of points -2 = 157

We are going to look for the *p*-value indicator with the *alpha* value in the following statistical table (`https://www.medcalc.org/manual/t-distribution-table.php`):

DF	A	0.80	0.90	0.95	0.98	0.99	0.995	0.998	0.999
	P	0.20	0.10	0.05	0.02	0.01	0.005	0.002	0.001
120		1.289	1.658	1.980	2.358	2.617	2.860	3.160	3.373
150		1.287	1.655	1.976	2.351	2.609	2.849	3.145	3.357
200		1.286	1.652	1.972	2.345	2.601	2.839	3.131	3.340

Figure 8.14 – The p-value statistical table – DF is the degrees of freedom, A is the alpha value, and P is the p-value

We find that the critical value to reject or accept the `null` hypothesis is *2.849*.

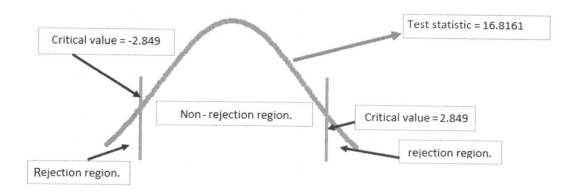

Figure 8.15 – The critical value

We have a test statistic value of *16.81616343*.

> **t-Statistics**
>
> The test statistic value is to the right of the critical value of 2.849. So, it falls in the rejection region. We accept the alternative hypothesis, and the slope is not equal to zero. There is a relationship between the variables, so we can build a predictive model.

We can also use the *p*-value to accept or reject the `null` hypothesis. For *99.99%* confidence to reject or accept the `null` hypothesis, use alpha = 0.01 (*100 - 99.99 = 0.01*). Then, get the *p*-value from the linear regression function in Excel, and if the *p*-value is less than the *alpha* value, reject the `null` hypothesis.

In this example, the *p*-value is *6.04735643294181E-37*, which is less than the *alpha* value.

Now, we can understand additional fields for the linear regression results returned by the function in Excel, R, or Python.

Figure 8.16 is the response from the linear function. It includes the following:

- *r* squared

- Unexplained and explained variations

- *t*-statistics

- *p*-value

With these values, we can interpret whether the regression model is useful for making predictions:

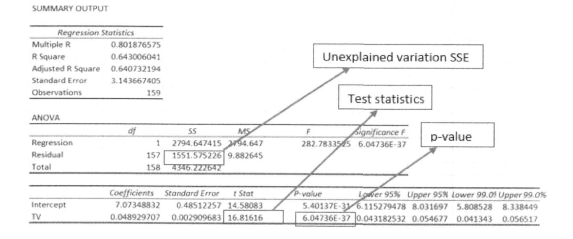

Figure 8.16 – The response from the linear regression function

The regression model's value ranges

As we have seen, the regression model is not an exact answer for our prediction's needs because it depends on the level of relationship between the causal variables and the Y result/effect variable.

Taking this into account, a more realistic model would be to present three possible prediction scenarios. The scenarios depend on the confidence level of the slope. We have the upper and lower scenario depending on the value assigned to the slope.

The formula for the confidence levels of the slope is as follows:

$$Confidence\ level\ of\ slope = Slope\ B1 \overset{+}{-} t_{alpha/2} * s_{b1}$$

From previous calculations of this example, we know the following:

$$t_{alpha/2} = 2.849$$

We also know this:

$$s_{b1} = 0.0029$$

The confidence level of the slope is between the upper values equal to 0.057219394 and the lower values equal to 0.04064002.

With this information, we can build a chart with three scenarios:

- The linear model without the confidence level
- The upper limit of the model
- The lower limit of the model

Let's look at this in the following figure:

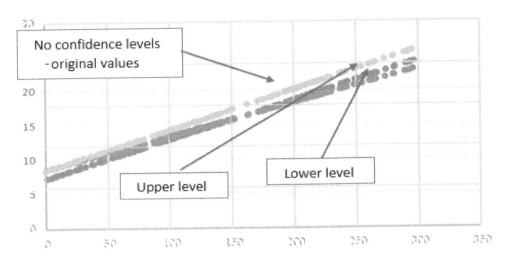

Figure 8.17 – The slope levels of confidence

Providing three scenarios of the linear model is the right approach for predicting models. The regression line is just an approximation of the values. Prediction values based on the past are also just a trend. Using multiple scenarios shows the range of possible values based on the past. It gives us an idea of the level of uncertainty we can expect if we use new values to predict the value of Y.

Summary

In this chapter, we learned how to plot variables to see whether they have a link before conducting statistical analysis. After this, we reviewed the differences between the expected values and the results from the linear model. These differences are the input for the formulas of the coefficient of determination and correlation, which show the variables' level of relationship and whether they are direct or inversely proportional.

Statistical methods such as t-statistics and the p-value tell us whether we can reject the null hypothesis. If the slope is zero, there is no relationship between the variables.

Once we have a level of confidence regarding the relationship between variables, we can conclude that the linear regression model is useful for building predictions. In the next chapter, we will write the formula of a simple (single-variable) regression model.

Questions

Here are a few questions and their answers to revisit what we have learned in this chapter:

1. How can we use our experience to see the level of relationship between variables to build a prediction model?

2. What is the input data for the formulas of the coefficient of correlation and determination?

3. How do we reject a `null` hypothesis using the *t*-statistic?

4. What is the SSE, and what is the other name for it?

5. What is the meaning of the slope sign in linear regression?

Answers

Here are the answers to the preceding questions:

1. Draw a chart of the variables and see whether there is a relationship by seeing whether the data points form a straight line with no scattered data.

2. The difference between the expected values and the results from the linear model.

3. Look in the *t*-statistics table for the critical value. If the calculated value of the *t*-statistic is greater than the critical value, we can reject the `null` hypothesis.

4. The SSE is the difference between the expected results of the training data and the results of the regression model, squared. The SSE is also called the unexplained variation.

5. A positive sign means a direct relationship. A negative sign means an inverse relationship.

Further reading

To further understand the concepts of this chapter, refer to the following sources:

- Read this scientific explanation of linear regression:

  `https://www.nku.edu/~intsci/sci110/worksheets/relation_between_variables.html`

- Read about correlation:

  `https://milnepublishing.geneseo.edu/natural-resources-biometrics/chapter/chapter-7-correlation-and-simple-linear-regression/`

9
Building, Training, and Validating a Linear Model

In the last chapter, we learned about statistical data tests to validate whether it is useful to build a predictive model. It depends on the strong relationship between the predictor variable, X, and the result variable, Y.

In this chapter, we will develop a prediction model to see whether the amount of fuel in miles per gallon is affected by motor horsepower. We will understand how to measure the difference between the expected values from the data source and the response given by the model.

The strong or weak relationship between the expected values and the linear regression is based on the difference between the training data and the regression model. We can use several tests to check whether the predictor variable and the result variable have a link. These statistical tests can be as follows:

- The coefficients of determination and correlation
- t-statistics
- The p-value
- f-statistics

t-statistics tell us whether we can reject the `null` hypothesis, *H0*, indicating that the slope is equal to zero. If it is zero, it indicates that there is no relationship between the variables.

To train and design the model, we will use 80% of the data source on horsepower and miles per gallon. Then, we will test the linear regression with the remaining 20% to see the percentage of error using known values. Finally, we will use the model to predict new values and the impact of the horsepower on miles-per-gallon performance.

Linear regression is not a single-response solution. It just gives trends of the prediction values. A more realistic approach is to present what the upper and lower ranges are where we can expect the linear prediction.

This chapter has the following sections:

- Calculating the intercept and slope with formulas
- Computing coefficient significance – *t*-statistics and the *p*-value
- Getting the residual standard error
- Calculating the *r*-squared
- Calculating the *f*-statistics
- Training and testing the model

Technical requirements

The technical requirements for this chapter are as follows:

- The `chapternineLinearModel` Excel file included with the book. Download the file from GitHub here: `https://github.com/PacktPublishing/Data-Forecasting-and-Segmentation-Using-Microsoft-Excel/blob/main/Chapter09/chapternineLinearModel.xlsx`.
- The statistical table found at this link: `https://www.medcalc.org/manual/t-distribution-table.php`.
- Download the `cars` dataset from here: `https://gist.github.com/noamross/e5d3e859aa0c794be10b`.

Calculating the intercept and slope with formulas

The main components of a linear model are as follows:

- Intercept
- Slope

The **regression slope** defines the difference between the expected values and those of the model. From here, we calculate the first check to determine whether the variables have a relationship and are useful to build a predictive model. We have accepted the hypothesis that the variables are related, and we can use them to build a predictive model. The first check includes the coefficients of determination and correlation.

The **slope** indicates whether the data has a direct or an inverse relationship. It is probable that the predictor value, X, grows, while the result variable, Y, decreases. In this case, we have an inverse relationship with a negative slope. A slope with a value equal to zero (flat) means there is no relationship between the model variables, predictors, and effects. We use the t-statistics test to probe the hypothesis that the slope is less or greater than zero, but *not* zero.

Also, we use **f-statistics** to see whether the difference between the average of the expected values and the actual results by the model provides enough evidence to check the relationship of the variables using the slope value.

The **intercept** indicates the effect on the Y variable when X is zero. Also, if the B1 slope has a value equal to zero, it means that there is no relationship between the X and Y variables.

For this chapter, we will develop a linear model for predicting what influence horsepower has on miles-per-gallon performance of cars. We will work on the full cycle until we put the model into practice. The steps to develop the machine learning predictive model are as follows:

1. Use the coefficients, t-statistics, and f-statistics tests to check the relationship between horsepower and miles-per-hour performance. Determine whether the data is strong enough to build a prediction model.
2. Train the model with test data.
3. Validate the model with known results data to see how the prediction is working.
4. Predict miles-per-hour performance using new values of horsepower.

The following chart shows the data for the effect of horsepower on miles-per-gallon consumption. The scattered points are source data.

The slope indicates that the linear regression is negative. This means that the relationship is inversely proportional. If we increase the motor's horsepower, it will travel fewer miles per gallon:

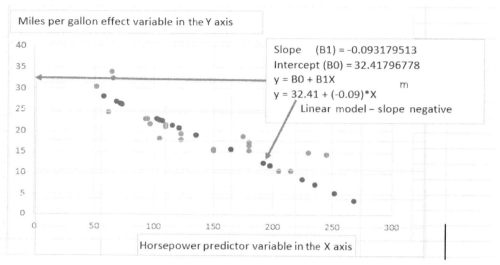

Figure 9.1 – Intercept and slope

The linear model has the following equation:

```
Y = Intercept (B0) + Slope (B1) * X
Y = 32.41 + (-0.09) * X
```

The negative slope indicates the trend of miles per gallon decreasing when horsepower (the *x* axis) grows.

The intercept represents the value of miles per gallon on the *y* axis when the horsepower is zero. When the horsepower is zero, the miles per gallon is *32.41*.

We will find out how to build the equation of the linear model when we look at coefficient significance in the *Training and testing the model* section. *Coefficient significance* is a statistical test to evaluate whether our regression model is good enough to work with.

It is more realistic to present a linear model with different scenarios. The model tries to predict trends, not the exact fit of the source data. The slope has an upper and lower range to consider in the prediction. The following chart shows the upper, lower, and normal linear models based on the data:

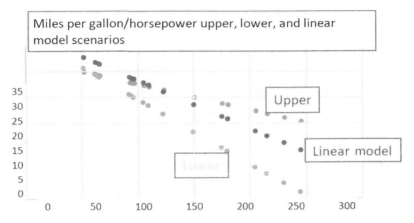

Figure 9.2 – Scenarios for the linear model

Upper and lower trends help us to understand what the possible linear regression thresholds are.

We use 80% of the data source to define and train the model. The remaining 20% we use to test and check how well it fits with the known values. The last step is to use the model to predict the unknown values of X:

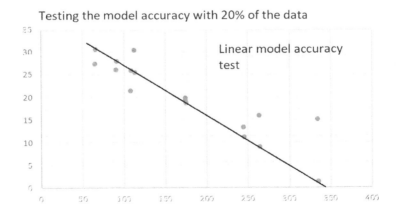

Figure 9.3 – The test model with 20% of the data

This gives us an idea of how well the model fits compared to predicted values. We predict the values using data that is unknown to the model:

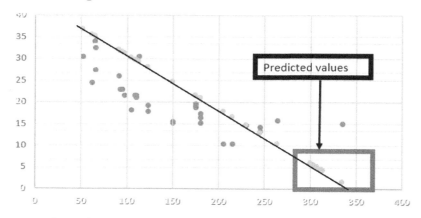

Figure 9.4 – The prediction model with new data – check whether the results make sense

Figure 9.2 shows what the possible ranges of values for the model are. The model just gives trends, not an exact prediction, and this figure shows the possible threshold. *Figure 9.3* tests the model with known input data to see how good the prediction is. The model is the straight line, and we can see the trend of the prediction. Finally, we input new values into the model in *Figure 9.4*. Review whether the result here matches the result from your experience. It is clear that the model predicts a decrease in miles-per-hour performance with more horsepower in the engine.

In the next chart, we see elements that determine how far the model is from the results we expect. Also, we will review the corresponding terms with the results obtained from the linear regression function in *R*, *Python*, or *Excel*:

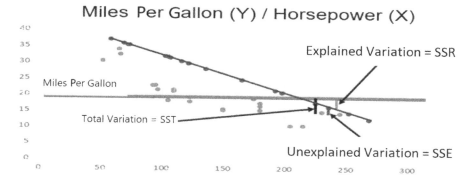

Figure 9.5 – Distance of the actual data from the model's values

Let's review, in this chart, the response from the linear regression function to understand the elements that represent the distance between the model and the original data:

- **Sum of Squares (SS) or Total Variation (SST)**: This is the distance from the data source point (the intersection of horsepower and miles per gallon) to the miles-per-gallon average line.

- **SS unexplained variation or residual error**: This is the distance between the data source point (intersection of horsepower and miles per gallon) and the value given by the linear model. This is known as the *error* of the linear model.

- **SS explained variation or regression**: This is the distance between the linear regression straight line and the miles-per-gallon average line.

> **Important Note**
>
> The SST is the sum of residual error (SSE) with the explained variation regression.

The results of the linear regression function are shown in *Figure 9.6*. In the **ANOVA** section, we review the errors of the unexplained difference between the expected results from the linear model. The regression, residual, and total results have formulas based on the distances explained in *Figure 9.5*:

SUMMARY OUTPUT

Regression Statistics	
Multiple R	0.853651
R Square	0.728721
Adjusted R Squa	0.715803
Standard Error	3.289136
Observations	23

ANOVA

	df	SS	MS	F	ignificance F
Regression	1	610.2775974	610.2775974	56.41099	2.23E-07
Residual	21	227.1867504	10.81841669		
Total	22	837.4643478			

	Coefficients	Standard Error	t Stat	P-value	Lower 95%	Upper 95%	Lower 99.0%	Ipper 99.0%
Intercept	32.41797	1.817807953	17.83354932	3.66E-14	28.63763	36.19831	27.27109986	37.56484
hp	-0.09318	0.012406194	-7.51072501	2.23E-07	-0.11898	-0.06738	-0.128305909	-0.05805

Figure 9.6 – The linear regression distance of the model from the actual data

The formula for SST is as follows:

```
SS Total (Total Variation SST) = Residual SS (Unexplained
Variation SSE) + Regression SS (Explained Variation SSR)
```

The formula for mean squared regression with a resulting value of `610.277` has the following components:

- Regression SS (explained variation SSR) with a resulting value of `610.27`.
- The regression degrees of freedom is the model's number of variables. In this case, it is 2 – miles per gallon and horsepower.

The formula for mean squared regression is as follows:

```
Mean Squared Regression = Regression SS (Explained Variation
SSR) / (Degrees of Freedom for Regression - 1)
Mean Squared Regression = 610.27 / (2 - 1) = 610.27 / 1 =
610.27
```

The formula for the mean squared residual with a resultant value of `10.8184` has the following components:

- Residual SS (unexplained variation SSE) with a resulting value of `227.1867`.
- The degrees of freedom for residual. This is the number of records of the linear regression. In this case, it is `22`.

The formula for the mean squared residual is as follows:

```
Mean Squared Residual = Residual SS (Unexplained Variation SSE)
/ (Degrees of Freedom for Residual - 1)
Mean Squared Residual = 227.1867 / (22 - 1) = 227.1867 / 21 =
10.818
```

The *f*-test is another statistical probe to check whether we can reject the `null` hypothesis that the slope is equal to zero or that there is no relationship between the variables. The *f*-test formula components are as follows:

- Regression mean squared error with a value equal to `610.27`
- Residual mean squared error with a value equal to `10.81`

The formula of the *f*-test is as follows:

```
F-Test = Regression Mean Squared Error / Residual Mean Squared
Error
610.27 / 10.81 = 56.41
```

We have to check in an *f*-test table to see whether the value of `56.41` falls in the rejection region of the `null` hypothesis. See *Figure 9.7* with the following parameters:

- **Numerator**: The regression degrees of freedom is the model number of variables. In this case, it is `2` – miles per gallon and horsepower.
- **Denominator**: The degrees of freedom for residual. They are the number of records of the linear regression. In this case, it is `22`.

We used the *f*-test table to see whether the value falls in the rejection region. The portion of the *f*-test table for 2 regression degrees of freedom and 22 degrees for residual is shown in *Figure 9.7*:

\	$df_1=1$	2	3
21	2.96096	2.57457	2.36489
22	2.94858	2.56131	2.35117

Figure 9.7 – The f-test value for 2 regression degrees of freedom and 22 degrees for residual

The *f*-test has a value of 56.41. It is greater than the critical value of 2.56. So, we can reject the null hypothesis that the slope is equal to zero. There is a relationship between miles per gallon and the predictor variable, the motor horsepower.

In this section, we learned the basic concepts of linear regression and statistical methods to check whether variables have a significant relationship in order to build a predictor model.

The main steps are as follows:

1. Build the regression model and review its range of values or thresholds.

2. Test the model with known values and do a prediction with new ones.

3. Explain the SS errors with charts and values. They are the unexplained differences between the expected values and the given linear regression results.

4. Use the coefficients of determination and regression to measure the relationship between variables.

5. Explain the formulas and calculations of the results given by the linear regression function. This is useful if you are using different statistical packages, such as R and Python.

In the next section, we will build the model and the statistic methods, calculating the results step by step.

Computing coefficient significance – t-statistics and p-value

In this section, we will see four statistical probes to verify whether the variables have a strong enough relationship to build a predictive model. First, we have to understand a chart with data variables, a linear regression model, and the separation between the data points and the straight line.

The statistical tests are as follows:

- Coefficient of determination
- Coefficient of correlation
- *t*-statistics
- *P*-value

Now, we are going to explain the basic concepts to test whether the variables have a relationship to build a predictive model. *Figure 9.8* shows the following:

- The distance between the expected values and the linear regression model. These are the errors of the model or the unexplained variations.
- The distance between the expected values' average line and the regression model. This is the explained variation.
- The total variation, which is the sum of the errors and the explained variation.

Look at *Figure 9.8* to review the distances between the linear model and the expected values of the miles-per-gallon dependency on the motor horsepower. See the linear model errors or unexplained variation of the distance between the miles-per-gallon results and the regression.

The linear model errors are the distance between the regression line and the miles per gallon:

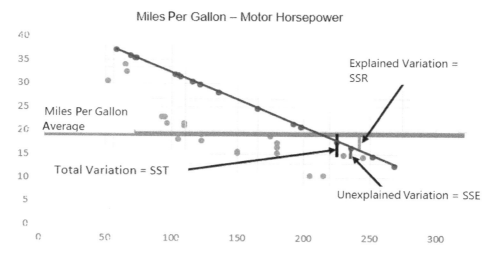

Figure 9.8 – The distance of the actual data from the linear model

The errors or unexplained variation and the explained variation distances are the input of statistical tests, such as t-test, p-value, and f-test, to check whether the data is useful to build a predictive model. The explanation for each concept is as follows:

- **SS total (the total variation, SST):** This is the distance from the data source point (intersection of horsepower and miles per gallon) to the miles-per-gallon average line.

- **SS unexplained variation or residual error SSE:** This is the distance between the data source point (intersection of horsepower and miles per gallon) and the value given by the linear model. This is known as the error of the linear model.

- **SS explained variation regression (SSR):** This is the distance between the linear regression straight line in gray and the miles-per-gallon average line.

The total variation (SST) is the sum of the residual error (SSE) and the explained variation regression.

Let's examine each of these elements with numerical values to show the relationship between the influence of horsepower and miles per gallon. The average of the miles per gallon or predicted variable, Y, is 19.77. It is represented by the horizontal straight line.

The unexplained variation or residual error (SSE) is the difference between the intersection of horsepower and the miles-per-gallon x and y axes and the value from the straight line of the model in gray.

For example, for 230 horsepower, the miles-per-gallon value is 14.70. The linear model value gave a result of 10.986. The difference between the data and the linear model is 3.71. Square this value to get the unexplained variation or residual error (SSE) equal to 13.788. The square is necessary to avoid any negative value due to subtraction (see *Figure 9.8*).

The explained variation regression (SSR) is the separation between the linear regression straight line and the Y average – in this case, the miles-per-gallon average line.

The total variation (SST) is the separation between the intersection of horsepower and the miles-per-gallon x and y axes and the miles-per-gallon average line (red line). In this example, for 230 horsepower, the miles-per-hour result is 14.70. The average miles per hour is 19.77. The subtraction of the miles-per-hour value and the average miles per hour is -5.07. Square this result to avoid all negative signs. The value for the total variation, SST, is equal to 25.74:

```
SST = Unexplained Variation or Residual Error (SSE) + Explained
Variation Regression (SSR)
```

We get the explained variation regression (SSR) with this formula:

```
Explained Variation Regression (SSR) = SST - Unexplained
Variation or Residual Error (SSE)
```

For this example, we have the following:

```
Explained Variation Regression (SSR) = 25.74 - 13.788 = 11.956
```

The following chart illustrates the SST, SRE, and SSR values and the calculations for each one:

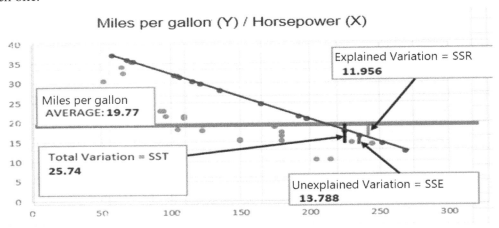

Figure 9.9 – The distance/variation of the actual data from the model's values

The sum of all the data source points (the intersection of horsepower and the miles-per-gallon x and y axes) for each variance gives the results of the SS of the linear regression function in *R*, *Excel*, or *Python*:

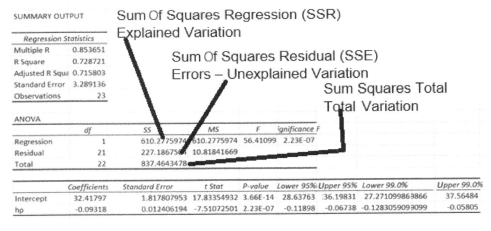

Figure 9.10 – The results of the linear regression function

The **ANOVA** section is a result of the linear regression model in *Figure 9.9*. *Figure 9.9* distances the data to the predictive values explained in *Figure 9.7*. One of the most important concepts to understand is the SS of the errors or the residual of the regression model (the unexplained variation). We will explain this in detail in the following paragraphs.

The ANOVA results from the linear regression function, which returns the values of the distances from the expected values to the model explained in *Figure 9.9*. The ANOVA results are in *Figure 9.10*.

ANOVA returns the following distance terms:

- **Regression** is the explained variation regression. **DF** is the **degrees of freedom** for regression. In this case, we have two variables – miles per gallon and horsepower. The degree of freedom is the number of variables minus 1 – in this example, *DF = 1*.

- **Residual** is the unexplained variation or residual error (SSE). The degree of freedom for the residual is the number of observations minus 2. In this example, the number of observations is 23. So, the degree of freedom for the residual is equal to 21.

Coefficient of determination

The **coefficient of determination** is the level of confidence to determine the *Y* value based on the *X* value. It is the percentage of trust for the relationship between horsepower and miles-per-gallon performance. The coefficient of determination formula is as follows:

```
SS Regression Explained Variation (SSR) divided by SST
```

You can see the SSR and the SST in the following chart:

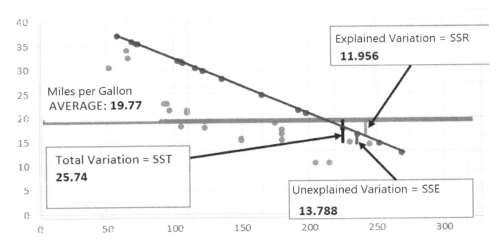

Figure 9.11 – SST, SSR, and SSE

We add all the points for the variance and get the results given by the linear regression function as follows:

SUMMARY OUTPUT

Regression Statistics	
Multiple R	0.853651
R Square	0.728721
Adjusted R Squa	0.715803
Standard Error	3.289136
Observations	23

ANOVA

	df	SS	MS	F	Significance F
Regression	1	610.2775974	610.2775974	56.41099	2.23E-07
Residual	21	227.1867504	10.81841669		
Total	22	837.4643478			

	Coefficients	Standard Error	t Stat	P-value	Lower 95%	Upper 95%	Lower 99.0%	Upper 99.0%
Intercept	32.41797	1.817807953	17.83354932	3.66E-14	28.63763	36.19831	27.27109986	37.56484
hp	-0.09318	0.012406194	-7.51072501	2.23E-07	-0.11898	-0.06738	-0.128305909	-0.05805

Figure 9.12 – The linear regression function results

We divide the explained variation regression (SSR) by the total variation (SST), and we get the coefficient of determination, r^2.

The formula for the coefficient of determination is as follows:

```
Coefficient of Determination, r2 = SSR / SST
r2 = 610.27 / 837.46 = 0.7287
```

The coefficient of determination (**R Square** in *Figure 9.13*) is *72%* of the horsepower data that determines miles-per-gallon performance:

SUMMARY OUTPUT

Regression Statistics	
Multiple R	0.853651
R Square	0.728721
Adjusted R Squa	0.715803
Standard Error	3.289136
Observations	23

ANOVA

	df	SS	MS	F	ignificance F
Regression	1	610.2775974	610.2775974	56.41099	2.23E-07
Residual	21	227.1867504	10.81841669		
Total	22	837.4643478			

	Coefficients	Standard Error	t Stat	P-value	Lower 95%	Upper 95%	Lower 99.0%	Ipper 99.0%
Intercept	32.41797	1.817807953	17.83354932	3.66E-14	28.63763	36.19831	27.27109986	37.56484
hp	-0.09318	0.012406194	-7.51072501	2.23E-07	-0.11898	-0.06738	-0.128305909	-0.05805

Figure 9.13 – The linear regression function results

In this section, we used the distance between the known values of miles per gallon influenced by motor horsepower to build a linear model and calculate its accuracy using the errors or the unexplained variation. These distance values are input to calculate the coefficient of determination, which gives an idea of how many points of motor horsepower directly influence miles-per-gallon performance. In the next section, we will see the coefficient of determination, which uses the sign of the slope to explain whether the relationship is direct or inverse.

Coefficient of correlation

The **coefficient of correlation** measures the strength of the relationship between the predictor variable, X (horsepower), and the prediction variable, Y (miles per gallon). It also says what the orientation of the slope is. It is helpful to know whether the relationship is proportional or inverse, depending on the slope sign. If the slope is positive, the relationship is direct. But if the slope is negative, the relationship is inverse. A direct relationship means that if the predictor variables grow (motor horsepower), the result also grows (miles per gallon). An inverse relationship is the opposite. In this case, the relationship is inverse because we see that the slope is negative. This means that as motor horsepower grows, miles-per-gallon performance decreases.

The formula for the coefficient of determination is as follows:

$$r_{xy=sign\ of\ b1}\sqrt{Coefficient\ of\ determination} = sign\ of\ b1\sqrt{r^2}$$

$$= -\sqrt{r^2} = -\sqrt{0.7287} = -0.8536$$

In the linear regression function results in *Figure 9.13*, the coefficient of determination term is **Multiple R**.

t-statistics and p-value

t-statistics and the **p-value** are tests to check whether the slope of the model is zero. If the slope is zero, it means that there is no relationship between the variables. A positive slope means a direct relationship between the variables. A negative slope means an inverse relationship. In this example, a negative slope says that greater horsepower means smaller miles-per-gallon performance. We are going to see how to calculate *t*-statistics and the *p*-value and check whether we can reject the `null` hypothesis that the slope is equal to zero. But first, we have to explain the residual standard error because it is an element of the *t*-test formula:

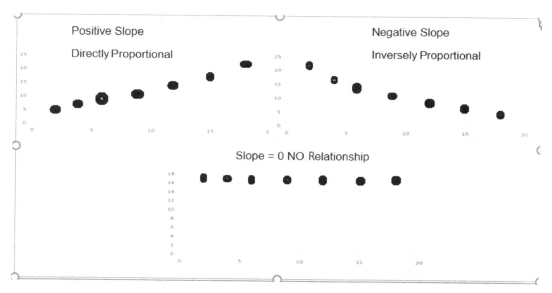

Figure 9.14 – A positive slope means a direct relationship, negative means an inverse relationship, and equal to zero means no relationship between variables

t-statistics give a value that can fall in the rejection region of the `null` hypothesis. The `null` hypothesis is that the slope is equal to zero, meaning that there is no relationship between the variables. If we reject that the slope is equal to zero, we conclude that there is a variable relationship, and we can use these values to make predictions:

$$Test\ Statistic = \frac{Slope\ B1}{S_{B_1}}$$

Here, we have the following:

$$S_{B_1} = \frac{s}{\sqrt{\Sigma(X_i - \overleftrightarrow{X})^2}}$$

The formula for *s* is as follows:

$$s = \sqrt{\frac{Unexplained\ variation\ SSE}{Number\ of\ elements - 2}}$$

s is the residual standard deviation. The residuals or errors are the differences between the expected values from the linear model. The best-case scenario is that the errors have a small standard deviation expressed by *s*. We are going to cover this in detail in the next section.

Getting the residual standard error

This term is used to calculate the *t*-statistics. The distance between the expected values is represented by the dots in *Figure 9.15*, and the straight line of the model is measured by the unexplained variation values. This best-case scenario for these unexplained variation values is to have a small residual standard deviation or a close distance between the expected values and the model:

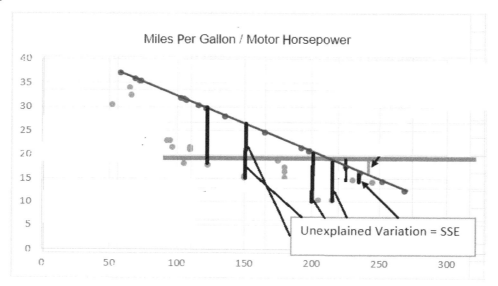

Figure 9.15 – Unexplained variation or SS errors

The unexplained variation distances have several points. The residual standard error says how scattered these points are. The ideal scenario is that we have a small average of unexplained variation and also a small standard deviation of unexplained variation. This means that the linear model fits the expected values of horsepower and miles per gallon.

Use the following distance measures between the model and the expected values to do a statistical analysis of the confidence of the values for horsepower and miles per gallon in order to build a prediction model:

- Unexplained variation
- Explained variation
- Total variation

To get these values, we need to calculate the intercept and the slope.

Next, we calculate the *t*-statistics to see whether we can reject the `null` hypothesis of *slope = 0*. The *t*-statistic value is an input for the ranges of the linear model. Presenting upper, medium, and lower scenarios of the predictions is more realistic than just one straight line.

Input data to build the prediction model and test whether the two variables have a strong relationship:

- **The x axis**: Horsepower – sum and average
- **The y axis**: Miles per gallon – sum and average

We will work with data for horsepower and miles per gallon to determine whether the predictor variable horsepower has a strong influence over miles per gallon and whether the data is useful to build a predictor model. *Figure 9.16* shows the data. The horsepower sum is `3,121.00` and the average is `135.69`. The miles-per-gallon sum is `454.8` and the average is `19.77`:

hp	mpg
110	21
110	21
93	22.8
110	21.4
175	18.7
105	18.1
245	14.3
62	24.4
95	22.8
123	19.2
123	17.8
180	16.4
180	17.3
180	15.2
205	10.4
215	10.4
230	14.7
66	32.4
52	30.4
65	33.9
97	21.5
150	15.5
150	15.2

sum	3121	454.8
avg	135.6956522	19.77391304

Figure 9.16 – Input data – the horsepower influence on miles per gallon

The linear model regression of the data in *Figure 9.16* is shown in *Figure 9.17*. Pay attention to the slope and the regression line to see how well they fit the values:

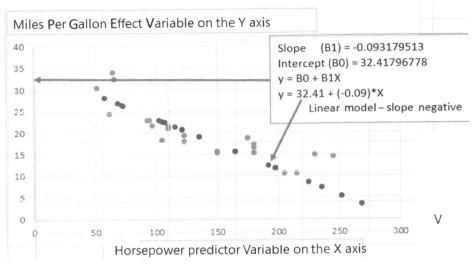

Figure 9.17 – Intercept and slope

The linear model has the following equation:

```
Y = Intercept (B0) + Slope (B1) * X
```

Here, the *B1* slope has the following formula:

$$Slope\ B1 = \frac{\Sigma(X_i - \bar{X})(Y_i - \overline{Y})}{\Sigma(X_i - \bar{X})^2}$$

In the numerator, we do the following:

- Subtract the average of *X* (horsepower) from every term in *X*.
- Subtract the average of *Y* (miles per gallon) from every term in *Y*.

In the denominator, we subtract the average value of X (horsepower) from every element of X and then apply exponent 2.

Calculations of the first row of the table in Figure 9.16 to show the operations

Let's calculate the distance of each predictor value (horsepower) from the average of all the horsepower points. Subtract each term from the average:

$(X_i - \bar{X}) = (110 - 135.69) = -25.695$

The next term is the difference between the Y result and its average:

$(Y_i - \bar{Y}) = (21 - 19.77) = 1.22$

Multiply the two terms described before – that is, the difference between the horsepower data and its average and the difference between the miles-per-gallon data and its average:

$(X_i - \bar{X}) \ (Y_i - \bar{Y}) = (-25.695) * (1.22) = -31.505$

Finally, square the difference between the horsepower and its average to avoid the negative symbol:

$\Sigma (X_i - \bar{X})2 = (110 - 136.69)2 = 660.266$

Use these calculated terms to get the slope:

$$Slope \ B1 = \frac{\Sigma \ (X_i - \bar{X})(Y_i - \bar{Y})}{\Sigma(X_i - \bar{X}) \ 2} = \frac{6549.48}{70288.86} = -0.09317951$$

We will provide an example to explain step by step how to build the linear regression model by calculating the intercept and the slope. *Figure 9.18* has the data and the source calculations for these terms:

hp	mpg	$(X_i - \bar{X})$	$(Y_i - \bar{Y})$	$(X_i - \bar{X})(Y_i - \bar{Y})$	$(X_i - \bar{X})^2$
	110	21	-25.69565217	1.226087	-31.50510397	660.2665406
	110	21	-25.69565217	1.226087	-31.50510397	660.2665406
	93	22.8	-42.69565217	3.026087	-129.2007561	1822.918715
	110	21.4	-25.69565217	1.626087	-41.78336484	660.2665406
	175	18.7	39.30434783	-1.07391	-42.2094518	1544.831758
	105	18.1	-30.69565217	-1.67391	51.38185255	942.2230624
	245	14.3	109.3043478	-5.47391	-598.3224953	11947.44045
	62	24.4	-73.69565217	4.626087	-340.9224953	5431.049149
	95	22.8	-40.69565217	3.026087	-123.1485822	1656.136106
	123	19.2	-12.69565217	-0.57391	7.286200378	161.1795841
	123	17.8	-12.69565217	-1.97391	25.06011342	161.1795841
	180	16.4	44.30434783	-3.37391	-149.479017	1962.875236
	180	17.3	44.30434783	-2.47391	-109.605104	1962.875236
	180	15.2	44.30434783	-4.57391	-202.6442344	1962.875236
	205	10.4	69.30434783	-9.37391	-649.6529301	4803.092628
	215	10.4	79.30434783	-9.37391	-743.3920605	6289.179584
	230	14.7	94.30434783	-5.07391	-478.4920605	8893.310019
	66	32.4	-69.69565217	12.62609	-879.9833648	4857.483932
	52	30.4	-83.69565217	10.62609	-889.3572779	7004.962193
	65	33.9	-70.69565217	14.12609	-998.6529301	4997.875236
	97	21.5	-38.69565217	1.726087	-66.79206049	1497.353497
	150	15.5	14.30434783	-4.27391	-61.13553875	204.6143667
	150	15.2	14.30434783	-4.57391	-65.4268431	204.6143667
sum	3121	454.8	2.55795E-13	1.07E-13	-6549.482609	70288.86957
avg	135.6956522	19.77391304	1.11215E-14	4.63E-15	-284.7601134	3056.037807

Figure 9.18 – Calculations for intercept and slope

The slope from *Figure 9.18* indicates an inverse relationship of the variables because it has a negative sign:

```
Slope B1 = -0.09317951
```

Now, we calculate the intercept. This value is the Y position when X is zero.

The formula is as follows:

```
Intercept B0 = Ȳ - Slope B1 * X̄
```

The average of the y axis (miles per gallon), minus the slope ($B1$), multiplied by the average of the x axis (horsepower) is as follows:

```
Intercept B0 = 19.77 - (-0.0931) * 135.695
Intercept B0 = 32.41796778
```

The linear model is represented by the following formula:

$$(Y) \text{ Miles per hour model} = \text{Intercept } B0 + \text{Slope } B1 * X$$

For the first row, we have the following:

$$(Y) \text{ Miles per hour model} = 32.4179 + (-0.0931) * 110 = 22.168$$

After developing the regression formula, we have the values returned by the model. The mpg^ column has the results of the regression formula. We are going to calculate the errors or the difference between the expected values in mpg and the results of mpg^ to see whether we can build predictions that are statistically confident:

hp	mpg	mpg^
110	21	22.16822
110	21	22.16822
93	22.8	23.75227
110	21.4	22.16822
175	18.7	16.11155
105	18.1	22.63412
245	14.3	9.588987
62	24.4	26.64084
95	22.8	23.56591
123	19.2	20.95689
123	17.8	20.95689
180	16.4	15.64566
180	17.3	15.64566
180	15.2	15.64566
205	10.4	13.31617
215	10.4	12.38437
230	14.7	10.98668
66	32.4	26.26812
52	30.4	27.57263
65	33.9	26.3613
97	21.5	23.37956
150	15.5	18.44104
150	15.2	18.44104

Expected results or data source for horsepower (hp) and miles per gallon (mpg)

Values for the linear model

Figure 9.19 – Calculations for the linear model

The chart representation of the source data and the linear model is as follows:

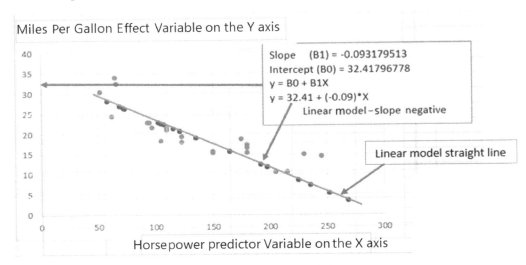

Figure 9.20 – Intercept and slope

The linear model says that when X (horsepower) equals zero, the miles per gallon is 32.41.

The model's straight-line distance from the expected values (the dots) determines whether there is a relationship between the variables. The statistical tests to prove this fact are as follows:

- Coefficient significance
- t-statistics and the p-value
- Residual standard error

To do the calculations of the statistical significance of the relationship between horsepower and miles per gallon, we have to remember the concepts of the distance from the expected values (data source) to the linear model:

- The explained variation (SS regression)
- The unexplained variation (SS errors)
- The total variation (SS total)

These terms are graphically represented in *Figure 9.21*. The most important element is the sum of unexplained variation because it measures how far the regression model is from the expected values:

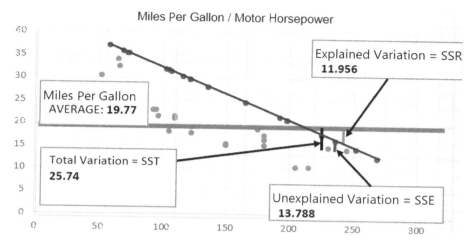

Figure 9.21 – SST, SSR, and SSE

The formula to calculate the SS due to error (the unexplained variation – SSE) is as follows:

$$SSE = \sum (Y_i - \hat{y}_i)^2$$

To calculate the SST or total variation, use the following formula:

$$SST = \sum (Y_i - \bar{Y}_i)^2$$

The value for each Y (miles per gallon) minus the average of Y squared is as follows:

```
Sum of Squares due to Regression (Explained Variation) = SST -
SSE (Unexplained Variation)
```

Figure 9.22 is a chart of the calculations. For the first row, the data for SSE is as follows:

```
SSE = (21 - 22.16)2 = 1.36
```

For the SSE of the previous chart with the distance's lines, we have this calculation:

```
SSE = (14.7 - 10.986)2 = 13.788
```

The explained variation calculation for the preceding distance chart is as follows:

```
Explained Variation Regression = SST - SSE = 24.74 - 13.788 =
11.956
```

For this example, we have `SSE = 227.18` and `SST = 837.46`.

The sum of squares regression (SST) is the result of the addition of the unexplained variation (errors) and the explained variation. To explain the formula, look at the values of the errors and the SST in *Figure 9.22*:

X	Y		Square Error- SSE	$\sum(\hat{y}_i - \bar{y})^2$
hp	mpg	mpg^	$\sum(Y_i - \hat{y}_i)2$	SumSquaresRegression(SST)
110	21	22.16822	1.364741215	1.503289225
110	21	22.16822	1.364741215	1.503289225
93	22.8	23.75227	0.906824065	9.157202268
110	21.4	22.16822	0.590164103	2.64415879
175	18.7	16.11155	6.700057514	1.153289225
105	18.1	22.63412	20.55823468	2.801984877
245	14.3	9.588987	22.19364174	29.96372401
62	24.4	26.64084	5.021354921	21.40068053
95	22.8	23.56591	0.586624376	9.157202268
123	19.2	20.95689	3.08665448	0.329376181
123	17.8	20.95689	9.965940111	3.896332703
180	16.4	15.64566	0.569035615	11.38328922
180	17.3	15.64566	2.736855705	6.120245747
180	15.2	15.64566	0.19860883	20.92068053
205	10.4	13.31617	8.504034	87.87024575
215	10.4	12.38437	3.937734474	87.87024575
230	14.7	10.98668	13.78874635	25.74459357
66	32.4	26.26812	37.59995301	159.4180718
52	30.4	27.57263	7.994003466	112.913724
65	33.9	26.3613	56.83200587	199.5463327
97	21.5	23.37956	3.532727199	2.979376181
150	15.5	18.44104	8.649721485	18.2663327
150	15.2	18.44104	10.50434602	20.92068053
sum	3121	454.8	227.1867504	837.4643478
avg	135.6956522	19.77391304	9.877684802	36.41149338

Figure 9.22 – Calculations for the SSE and the SST

The sum for SS errors is `227.18` and the sum for the SS total is `837.46`.

We can calculate the *t*-statistic to see whether we can reject the `null` hypothesis that the slope is equal to zero. Remember the formula for *t*-statistics:

$$Test\ Statistic = \frac{Slope\ B1}{S_{B_1}}$$

Here, we have the following:

$$S_{B_1} = \frac{s}{\sqrt{\Sigma(X_i - \overleftrightarrow{X})^2}}$$

Subtract each X_i value from the average of all the X values and then apply an exponent of 2.

The term s is the residual standard error.

The formula for s is as follows:

$$s = \sqrt{\frac{Unexplained\ variation\ SSE}{Number\ of\ elements - 2}}$$

Remember that the unexplained variation (SSE) is the separation distance between the data and the linear model values.

The chart in *Figure 9.23* shows the standard deviation of the distance between the expected values and the linear regression model. The vertical lines are the unexplained variation values:

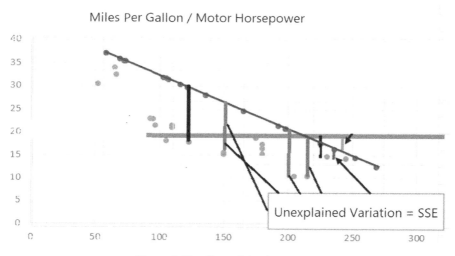

Figure 9.23 – Unexplained variation

The unexplained variation distances have several points. The residual standard error indicates how scattered these points are. The ideal case is that we have a small average of unexplained variation and also a small standard deviation of unexplained variation. This means the linear model fits the expected values of horsepower and miles per gallon.

The number of elements of the SSE or residual is the number of points minus 2. In this example, it is 23 – 2 = 21. The SSE unexplained variation calculated is 227.186:

$$s = \sqrt{\frac{227.186}{21}}$$

The result is s = 3.213.

Then, we calculate the following:

$$S_{B_1} = \frac{s}{\sqrt{\sum(X_i - \vec{X})^2}}$$

$$S_{B_1} = \frac{3.213}{\sqrt{70288.86957}}$$

$$S_{B_1} = 0.012120956$$

$$Test\ Statistic = \frac{Slope\ B1}{S_{B_1}}$$

$$Test\ Statistic = \frac{-0.09317951}{0.012120956}$$

$$Test\ Statistic = -7.687472133$$

We can find a *t*-statistics table here: https://www.medcalc.org/manual/t-distribution-table.php.

The *t*-statistics value is -7.68, so we have to evaluate whether it falls in the rejection area to accept the alternative hypothesis that the slope is not equal to zero and there is a relationship between horsepower and miles-per-gallon performance:

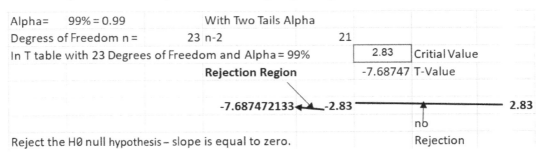

Figure 9.24 – Reject the H0 null hypothesis – the slope is not equal to zero

There is a relationship between the variables because we reject the `null` hypothesis. The slope is *not* equal to zero.

The critical values are `2.83` and `-2.83`. The *t*-statistic value is `-7.68`, so it is in the rejection region. We accept the alternative hypothesis, and the slope is *not* equal to zero. This means there is a relationship between miles per gallon and horsepower.

Using the *p*-value approach, we look for the `7.68` (absolute value) and 21 degrees of freedom values in the table. The alpha value is `0.01`. To reject the `null` hypothesis, we need a *p*-value that is less than `0.01`.

We see that the *p*-value is less than `0.001`. We multiply `0.001` by 2 because we want the rejection region to be at both tails of the bell curve. The result of the multiplication for the *p*-value is `0.002`.

The *p*-value (`0.002`) is less than the alpha value (`0.01`), so we reject the `null` hypothesis and accept the alternative. The slope is *not* equal to zero:

p-value				
t (statistic) =	b1/Sb1	-7.687472133	alpha = 0.01	
Degrees of freedom n =	23 n-2		21	
For the T table with 23 degrees of freedom, look for p-value			-7.68747 Moving to the right, the p-value is less than 0.001	
			For two tail the p-value*2 (0.001*2) =	0.002
	Remember to take the absolute value = 7.68		Reject H0 if p-value < alpha	0.002 < 0.01
			0.002 < 0.01	
	0.01-0.002=		0.008	
			Accept H1 – there is a relationship between the two datasets	

Figure 9.25 – The p-value rejects the null hypothesis H0 – the slope is not equal to zero

In this section, we used the *t*-statistics and *p*-value to see whether we can reject the `null` hypothesis that the slope is equal to zero. This fact means that there is no relationship between the variables. In the next section, we will see another coefficient that tells us the level of statistical significance that the predictor variables have over the results of the *Y* value.

Calculating the r-squared

The *r*-squared is the coefficient of determination that was calculated earlier. It tells us the factor of separation between the *Y* value (miles per gallon) of the dataset (the blue dots) and *Y'* (miles per gallon calculated by the model – the gray line) from the average of *Y* (the red line) as an origin line. Consult the chart to understand this relationship.

This is the explained variation (SSR) divided by the total variation (SST):

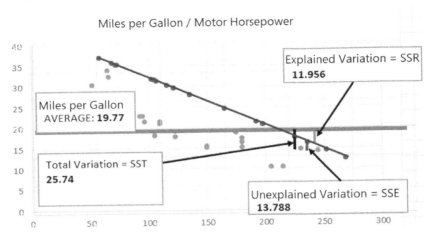

Figure 9.26 – SST, SSR, and SSE

The coefficient of determination

The coefficient of determination is one of the indicators of the relationship strength between the variables:

```
r2 = Explained Variation Regression Sum of Squares SSR divided
by Total Variation Sum of Squares SST
```

For our example, we calculated these variations:

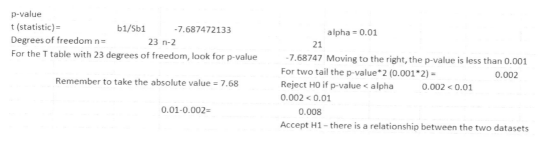

X	Y		Square Error – SSE	$\Sigma(\hat{y}_i - \bar{y})^2$
hp	mpg	mpg^	$\Sigma(Y_i - \hat{y}_i)2$	Sum Squares Regression (SST)
110	21	22.16822	1.364741215	1.503289225
110	21	22.16822	1.364741215	1.503289225
93	22.8	23.75227	0.906824065	9.157202268
110	21.4	22.16822	0.590164103	2.64415879
175	18.7	16.11155	6.700057514	1.153289225
105	18.1	22.63412	20.55823468	2.801984877
245	14.3	9.588987	22.19364174	29.96372401
62	24.4	26.64084	5.021354921	21.40068053
95	22.8	23.56591	0.586624376	9.157202268
123	19.2	20.95689	3.08665448	0.329376181
123	17.8	20.95689	9.965940111	3.896332703
180	16.4	15.64566	0.569035615	11.38328922
180	17.3	15.64566	2.736855705	6.120245747
180	15.2	15.64566	0.19860883	20.92068053
205	10.4	13.31617	8.504034	87.87024575
215	10.4	12.38437	3.937734474	87.87024575
230	14.7	10.98668	13.78874635	25.74459357
66	32.4	26.26812	37.59995301	159.4180718
52	30.4	27.57263	7.994003466	112.913724
65	33.9	26.3613	56.83200587	199.5463327
97	21.5	23.37956	3.532727199	2.979376181
150	15.5	18.44104	8.649721485	18.2663327
150	15.2	18.44104	10.50434602	20.92068053
sum	3121	454.8	227.1867504	837.4643478
avg	135.6956522	19.77391304	9.877684802	36.41149338

Figure 9.27 – Calculations for SSE and SST – the sum of the SS errors is 227.18 and the sum for the SS total is 837.46

Calculate the linear regression terms using the values of *Figure 9.27*:

```
Explained Variation (SSR) = Total Variation Sum of Squares
(SST) - Unexplained Variation Residual Sum of Squares (SSE)
Explained Variation (SSR) = 837.4643 - 227.186 = 610.2783
Coefficient of Determination, r2 = Explained Variation
Regression Sum of Squares (SSR) / Total Variation Sum of
Squares (SST)
rr squared = 610.2783 / 827.4643 = 0.7375
```

This means *73%* of the distance (see *Figure 9.27*) from the average of the data source to the model, which is acceptable.

The coefficient of determination is the r-squared result returned by the linear regression formula in *Figure 9.28*. It has a value of 0.7287:

SUMMARY OUTPUT

Regression Statistics	
Multiple R	0.853651
R Square	0.728721
Adjusted R Square	0.715803
Standard Error	3.289136
Observations	23

ANOVA

	df	SS	MS	F	Significance F
Regression	1	610.2775974	610.2775974	56.41099	2.23E-07
Residual	21	227.1867504	10.81841669		
Total	22	837.4643478			

	Coefficients	Standard Error	t Stat	P-value	Lower 95%	Upper 95%	Lower 99.0%	Upper 99.0%
Intercept	32.41797	1.817807953	17.83354932	3.66E-14	28.63763	36.19831	27.27109986	37.56484
hp	-0.09318	0.012406194	-7.51072501	2.23E-07	-0.11898	-0.06738	-0.128305909	-0.05805

Figure 9.28 – The response from the linear model function

The r-squared value in the response from the linear function is 0.7287. The difference between the function results of *Figure 9.28* and the previous r-squared calculation is because of the decimals in the calculation.

Calculating the f-statistics

The f-statistics are another test to see whether the slope is equal to zero. The `null` hypothesis is that the slope is zero. The f-statistics test whether we can reject this. To calculate it, we have to define the mean squared error first.

The regression for the mean squared error is the explained variation regression (SSE) divided by the regression degrees of freedom minus 1. In this example, we have the regression for two variables. The degree of freedom is 1:

```
Regression Mean Squared Error = SSR / Regression Degrees of
Freedom
Regression Mean Squared Error = 610.277 / 1 = 610.277
```

The residual mean squared error is the unexplained variation residual sum of squares (SSE) divided by the degrees of freedom of the residuals. The residual degrees of freedom are the number of records of the data source minus 2. In this case, we have 23 records. The degrees of freedom are 21:

```
Residual Mean Squared Error = Unexplained Variation Residual
Sum of Squares (SSE) / Residuals Degrees of Freedom
Residual Mean Squared Error = 227.186 / 21 = 10.818
```

The f-statistics formula is as follows:

```
F-Statistics = Regression Mean Squared Error / Residual Mean
Squared Error
F-Statistics = 610.277 / 10.8184 = 56.41
```

The f-statistics are the F term of the linear regression function response in *Figure 9.29*. It is the result of dividing the mean squared regression by the mean squared residual:

SUMMARY OUTPUT

Regression Statistics	
Multiple R	0.853651
R Square	0.728721
Adjusted R Square	0.715803
Standard Error	3.289136
Observations	23

ANOVA

	df	SS	MS	F	Significance F
Regression	1	610.2775974	610.2775974	56.41099	2.23E-07
Residual	21	227.1867504	10.81841669		
Total	22	837.4643478			

	Coefficients	Standard Error	t Stat	P-value	Lower 95%	Upper 95%	Lower 99.0%	Upper 99.0%
Intercept	32.41797	1.817807953	17.83354932	3.66E-14	28.63763	36.19831	27.27109986	37.56484
hp	-0.09318	0.012406194	-7.51072501	2.23E-07	-0.11898	-0.06738	-0.128305909	-0.05805

Figure 9.29 – The response from the linear model function

We look for the degrees of freedom of regression and residual in an f-table. df_1 is 1 and df_2 is 21. The critical value for f-statistics is 2.96:

\	df_1=1	2	3	4
df_2=1	39.86346	49.50000	53.59324	55.83296
2	8.52632	9.00000	9.16179	9.24342
3	5.53832	5.46238	5.39077	5.34264
4	4.54477	4.32456	4.19086	4.10725
5	4.06042	3.77972	3.61948	3.52020
19	2.98990	2.60561	2.39702	2.26630
20	2.97465	2.58925	2.38009	2.24893
21	2.96096	2.57457	2.36489	2.23334

Figure 9.30 – The f-statistics table

The f-statistics value is 56.41. It is greater than the critical value of 2.96. Reject the null hypothesis that the slope is zero. Choose the alternative hypothesis and you will see that the slope is different than zero. So, there is a relationship between the two variables.

Training and testing the model

Now that we have done statistical tests to see whether there is a significant relationship between the predictor variable (horsepower) and the result variable (miles per gallon), we are ready to test the model with known values and see how well it fits. The tests we did are as follows:

- The coefficient of determination
- The coefficient of correlation
- t-statistics
- The p-value
- f-statistics

We will provide a summary of them in the following paragraphs.

The **coefficient of determination** is the level of confidence to determine the Y value based on the X value. It is the percentage of trust in the relationship between horsepower and miles-per-gallon performance. For this example, it has a value of 0.7287, meaning that *72%* of the predictor values (horsepower) determine the result of miles per gallon.

The **coefficient of correlation** measures the strength of the relationship between the X predictor variable (horsepower) and the Y prediction variable (miles per gallon).

In this example, it has a value of 0.8536, or *85%*, meaning that the predictor variables have a strong influence over the Y result variable or miles-per-gallon performance.

t-statistics check that the slope is *not* equal to zero. That indicates the existence of a relationship between the variables. Miles per gallon are impacted by horsepower. In our example, the *t*-statistics value falls in the rejection region. So, we reject the `null` hypothesis and accept the alternative. The slope is not zero. Also, the **p-value** indicates that the slope is not zero.

f-statistics also check that the slope is not zero.

The calculation for *f*-statistics is `regression mean squared / residual mean squared`:

```
Regression degrees of freedom = 1
Residual degrees of freedom = 21
```

Look at an *f*-distribution table and search for 1 in the first degrees of freedom column and 21 in the second degrees of freedom column. We know that the critical value for the *f*-distribution is 2.96096. The *f*-statistical value is 56.4109. This value is greater than 2.96096, so we can accept the alternative hypothesis. The slope is *not* zero. There is a relationship between the variables.

This is supervised machine learning because we get and train the model with known values. These known values are, for example, *80%* of the data source. Then, we use the remaining *20%* to test the linear model and see whether it fits the expected values.

Test the following linear model that we get after calculating with known values. Next, you need to review the separation values between the expected values and what the model calculated. The linear model is calculated with the following formula:

```
y = Intercept B0 + Slope B1 * X
y = 32.41 + (-0.09) * X
```

Figure 9.31 shows the values calculated by the model. The headings are as follows:

- **hp** (the *x* axis) = horsepower

- **mpg** (the *y* axis) = miles per gallon

- **mpg^** = miles per gallon calculated by the model

- Y_i-$Y^\wedge_i$ = the difference between the expected value and the calculation from the model

See the chart test model in *Figure 9.31* with 10 known data points. For the first row, the calculation is as follows:

```
Miles per gallon (y), mpg^ = 32.41 + (-0.09) * X (horsepower)
Miles per gallon (y), mpg^ = 32.41 + (-0.09) * 245 (horsepower)
Miles per gallon (y), mpg^ = 9.588
```

Having designed the model with *80%* of the data, we will now test its accuracy using the remaining *20%*, which is unknown to the regression model, and we will see how accurate it is in predicting. These data values are shown in *Figure 9.31*:

X	Y		Error	
hp	mpg		mpg^	Yi-Y^i
245	13.3		9.588987	3.711012814
175	19.2		16.11155	3.088446931
66	27.3		26.26812	1.031880055
91	26		23.93863	2.061367871
113	30.4		21.88868	8.511317148
264	15.8		7.818576	7.981423554
175	19.7		16.11155	3.588446931
335	15		1.202831	13.79716895
109	21.4		22.2614	-0.861400902

Figure 9.31 – 20% of the data source testing the model

In *Figure 9.32*, you can see that we tested the model with 10 known data points, and we see the linear regression straight line in red. The expected values are in blue. We see that values between 13 and 15 miles per hour impacted by horsepower between 250 and 350 have a large distance from the linear model.

We get the error of the separation between the linear model and expected values with the following formula:

```
Error Yi-Y^i = 13.3 - 9.588 = 3.711
```

See the separation distance in the chart between the expected values and the linear model. We create a coordinates chart with these distances and check four points that have a large distance from the expected values:

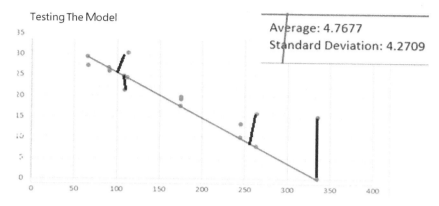

Figure 9.32 – The linear test model for 20% of the data

The vertical lines represent the errors or unexplained variations of the model. These variations have an average of 4.7677 and a standard deviation of 4.2709.

The average for the separation is 4.7677 and the standard deviation is 4.2709. This large standard deviation indicates that the model error from the expected values is scattered. The model does not generate compact values.

After doing the machine learning steps to build a predictive model, do the following:

- Define the model and validate that the data is useful for predicting.
- Train the linear regression with known data.
- Test the linear model to check whether it fits the expected values.
- Generate predictions of values using the linear regression model.

We are ready to build predictions and see whether the results make sense based on our experience. The calculation of the first row of the predicted values is as follows:

```
Miles per gallon (y), mpg^ = Intercept B0 + Slope B1 * X
Miles per gallon (y), mpg^ = 32.41 + (-0.09) * X
Miles per gallon (y), mpg^ = 32.41 + (-0.09) * 300
Miles per gallon (y), mpg^ = 4.4641
```

Now, we will use unknown values for the regression model to test its ability to predict new scenarios. We have to use our know-how and experience to evaluate whether the model is doing good work in making predictions or whether we are still missing something, even when the statistical tests prove that there is a relationship among the variables:

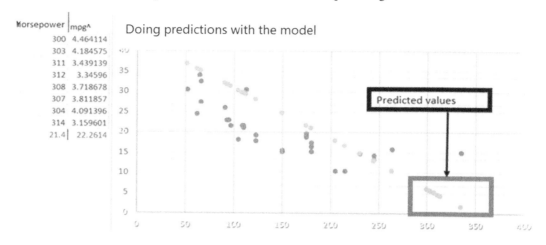

Figure 9.33 – The predicted values chart and table

Check the predicted values in the red box. Note the miles-per-gallon outlier value of 15 when horsepower is at 345. It goes against the trending downloading downward slope.

In this section, we used unknown values to test the prediction model. Use your judgment to determine whether the regression is working or whether it is returning inaccurate values. The model gives just an approximation of what can happen; it is not an exact reflection of the future. In the next section, we are going to see how to build distinct scenarios of the probable predictions of the regression model.

Doing prediction scenarios with the regression model

As we saw earlier, the regression model is not an exact answer for our prediction's needs because it depends on the level of the relationship between the causal variables and the Y result/effect variable.

Taking this into account, a more realistic answer is to present three scenarios of the prediction model. The scenarios depend on the confidence level of the slope. We have the upper and lower scenarios, depending on the value assigned to the slope. These scenarios exhibit the different value range for miles-per-gallon performance, depending on the variation of horsepower from *0* to *150*:

- **Linear model scenario**: Miles-per-gallon performance goes from *34* to *14*

- **Upper scenario**: Performance of miles per gallon has a range between *30* and *17*

- **Lower scenario**: Performance of miles per gallon goes from *30* to *0*

The formula for the confidence level of the slope is as follows:

$$Confidence\ level\ of\ slope = Slope\ B1 \pm t_{alpha/2} * s_{b1}$$

From previous calculations of this example, we know the following:

$$t - statistic = t_{alpha/2} = 2.83$$

We also know the following:

$$s_{b1} = 0.0121$$

The confidence level of the slope is as follows:

```
Upper value = -0.058877207
Lower value = -0.127481819
```

The chart for the range scenarios is as follows. We have three scenarios for the prediction model – the upper, lower, and original linear model without ranges:

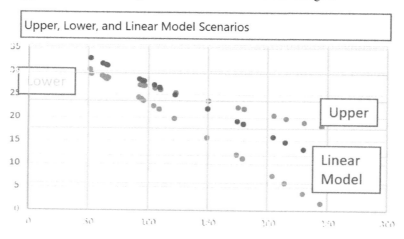

Figure 9.34 – The range scenarios

We learned how we can see the upper and lower trending values predicted by the model. With these results, we can get an idea of the ranges for possible future values. In the next chapter, we are going to start a new topic. We will see how a time series can help us to identify season-dependable data and how to do predictions with information that depends on a time variable.

Summary

In this chapter, we learned how to build a linear regression formula and, beyond this, how to visualize the distances between expected values and a model. These distances are input for statistical tests to find out whether the model is good enough to predict new values.

The machine learning workflow to use a model for prediction starts by doing a definition of the target information we expect and data validation, using a chart to see the possible relationships between the variables. We use 80% of the known data to train the model and see whether it returns values that make sense to our experience. With the remaining 20% of the data, we test the model and see whether it fits the data that was not part of the training. Finally, we predict new values. We have to apply our judgment to see whether the regression is working or not.

This knowledge is useful to apply statistical tests that reject the `null` hypothesis that the slope of the linear model is equal to zero. A slope greater than zero means a relationship between variables and their ability to predict new values.

We use the coefficient of determination and correlation to see the level of influence of the predictor variables over the results of Y, as well as seeing whether the relationship is directly or inversely proportional, depending on the sign of the slope. The t-statistics, p-value, and f-statistics check whether we can reject the `null` hypothesis that there is no relationship between the variables. If we can reject the `null` hypothesis, that means the slope is equal to zero.

If the model is successfully tested to make predictions, we can generate upper and lower scenarios to see the range of values.

All these concepts give the possible behavior of the predictions because the model gives trends, not exact results.

The model definition, understanding of the variables' relationships, training, and validation with statistical methods of the simple linear model, which we learned in this chapter, are applied to multiple regression in the next chapter. We will design predictions for three or more variables.

Questions

Here are a few questions and their answers to revisit the concepts we learned in this chapter:

1. What are the input values for the coefficient of correlation? Explain each of them.
2. What is the application of t-statistics in a linear model?
3. Why do we need to build different scenarios for the regression model?
4. What is the worst-case scenario for the residual standard error?

Answers

Here are the answers to the preceding questions:

1. The first input value is the coefficient of determination. Its formula is the explained variation divided by the total variation. The second input value is the sign of the slope. If it is positive, the relationship is direct. If not, the relationship is inverse.
2. t-statistics tell us whether the `null` hypothesis that the slope is equal to zero can be rejected. The slope with a non-zero value means a relationship between the variables. This is the alternative hypothesis.

3. The model just gives trends, not exact results. The scenarios give us an idea of the range of values that the model predicts. It helps to analyze whether the results make sense or not, based on our experience.

4. The unexplained variation or errors of the linear model is the distance of the model from the expected values. These distances must be short to have an effective predictor model. If it is not, the worst-case scenario is a high standard deviation of the errors. The model gives scattered results that can lead to bad predictions.

10
Building, Training, and Validating a Multiple Regression Model

In this chapter, we are going to apply our knowledge of the statistical tests of relationship confidence to build a predictive model.

Because we are now working with a multivariable regression model, we have to explore the most influential variables to build the best prediction case.

We will work with a case with several values, and we will use our judgment and statistical tests to ascertain which two variables have more influence over the prediction that we are looking for.

We have to apply our judgment because it could be the case that the f-statistics and p-value accept the null hypothesis that the slope is equal to zero for a variable. However, the relationship is validated by the coefficients of determination and correlation, as well as by the f-statistics. f-statistics is a test to reject the hypothesis that the slope is equal to zero, meaning that there is no relationship between the regression variables, so the data is not useful in terms of building a prediction model. The p-value also tests the relationship among regression variables.

That is why, besides the statistical tests, we have to visualize the relationship of the variables with a chart.

The topics covered in this chapter are as follows:

- Exploring the variables with more influence
- Calculating t-statistics and p-values
- Calculating residuals standard error and f-statistics
- Training and testing the model

After we validate the relationship between the variables in this chapter, we will learn how to apply the steps of the **machine learning** (**ML**) model by training and writing the regression function with 80% of the data and testing the model with the remaining 20%. Finally, we will use the model to predict with new input predictor values.

Technical requirements

Download the Excel file for this chapter here: `https://github.com/PacktPublishing/Data-Forecasting-and-Segmentation-Using-Microsoft-Excel/blob/main/Chapter10/chapterTenMultiRegression.xlsx`.

Exploring the variables with more influence

In this section, we will undertake a multi-regression exercise exploring the variables that could influence the sales revenue of a business. Please download the Excel worksheet from the *Technical requirements* section at the beginning of this chapter. Open the **Sales inventory** sheet. The first task of the job is to find which are the two most influential variables, *X* and *Y*, over a `sales-revenue` results variable. The variables on the worksheet that could influence sales and revenue are as follows:

- Number of hours out of service
- Material rotation
- Online marketing

- Sector sales

- Distance (Km) to competing stores

To find the two most influential variables, follow this process:

- Use the t-statistics and the p-value analysis returned by the regression function. To validate the variables, examine the 3D chart and ascertain whether there is an obvious relationship between them.

- Understand the influence of each predictor variable on the Y result (sales revenue) by plotting each variable in a simple regression chart.

The regression function returns the t-statistics, p-value, and f-statistics for multiple variables to identify the level of relationship among them and the result variable. However, it is better to run the regression function using each variable and the result variable to measure the influence of each one independently.

The dataset for sales revenue and possible influence variables is as follows:

Revenue-Sales	Hours Out Of Service	Material Rotation	Online Marketing	Sector Sales	Kms. To Store Competition
92.4	1.2	117.6	3.279999924	3.279999924	4.4
62.4	0.880000019	92.8	2.760000038	1.639999962	4.8
4	0.2	59.6	1.2	1.720000076	6
207.6	2.2	240	4.8	6.440000152	0.4
174.8	1.760000038	226.8	4.240000152	5.640000152	2
194.8	1.920000076	228.4	4.720000076	5.079999924	1.6
119.6	1.239999962	204.8	3.24	4.040000152	4
78	1	138.8	3.079999924	3.36	4.8
8	0.480000019	84.8	1.319999981	0.839999962	6
27.2	0.24000001	40.8	1.960000038	1.879999924	3.2
228	2.160000038	315.2	6.959999848	4.920000076	0.4
171.2	1.679999924	230.8	4.2	5.6	2.8
185.6	1.879999924	214	4.520000076	6	1.2
6	0.24000001	65.2	1	1	5.6
26	0.480000019	67.2	1.879999924	1.319999981	4.4
39.2	0.64000001	60.4	1.839999962	1.080000019	4
159.2	1.720000076	136.8	2.2	6.4	1.6
64.4	1.039999962	78.4	2.879999924	2.520000076	5.2
158.8	1.519999981	181.2	4.159999848	5.559999848	2.8
198.8	2.120000076	207.2	4.6	6.519999696	0.4
211.2	2.239999962	246	4.920000076	6.4	0
39.6	0.320000005	111.2	1.119999981	2.6	5.6
0.2	0.44000001	56.8	1.239999962	0.64000001	4.8
138.8	1.439999962	184.4	3.84	4.520000076	2.4
136.4	1.4	152.8	3.920000076	4.6	2
202.8	2.039999962	236	4.8	6.279999924	0
160	3.44	206.8	2.8	4.8	3.2

Figure 10.1 – A possible predictor variable for sales revenue

Use the p-value to find which variables have more influence. The alpha value is 0.01 because we look at a 99.99 level of confidence. So, the p-value must be less than 0.01 to accept the relationship between the analyzed variable and the sales revenue.

To execute the regression function in Excel, go to the **DATA** option in the upper panel. Then, click **Data Analysis** and select **REGRESSION**. Refer to *Figure 10.1* for the input parameters:

- **Input Y Range**: The sales revenue results variable.
- **Input X Range**: The predictor variables.
- Check the **Labels** box.
- Input 99% for **Confidence Level**.
- **Output Range** selects the cell to store the results.

The Excel regression function result elements are in *Figure 10.2*:

Revenue-Sales	Hours Out Of Service	Material Rotation	Online Marketing	Sector Sales	Kms. To Store	Competition
92.4	1.2	117.6	3.279999924	3.27999992		4.4
62.4	0.880000019	92.8	2.760000038	1.63999996		4.8
4	0.2	59.6	1.2	1.72000008		6
207.6	2.2	240	4.8	6.44000015		0.4
174.8	1.760000038	226.8	4.240000152	5.64000015		2
194.8	1.920000076	228.4	4.720000076	5.07999992		1.6
119.6	1.239999962	204.8	3.24	4.04000015		4
78	1	138.8	3.079999924	3.36		4.8
8	0.480000019	84.8	1.319999981	0.83999996		6
27.2	0.24000001	40.8	1.960000038	1.87999992		3.2
228	2.160000038	315.2	6.959999848	4.92000008		0.4
171.2	1.679999924	230.8	4.2	5.6		2.8
185.6	1.879999924	214	4.520000076	6		1.2
6	0.24000001	65.2	1	1		5.6
26	0.480000019	67.2	1.879999924	1.31999998		4.4
39.2	0.64000001	60.4	1.839999962	1.08000002		4
159.2	1.720000076	136.8	2.2	6.4		1.6
64.4	1.039999962	78.4	2.879999924	2.52000008		5.2
158.8	1.519999981	181.2	4.159999848	5.55999985		2.8
198.8	2.120000076	207.2	4.6	6.5199997		0.4
211.2	2.239999962	246	4.920000076	6.4		0
39.6	0.320000005	111.2	1.119999981	2.6		5.6
0.2	0.44000001	56.8	1.239999962	0.64000001		4.8
138.8	1.439999962	184.4	3.84	4.52000008		2.4
136.4	1.4	152.8	3.920000076	4.6		2
202.8	2.039999962	236	4.8	6.27999992		0
160	3.44	206.8	2.8	4.8		3.2

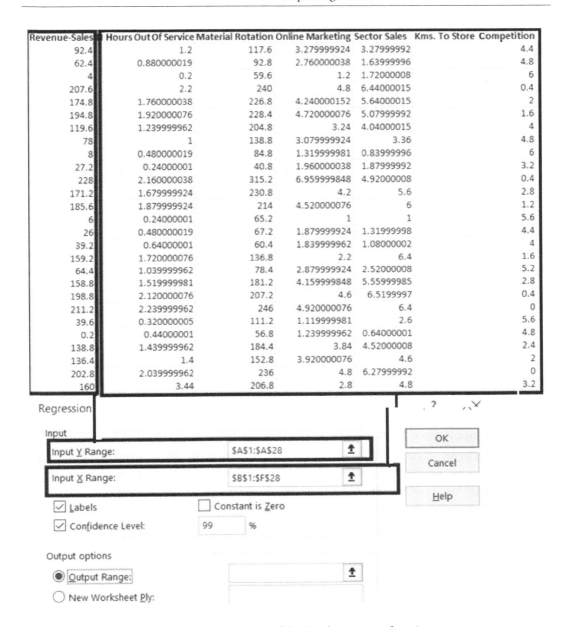

Figure 10.2 – Execution of the Excel regression function

After running the regression function of Excel using the preceding data, the following results are obtained:

SUMMARY OUTPUT

Regression Statistics	
Multiple R	0.996583914
R Square	0.993179497
Adjusted R Square	0.991555568
Standard Error	7.059696658
Observations	27

ANOVA

	df	SS	MS	F	ignificance F
Regression	5	152406.2	30481.24613	611.5904	5.4E-22
Residual	21	1046.626	49.8393169		
Total	26	153452.9			

	Coefficients	andard Err	t Stat	P-value	Lower 95%	Upper 95%	ower 95.0%	pper 95.0%
Intercept	-7.543765663	12.06009	-0.625514812	0.538372	-32.6241	17.53656689	-32.6241	17.53657
Hours out of service	16.20157356	3.544437	4.570986073	0.000166	8.830513	23.57263445	8.830513	23.57263
Material Rotation	0.174635154	0.057606	3.031540961	0.006347	0.054837	0.294433531	0.054837	0.294434
Online marketing	11.52626903	2.532103	4.55205324	0.000174	6.260472	16.79206611	6.260472	16.79207
Sector Sales	13.5803129	1.770457	7.670514392	1.61E-07	9.898447	17.26217897	9.898447	17.26218
Kms. To store competion	-5.31097141	1.705427	-3.114160174	0.005249	-8.8576	-1.764342766	-8.8576	-1.76434

Figure 10.3 – Regression function results' p-values

Review the p-values returned by the regression function. The five variables have a p-value less than *alpha=0.01*. We are using 99.99 of tolerance, so the alpha value is 0.01.

We will choose two variables:

- Material rotation
- Online marketing

This is because their p-value is less than the alpha of 0.01.

For the 99.99 tolerance, we have two predictor variables with a p-value less than the alpha rate of 0.01. These two variables influence the prediction of the result variable. Look at *Figure 10.3* and use these variables for the analysis:

- Predictors: Material rotation and online marketing
- Result: Sales revenue

Execute the multi-regression model and visualize it with the two predictors, material rotation and online marketing, to determine the result variable, sales revenue, with a 3D chart.

Execute a single regression analysis with these pairs:

- Material rotation and revenue
- Online marketing and revenue

Then, visualize it with a two-variables (2D) chart.

This regression analysis provides a complete understanding of the relationship of the variables and whether they are good candidates for building a predictor model.

Figure 10.4 shows the results of the multi-regression model of the three variables:

- Material rotation
- Online marketing
- Sales revenue

Figure 10.4 shows the results of the regression function results using the two predictors and the result variable incidence. The R-squared, p-value, and t-statistics results will help to determine whether the relationship is enough to build a predictor model.

Revenue-Sales	Material Rotation	Online marketing
92.4	117.6	3.279999924
62.4	92.8	2.760000038
4	59.6	1.2
207.6	240	4.8
174.8	226.8	4.240000152
194.8	228.4	4.720000076
119.6	204.8	3.24
78	138.8	3.079999924
8	84.8	1.319999981
27.2	40.8	1.960000038
228	315.2	6.959999848
171.2	230.8	4.2
185.6	214	4.520000076
6	65.2	1
26	67.2	1.879999924
39.2	60.4	1.839999962
159.2	136.8	2.2
64.4	78.4	7.879999924
158.8	181.2	4.159999848
198.8	207.2	4.6
211.2	246	4.920000076
39.6	111.2	1.119999981
0.2	56.8	1.239999962
138.8	184.4	3.84
136.4	152.8	3.920000076
202.8	236	4.8
160	206.8	2.8

SUMMARY OUTPUT

Regression Statistics

Multiple R	0.955127
R Square	0.912269
Adjusted R	0.904958
Standard E	23.68425
Observatic	27

ANOVA

	df	SS	MS	F	ignificance F
Regressior	2	139990.2	69995.11	124.781	2.08E-13
Residual	24	13462.64	560.9435		
Total	26	153452.9			

	Coefficients	andard Err	t Stat	P-value	Lower 95%	Upper 95%	ower 99.99	pper 99.99%
Intercept	-40.1985	10.99758	-3.65522	0.001253	-62.8964	-17.5007	-91.3855	10.98839
Material R	0.658672	0.143675	4.58447	0.000119	0.362142	0.955202	-0.01004	1.327389
Online ma	16.27743	7.276695	2.236926	0.034844	1.259071	31.29579	-17.5911	50.14594

Figure 10.4 – Two variables predicting sales revenue and regression results

Observe that the p-value for material rotation is 0.000119, but for online marketing, this figure is 0.034. This value is greater than the *alpha=0.01*. However, we can still use these variables to predict the sales revenue because the R-squared value is 0.91. Remember that R-squared measures the degree of the relationship between the predictors and the sales revenue.

Test the relationship by doing a 2D chart for each of the predictors against the objective variable's sales revenue. It is better to do a separate chart for each predictor variable with the result and visualize independently how they are related to each other. Look at *Figure 10.5* and the relationship between online marketing and sales revenue. The next chart is the incidence of inventory rotation in sales revenue:

Figure 10.5 – Sales revenue influenced by online marketing

Look at *Figure 10.5* and review that even the p-value of **Online Marketing** is **0.03**, greater than *alpha = 0.01*, hence the relationship between *X* and sales marketing is clear. So, we can accept **Online Marketing** as a predictor variable for sales revenue.

Now, we plot the material rotation influence over sales revenue by testing the following pairs:

- Online marketing with sales revenue
- Inventory rotation with sales revenue

Using 2D charts, we visually verify that the variables are useful for predicting sales revenue:

Figure 10.6 – Inventory rotation influence over sales revenue

Figure 10.6 probes the relationship between **Inventory rotation** and **Revenue-Sales**. It is confirmed by the p-value of 0.00011, less than *alpha=0.01*.

In conclusion, we can use inventory rotation and online marketing to predict sales revenue because visually, the 2D charts probe the relationship among the variables. Consider that we have to perform several tests to accept or reject whether the variables are useful for the model. If we do just one test, we are discarding a good predictor variable. For example, online marketing does not pass the p-value to reject the null hypothesis that the slope is not zero. However, the 2D chart visually probes the relationship between online marketing and sales revenue. Also, the R-squared value is high with a value greater than 0.9.

As a final test, we do a 3D chart of the three variables and we check that the relationship among them is visually acceptable:

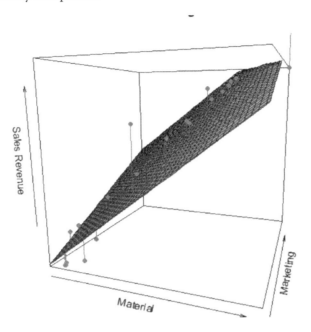

Figure 10.7 – 3D chart showing the influence of material rotation and online marketing over sales revenue

The square plane represents the equation of the linear regression model. It is clear that as inventory rotation and online marketing grow, their effect is directly proportional to sales revenue. In this lesson, we learned how to identify what the more useful variables are when it comes to building a predictor model using these methods:

- Execute the multi-regression function and select the variables with a p-value less than the alpha value.

- Run a single regression model with two pairs of variables each time.

- Research the relationship with two and three variables using 2D and 3D charts.

In the next section, we will learn how to know the statistical confidence of the variables to build a predictor model for a multi-linear regression variable.

Calculating t-statistics and p-values

In this section, we will apply our knowledge of how to ascertain whether the variables have a strong relationship to predict new values with a regression model. The complexity, in this case, is that we are not working with just one predictive variable. Now, we are working with two or more variables in a multiple linear regression model.

The statistical probes to determine the significance of the relationship are as follows:

- Determination coefficient
- Correlation coefficient
- t-statistics
- p-value

To find the coefficients, we have to review the distances between the average of the expected values and the linear model.

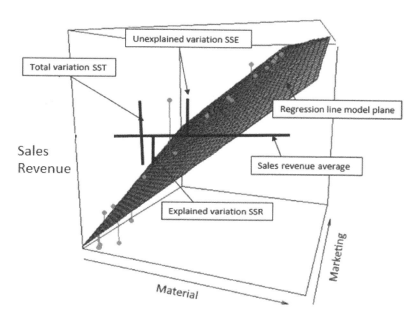

Figure 10.8 – 3D chart distances; linear model to expected results

Figure 10.8 is the 3D chart of the variations we saw in the previous chapter. The errors or unexplained variations (**sum of squares errors (SSEs)**) are the distance between the expected values and the linear regression model. The total variation is the sum of the explained and unexplained variations.

Determination coefficient

Figure 10.8 shows the elements for calculating the coefficients of regression and correlation:

- **Explained variation SSR** is the distance between the linear regression model plane and the average of the sales revenue values.

- **Unexplained variation SSE** is the separation between the linear regression model plane and the expected value, also known as the **sum of square residual error**.

- **Total variation SST** is the sum of the explained and unexplained variations.

The coefficient of determination $r^2 = SSR / SST$ equates to the following:

> Explained variation of the sum of squares regression / Total
> variation in the total sum of squares

The linear regression function analyzes the multivariable regression and returns the R-squared (coefficient of determination) and Multiple-R (coefficient of correlation) values. See *Figure 10.9* for the regression function results in Excel:

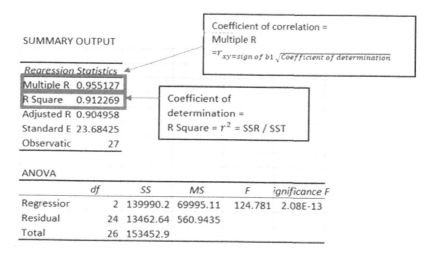

Figure 10.9 – Regression function results for the example involving three variables

From *Figure 10.9*, we have the following results from the regression function:

> Explained variation in the sum of squares regression = 139990.2
> Total variation in the total sum of squares = 153452.9
> Coefficient of determination = R-square = r² = SSR / SST =
> 139990.2/153452.9 = 0.9122

This result appears in the R-square line of the regression function results.

Correlation coefficient

The formula for the *correlation coefficient* is as follows:

$$r_{xy} = sign\ of\ b1\ \sqrt{Coefficient\ of\ determination} = sign\ of\ b1\sqrt{r^2}$$

We deduce from *Figure 10.8* that the slope is positive because the linear regression plane increases with the *y* axis value. The two variables have a direct relationship with sales revenue. So, the sign of the slope is positive. The result for the coefficient of determination is as follows:

$$r_{xy} = sign\ of\ b1\sqrt{r^2} = +\sqrt{0.9122} = 0.955$$

The coefficient of determination appears as a multiple R-value in the results from the linear regression function terms in *Figure 10.8*.

Both coefficients are above 0.9, meaning that 90% of the inventory and online marketing points affect the sales revenue result. The data is useful for building a predictive model.

t-statistics

Use the t-statistic for every predictor variable to check whether we can reject the null hypothesis (the slope equals zero). Hence, we can accept the alternate hypothesis, that the slope is not zero and that there is a relationship between the variables. Remember that when a slope equals zero, this means that there is no relationship among the three variables.

From *Figure 10.10*, we get the t-statistics for the two variables, inventory and marketing:

	Coefficients	Standard Err	t Stat	P-value	Lower 95%	Upper 95%	Lower 99.99	Upper 99.99%
Intercept	-40.1985	10.99758	-3.65522	0.001253	-62.8964	-17.5007	-91.3855	10.98839
Material R	0.658672	0.143675	4.58447	0.000119	0.362142	0.955202	-0.01004	1.327389
Online mar	16.27743	7.276695	2.236926	0.034844	1.259071	31.29579	-17.5911	50.14594

Figure 10.10 – Regression function t-statistics results for two variables

We test each variable to see whether the slope is not equal to zero. The variables tested are as follows:

- Inventory rotation
- Online marketing

The t-statistics parameters are as follows:

- 99% of confidence
- *Number of degrees of freedom = number of data – 1 = 26 – 1 = 25*

For the critical value of inventory rotation, we look at the t-statistics table here:
`https://www.medcalc.org/manual/t-distribution-table.php`.

DF	A	0.80	0.90	0.95	0.98	0.99	0.995	0.998	0.999
	P	0.20	0.10	0.05	0.02	0.01	0.005	0.002	0.001
25		1.316	1.708	2.060	2.485	2.787	3.078	3.450	3.725

Figure 10.11 – t-statistics table results

The critical value for inventory rotation is 2.787.

The inventory rotation t-statistics value is 4.58 according to the regression results of *Figure 10.10*. This value is greater than the critical value of 2.787, so, for this variable, we conclude that the slope is not equal to zero.

Contrary to inventory rotation, the t-statistics value for online marketing is less than the critical value of 2.787; it is 2.23. So, if we apply just this criterion, we have to accept the null hypothesis and that the slope is equal to zero. However, we have to understand the whole context. Remember that the coefficients have a value above 0.9. So, we can accept that online marketing is useful for a prediction model. We use the t-statistics value from the regression function response to see whether it falls in the rejection region. We look to reject the null hypothesis that the slope is equal to zero and probe the fact that there is a relationship between the predictor variable and the result variable. If the t-statistics value is greater than the critical value found on the t-statistics table, we can accept the alternate hypothesis and the fact that there is a relationship between the variables. In the next section, we will use the p-value to reject the null hypothesis.

p-value

Use the p-value approach to see whether we reject the null hypothesis for each of the inventory rotation and online marketing variables. We want a degree % of confidence of 99, meaning the value of alpha is equal to 0.01.

The p-value according to the regression results of *Figure 10.9* is as follows:

- Material rotation: 0.0001
- Online marketing: 0.0348

The material rotation has a p-value less than *alpha=0.01*. So, we can reject the null hypothesis with this variable.

This is not the case with online marketing. The value is greater than 0.01, so we have to accept the null hypothesis. As we explained before, due to the high value of the coefficients, we are going to accept the online marketing value as valid when building a predictor model.

With a level of confidence of *99.99%*, the alpha value is equal to 0.01. So, we look out for the fact that the p-value is less than 0.01 to reject the null hypothesis.

In the next section, we will ascertain the meaning of the SSE from the regression function and how to calculate the f-statistics.

Calculating residuals standard error and f-statistics

The residuals, or errors, are the unexplained variations of the model. It is the separation of the expected value to the response given by the linear regression.

f-statistics is another test for rejecting the possibility of the slope being equal to zero.

To calculate the residuals, we will write down the equation for a multivariable regression model. Then, we will calculate how well the model fits the expected values. The difference between the expected values (sales revenue) and the results from the regression model is the errors or unexplained variation. Remember that this variation is supposed to be small, with a small standard deviation to have a model useful for prediction.

f-statistics come from the explained and unexplained variations of the expected values and the linear model. We will calculate the f-statistics and then check whether the value is in the region of rejection for accepting the alternate hypothesis that the slope is not zero, meaning that there is a relationship between the predicting variables and the sales revenue.

The regression formula for multiple variables has this general form:

$$Y' = B0 + B1X1 + B2X2 + BnXn$$

For this example, we have the following variables:

- $X1$ = Material rotation
- $X2$ = Online marketing

We get the intercepts *B0*, *B1*, and *B2* from the coefficients of the linear regression response function:

	Coefficients
Intercept	-40.19854635
Material Rotation	0.658672105
Online marketing	16.27743177

Figure 10.12 – Linear regression function coefficients' response

From *Figure 10.12*, we get these function coefficients:

- Intercept *B0* = -40.1985
- *X1* material rotation = 0.6586
- *X2* online marketing = 16.2774

The formula for the regression model is as follows:

$$Y' = -40.1985 + (0.6586) * Material\ Rotation_i + (16.2774) * Online\ marketing_i$$

We will do the calculation for the first row of *Figure 10.12*. This is the first data for the regression model. The first row of the Excel linear regression calculation is as follows:

$$Y' = -40.1985 + ((0.6586) * 117.6) + (16.2774) * 3.279 = 90.65$$

Here is the result:

Revenue-Sales	Material Rotation	Online Marketing	Model Revenue Sales
92.4	117.6	3.279999924	90.651268119
62.4	92.8	2.760000038	65.85193726
4	59.6	1.2	18.59122921
207.6	240	4.8	196.0144313
174.8	226.8	4.240000152	178.2046002
194.8	228.4	4.720000076	187.0716415
119.6	204.8	3.24	147.4363796
78	138.8	3.079999924	101.3596304
8	84.8	1.319999981	37.14305775
27.2	40.8	1.960000038	18.5790424
228	315.2	6.959999848	280.7058237
171.2	230.8	4.2	180.1881888
185.6	214	4.520000076	174.3312769
6	65.2	1	19.02430664
26	67.2	1.879999924	34.66578956
39.2	60.4	1.839999962	29.5357226
159.2	136.8	2.2	85.71814746
64.4	78.4	2.879999924	58.3203489
158.8	181.2	4.159999848	146.8669527
198.8	207.2	4.6	171.1544999
211.2	246	4.920000076	201.9197569
39.6	111.2	1.119999981	51.27651496
0.2	56.8	1.239999962	17.39804397
138.8	184.4	3.84	143.7659277
136.4	152.8	3.920000076	124.254085
202.8	236	4.8	193.3797428
160	206.8	2.8	141.5916538

First Row of calculation

Figure 10.13 – Y' model sales revenue linear regression results

The Y' results represent the linear regression model. Y' is the linear model plane of *Figure 10.8.*

In this section, we use the regression formula with two variables:

- Online marketing
- Inventory rotation to predict the sales revenue

This is a more complex case compared with a single regression. In the next section, we will find the variation from the expected values and the results from the regression model, or errors.

Calculating residuals standard errors

Now, we are going to calculate the explained and unexplained variations. The unexplained variations are the SSE values. These values are in the response to the linear regression function in *Figure 10.13*:

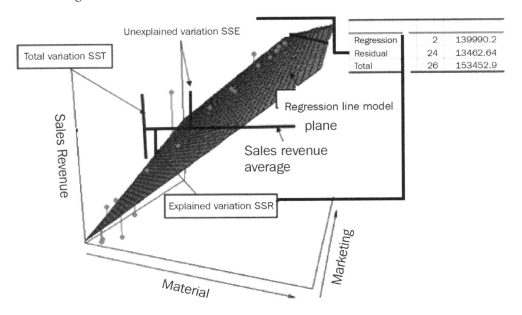

Regression	2	139990.2
Residual	24	13462.64
Total	26	153452.9

Figure 10.14 – Linear regression function coefficients' response

Figure 10.14 is the graphic representation of the distance from the expected values, their average, and the linear regression model plane:

- *Sum of squares regression*: The explained variation is the distance of the linear regression plane to the average line of the expected values.

- *Sum of squares residual or standard errors*: The unexplained variation. The distance between the expected value and the linear regression model calculation.

The first line of the sum of squares regression or the explained variance is calculated as follows:

```
Sum of squares regression = (model revenues sales - expected
sales revenue average) ^ 2
Sum of squares regression = (90.65 - 114.62) ^ 2 = (-23.97)^2 =
574.96
```

The rest of the values can be seen in *Figure 10.15*:

Revenue-Sales	Material Rotation	Online marketing	Model Revenue Sales	SSR			df	SS
92.4	117.6	3.279999924	90.65126811	574.9618	Regression		2	139990.2
62.4	92.8	2.760000038	65.85193726	2379.263	Residual		24	13462.64
4	59.6	1.2	18.59122921	9223.374	Total		26	153452.9
207.6	240	4.8	196.0144313	6623.486				
174.8	226.8	4.240000152	178.2046002	4041.777				
194.8	228.4	4.720000076	187.0716415	5247.845				
119.6	204.8	3.24	147.4363796	1076.283				
78	138.8	3.079999924	101.3596304	176.0929				
8	84.8	1.319999981	37.14305775	6004.169				
27.2	40.8	1.960000038	18.5790424	9225.715				
228	315.2	6.959999848	280.7058237	27581.3				
171.2	230.8	4.2	180.1881888	4297.925				
185.6	214	4.520000076	174.3312769	3564.287				
6	65.2	1	19.02430664	9140.378				
26	67.2	1.879999924	34.66578956	6394.216				
39.2	60.4	1.839999962	29.5357226	7240.973				
159.2	136.8	2.2	85.71814746	835.8738				
64.4	78.4	2.879999924	58.3203489	3170.735				
158.8	181.2	4.159999848	146.8669527	1039.245				
198.8	207.2	4.6	171.1544999	3195.061				
211.2	246	4.920000076	201.9197569	7619.566				
39.6	111.2	1.119999981	51.27651496	4013.617				
0.2	56.8	1.239999962	17.39804397	9453.981				
138.8	184.4	3.84	143.7659277	848.9239				
136.4	152.8	3.920000076	124.254085	92.63014				
202.8	236	4.8	193.3797428	6201.58				
160	206.8	2.8	141.5916538	726.9507				
114.6296296	Revenue Sales average		**Sum of SSR Regression**	139990.2				

Figure 10.15 – Calculation of the sum of squares regression

The result in the linear regression function is equal to the sum of the SSR results of the Excel worksheet. The number of **degrees of freedom (DF)** for regression is two because we have two predictor variables:

- Online marketing
- Material rotation

The DF for the residual or sum of squares error is 24.

The first line of the sum of squares residual or the unexplained variance is calculated as follows:

```
Sum of squares residual = (model revenues sales - expected
sales revenue) ^ 2
Sum of squares residual = (92.4 - 90.65) ^ 2 = (1.75)^2 = 3.058
```

The rest of the values can be seen in *Figure 10.16*:

Y' Model Revenue Sales	Revenue-Sales	SSE			df	SS
90.65126811	92.4	3.058063226	Regression		2	139990.2
65.85193726	62.4	11.91587083	Residual		24	-13462.64
18.59122921	4	212.9039698	Total		26	153452.9
196.0144313	207.6	134.2254033				
178.2046002	174.8	11.59130221				
187.0716415	194.8	59.72752462				
147.4363796	119.6	774.8640299				
101.3596304	78	545.6723313				
37.14305775	8	849.3178148				
18.5790424	27.2	74.32090992				
280.7058237	228	2777.903848				
180.1881888	171.2	80.78753841				
174.3312769	185.6	126.984121				
19.02430664	6	169.6325635				
34.66578956	26	75.09590873				
29.5357226	39.2	93.39825758				
85.71814746	159.2	5399.582653				
58.3203489	64.4	36.96215751				
146.8669527	158.8	142.3976181				
171.1544999	198.8	764.2736778				
201.9197569	211.2	86.12291149				
51.27651496	39.6	136.3410016				
17.39804397	0.2	295.7727163				
143.7659277	138.8	24.66043827				
124.254085	136.4	147.5232509				
193.3797428	202.8	88.741245				
141.5916538	160	338.86720				
Sum of SSE Sum Squares Errors		13462.6443				

Figure 10.16 – Calculation of the sum of squares residual

The sum of squares error or residual is the separation between the linear regression model plane and the expected sales revenue value. This term is the unexplained variation in the model.

Calculating f-statistics

f-statistics is another test for rejecting the fact that the slope is equal to zero or that there is no relationship among the variables.

To calculate f-statistics, we first need to get the **mean squares (MS)** of the **sum of squares regression (explained variation)** and **residual (error unexplained variation)**. The formula for this calculation is as follows:

```
Mean squares regression = sum of squares regression/degrees of
freedom
```

The number of DF for regression is the number of predictor variables.

In this example, we have two predictor variables:

- Material rotation
- Online marketing

Remember that the sum of squares regression is the distance between the regression model and the average of the result variable. The other name for this term is **explained variation**. To calculate the mean squares regression, we divide the explained variation into the number of predictor variables. In this case, the prediction variables are two:

```
Mean squares regression = 139990.212/2 = 69995.10598
Mean squares residual errors = sum of squares residual/degrees
of freedom
```

The DF for residual is 24:

```
Mean squares residual errors = 13462.64434/24 = 560.943514
```

The formula for f-statistics is as follows:

```
f-statistics = mean squares regression / mean squares residual
errors
f-statistics = 69995.10598 / 560.943514 = 124.78
```

The results from the linear regression function in Excel can be seen in *Figure 10.17*:

	df	SS	MS	F
Regression	2	139990.2	69995.11	124.7810238
Residual	24	13462.64	560.9435	
Total	26	153452.9		

Figure 10.17 – Calculation of the sum of squares residual

Now, we have to check whether the f-statistics value of 124.78 falls within the rejection region of the null hypothesis that the slope is equal to zero. For this purpose, we use the f-statistics table in *Figure 10.18*:

\	$df_1=1$	2	3	4
$df_2=1$	39.86346	49.50000	53.59324	55.83296
21	2.96096	2.57457	2.36489	2.23334
22	2.94858	2.56131	2.35117	2.21927
23	2.93736	2.54929	2.33873	2.20651
24	2.92712	2.53833	2.32739	2.19488
25	2.91774	2.52831	2.31702	2.18424

Figure 10.18 – f-statistics table

In the table in *Figure 10.18*, we look for the DF of regression and 24 DF of residuals.

The f-statistics value of 124.78 is bigger than the critical value of 2.53 given by the table, so we can reject the null hypothesis that the slope is equal to zero. We accept the alternate hypothesis that the slope is not zero, meaning there is a relationship among the variables.

Remember *Figure 10.9*, where the online marketing variable t-statistics and p-values say that there was not a relationship between online marketing and sales revenue. We keep this variable because the coefficients of determination and correlation values were above 0.9, indicating that the relationship exists. Now, we have other evidence with f-statistics that the relationship among the variables has a statistical significance. This means that we have to look for several statistical tests to check whether the model variables are useful for predicting values.

In the next section, we are going to train this model with 80% of the data, and then we will test whether it fits the expected values.

Training and testing the model

To predict new values using the data that we have, we will follow these steps:

- Use 80% percent of the data to train and generate the linear regression model.

- Give the upper and lower models ranges of uncertainty. Remember that a model is just a trend and approximation of the prediction values.

- Test the linear model with the remaining 20% of the data and see how the model fits with these expected values.

- Use the model to predict new values using unknown data.

Build the linear model formula with 80% of the data in *Figure 10.19*:

Revenue-Sales	Material Rotation	Online marketing
92.4	117.6	3.279999924
62.4	92.8	2.760000038
4	59.6	1.2
207.6	240	4.8
174.8	226.8	4.240000152
194.8	228.4	4.720000076
119.6	204.8	3.24
78	138.8	3.079999924
8	84.8	1.319999981
27.2	40.8	1.960000038
228	315.2	6.959999848
171.2	230.8	4.2
185.6	214	4.520000076
6	65.2	1
26	67.2	1.879999924
39.2	60.4	1.839999962
159.2	136.8	2.2
64.4	78.4	2.879999924
158.8	181.2	4.159999848
198.8	207.2	4.6

SUMMARY OUTPUT

Regression Statistics

Multiple R	0.945273
R Square	0.893542
Adjusted R	0.881017
Standard E	26.73501
Observatic	20

ANOVA

	df	SS	MS	F	ignificance F
Regressior	2	101986.9466	50993.47	71.34341	5.38E-09
Residual	17	12150.93336	714.7608		
Total	19	114137.88			

	Coefficients	Standard Error	t Stat	P-value	Lower 95%	Upper 95%	ower 95.0%	pper 95.0%
Intercept	-34.8789	14.39088307	-2.42368	0.026809	-65.241	-4.51683	-65.241	-4.51683
Material R	0.630476	0.206468617	3.053614	0.007183	0.194865	1.066086	0.194865	1.066086
Online mar	15.69945	10.78734332	1.455359	0.163788	-7.05985	38.45876	-7.05985	38.45876

Figure 10.19 – Linear regression coefficients for building a formula model

Writing a linear regression model formula

Using the coefficients of the linear model, we build the formula for the regression line:

```
Intercept B0 = -34.8789
B1 material rotation = 0.63
B2 online marketing = 15.699
Predicted sales revenue from model = Intercept B0 + (B1 *
material rotation) + (B2 * online marketing)
```

The linear model formula is as follows:

```
Predicted sales revenue from model = Intercept B0 + (0.63 *
material rotation) + (15.699 * online marketing)
```

The first line of the model results in *Figure 10.19* are calculated as follows:

```
Predicted sales revenue from model = Intercept B0 + (B1 *
material rotation) + (B2 * online marketing)
Predicted sales revenue from model = -34.8789 + ( 0.63 * 117.6)
+ (15.699 * 3.27) = -34.8789 + 74.088 + 51.33573 = 90.54483
```

Now, we are going to use the regression formula and the source data values of online marketing and inventory rotation to get the values of the model. These initial values are used as trainers for the regression. We will test this model with the remaining 20% of the data and then we will predict new values with this trained and tested model.

Revenue-Sales	Material Rotation	Online marketing	Model Training
92.4	117.6	3.279999924	90.75918957
62.4	92.8	2.760000038	66.9596825
4	59.6	1.2	21.53674746
207.6	240	4.8	191.792565
174.8	226.8	4.240000152	174.6785967
194.8	228.4	4.720000076	183.2230938
119.6	204.8	3.24	145.1086795
78	138.8	3.079999924	100.9853804
8	84.8	1.319999981	39.30866506
27.2	40.8	1.960000038	21.61539219
228	315.2	6.959999848	273.1151414
171.2	230.8	4.2	176.5725183
185.6	214	4.520000076	171.0043554
6	65.2	1	21.92751988
26	67.2	1.879999924	37.00398835
39.2	60.4	1.839999962	32.08877718
159.2	136.8	2.2	85.90891191
64.4	78.4	2.879999924	59.76476731
158.8	181.2	4.159999848	144.6729512
198.8	207.2	4.6	167.9730768

Figure 10.20 – Model training results applying the linear regression formula

In the `Model Training` column, we have the results of the linear model formula. Now that we have the formula, we will test the regression with the remaining *20%* of the data and we will see how well or badly it fits. *20% of the data is used in Figure 10.21*:

Revenue-Sales	TestModel	Diff.in Tests	PredictValues
211.2	140.8375	70.3625028	
39.6	52.049395	-12.449395	
0.2	17.871525	-17.671525	
138.8	100.9202	37.879796	
136.4	81.077177	55.3228229	
202.8	134.41274	68.3872583	
160	114.00286	45.997144	
		35.4040863	Diff. Tests Avg.
		31.4882017	Diff. Tests STD.

Figure 10.21 – 20% of the data to test the linear model

The TestModel column has the results given by the regression model. Diff.in Tests shows the difference between the expected value and what the result from the model was.

The difference between the test model and the average of the expected values is 35.4, meaning that is the average failure of the model in fitting the expected values. The standard deviation is 31.48, far removed from the average. This means that the difference is scattered and that the points of difference are not together. We can see this representation in *Figure 10.22*:

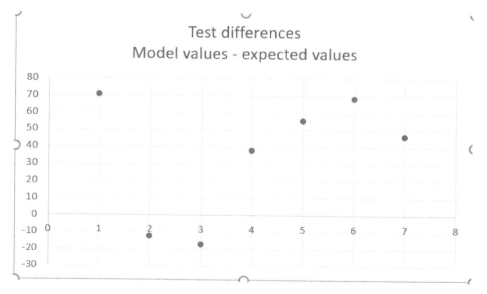

Figure 10.22 – Chart of scattered differences between the model and expected test values

From *Figure 10.22*, we can review that the model is *65%* accurate with the test values. This is because the separation has an average of *35%*. Here, we can see that even the relationship has a 0.90 value according to the coefficients. The model does not have a high accuracy of prediction. Remember that a model just gives a trend and is not supposed to be exact. We probably need more data to design a more exact model than we have at present. With this % test using 65% of the data, we can use the model with new values to make a prediction.

Building the prediction model

Use the model to predict new values and see whether the results make sense with your business or research know-how.

Perform the test with new data points to see how the model behaves. These new data points are for online marketing and inventory rotation. The data input for the model is available in *Figure 10.23*.

For the first line of the predicted results in *Figure 10.23*, we perform this calculation:

```
Predicted sales revenue from model = -34.8789 + ( 0.63 * 321) +
(15.699 * 7.4) = -34.8789 +202.23+116.17=283.6796
```

Figure 10.23 shows the complete prediction values of the linear model:

Material Rotation	Online marketing	PredictValues
321	7.4	283.6796612
318	7	275.5084535
321	8.2	296.2392236
325	7.1	281.4917275
330	9.1	316.0430111
341	8	305.7088438
351	8.1	313.5835444

Figure 10.23 – Predicted values from new input data of the material rotation and online marketing variables

The predicted values are just an approximation because the linear model just gives trends and does not predict exact values.

These are the results from the prediction model. We see that if we invest `9.1` in online marketing with an inventory rotation of `330`, we get a sales revenue of `316.04`. As a matter of comparison, refer to *Figure 10.19*, containing the known training data for the model. With an online marketing value of `6.95`, and a material rotation value of `315.2`, we get a sales revenue of `228`. The model for this data gave a result of `273`, enabling us to conclude that the predicted value of sales revenue of `316.04` makes sense with the trending information we use for training and testing the model.

Summary

In this chapter, we learned to choose which variables have a greater influence over the prediction variable, *Y*. Statistical methods to search for these high influence variables include the coefficient of determination and correlation, which indicates a percentage of the relationship of the variables by measuring their variances, and also whether the relationship is direct or inverse depending on the slope sign. t-statistics, f-statistics, and the p-value determine whether we can reject the null hypothesis that the slope is equal to zero.

These tests help to get the statistical confidence of the variables to generate a prediction model while helping to reject the null hypothesis that the slope is equal to zero.

It is important to evaluate all the statistical tests. Sometimes, f-statistics and the p-value indicate that a variable could affect the model with a slope equal to zero. However, we have to understand all the evaluation methods to include the variables that influence the prediction variable.

Build the linear model equation and follow the steps of the ML process. Build the model by writing the linear regression equation. Train the model with 80% of the given data. This data is useful for understanding the relationship among the variables. Test the model with 20% of the data. Do a chart of the scattered data of the model that did not fit the expected values. That gives an idea of how good the predictive model is. Run the model with unknown values of the predictor variables.

After running the model, review the results with the data used for training and testing. Be sure that the result given by the model makes sense in terms of the results of the training and testing phases.

In the next chapter, we will start with a new topic. We will see how to predict future values based on temporary or time-series data. Time series is a different algorithm because the data changes over the seasons. It does not have a linear trend like regression. It exhibits sinusoidal behavior that could be up or down depending on the season of the year.

Questions

Here are a few questions and their answers to revisit what we have learned in this chapter:

1. How do we identify the variables with more influence on the result variable?

2. What is the unexplained variation?

3. What is the alpha for the p-value with a tolerance of 99.99%? Does the p-value have to be greater or smaller than the alpha?

4. What are the degrees of freedom?

5. What are the input predictor values for running the model?

Answers

Here are the answers to the preceding questions:

1. We identify the variables with more influence on the result variable:

   - By charting each predictor variable with the result variable independently

   - By running the regression model function for each predictor variable and measuring the p-value and t-statistics

2. It is the distance between the regression model and the expected values.

3. alpha = 0.01. The p-value has to be smaller than the alpha.

4. They are the number of predictor variables.

5. We use different values for the predictor variables to see whether the model results make sense given our experience with the data.

Further reading

To further understand the concepts of this chapter, refer to the following sources:

- *Easy statistics: Linear regression [Video]*:

  https://www.packtpub.com/product/easy-statistics-linear-regression-video/9781800565593

- *Regression analysis with R*:

  https://www.packtpub.com/product/regression-analysis-with-r/9781788627306

Part 4 – Predicting Values with Time Series

Time series is data that is used to predict values based on past stationary data. It does not rely on multiple variables. We will use time series data to validate a model and see whether it is able to predict values based on past stationary data.

This part includes the following chapters:

- Chapter 11, Testing Data for Time Series Compliance
- Chapter 12, Working with Time Series Using the Centered Moving Average and a Trending Component
- Chapter 13, Training, Validating, and Running the Model

11
Testing Data for Time Series Compliance

Predicting values with a time series requires that we have historical data to analyze whether past values have a relationship with present ones and whether this relationship can be useful to predict future values. To validate this, we have to test the autocorrelation of the data. This chapter's purpose is to train professionals responsible for doing purchase planning and inventories, as well as those who need to do forecasts. To do effective planning based on data, we first have to validate that we have a good fit to do this kind of analysis. We need data to contain past values that correlate with present ones to predict future ones. We can create charts to see whether there is predictable behavior in our data and then run a statistical test to confirm that. To do this research, we will be doing the following in this chapter:

- Visualizing seasonal trends
- Researching autocorrelation – past values' influence over present values
- Performing the Durbin-Watson autocorrelation test

A chart is a standard way to present data; in this case, we can visualize a chart of data to see whether the present has some influence on the past. We test this influence of autocorrelation with the **Durbin-Watson statistical test**, which we will learn about in this chapter. Generally, if we have periodic behavior of data in a time frame, we can accept that the data can predict the future. The Durbin-Watson test determines statistically whether there is autocorrelation (that is, whether there is a past-present relationship) using the residuals of linear regression.

Technical requirements

Download the Excel file for this chapter here:

```
https://github.com/PacktPublishing/Data-Forecasting-and-
Segmentation-Using-Microsoft-Excel/blob/main/Chapter11/
chapterElevenTimeSeriestoUPLOADSeries.xlsx
```

Visualizing seasonal trends

We are going to do a new type of prediction involving the time variable. Before we build our model, we want to see whether the data is useful for making predictions. Our data must be such that present values have a relationship with past values. This characteristic is known as **autocorrelation**.

To make predictions, we need the following elements:

- Time-series data
- A trend line from the data linear regression
- Errors of the data linear regression

We will use an 8-year *air passenger sales* dataset to do a time-series analysis. In the following screenshot, look at the plot of the aforementioned elements. We can see that the data is probably useful enough for us to do a 1-year forecast. We will look at a prediction for **Year 9** and see whether the **Year 9** forecast makes sense based on past behavior and our data experience. Remember that everything can be validated, but ultimately, we have to judge whether the results make sense or not using our common sense. To do our statistical test, we will use a Durbin-Watson probe. We are going to develop this test step by step in the next section:

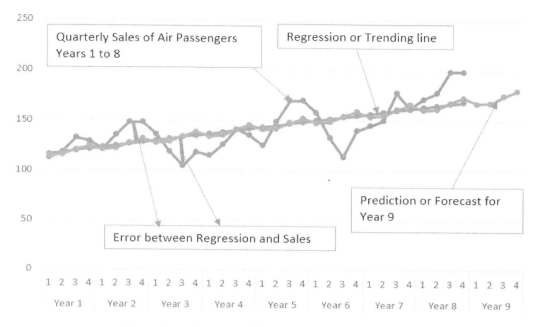

Figure 11.1 – Elements of the time-series prediction model

In *Figure 11.1*, we can see the probable air ticket sales' seasonal trend, which is characteristic of most time-series data. We test this apparent trend with Durbin-Watson to see the data autocorrelation and whether the data has an application to create a predictor model. The steps to decide whether the data is useful for forecasting are as follows:

1. Build a data plot using a chart.
2. Judge visually whether the data has autocorrelation.

The chart element that we will use to perform the Durbin-Watson test is in the form of **linear regression errors**. To find the autocorrelation, we will test whether the errors have periodic behavior along with the time frame. See the error chart in the following screenshot. Remember that the linear regression error is the *unexplained* difference in the model. It is the distance between the regression and the expected values:

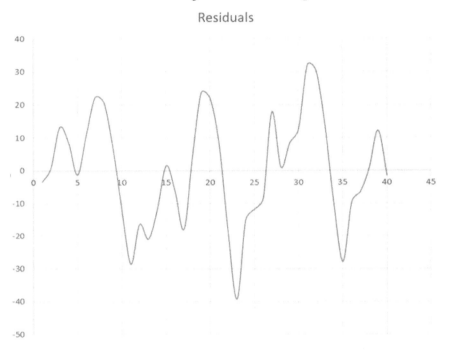

Figure 11.2 – The linear regression residuals of air ticket sales

We can see seasonal up-and-down trends in the error chart in *Figure 11.2*. That gives us an idea that the Durbin-Watson test will accept the alternative hypothesis of autocorrelation of the airplane passenger sales data.

This seasonal autocorrelated data probed by Durbin-Watson shows that the data is useful for building a prediction model because past data has a relationship with present data.

Not all sales data has seasonal behavior to do forecasting predictions. That's why we have to do the Durbin-Watson test before designing any predictions – to avoid reaching doubtful and wrong conclusions. This is useful advice for purchase planners and inventory managers. First, they have to identify products with predictable performance and then apply a time-series **Machine Learning** (**ML**) algorithm. Products with scattered sales are not eligible for forecasting. You have to design a specific purchase-and-sales strategy for them.

For example, let's take the example we developed in *Chapter 6, Finding the Optimal Number of Multi-Variable Groups.* We identify that the first group has the highest profit. For this group, we take the profits for Canada to see whether we can forecast with this data. The data plot is shown here – it includes 4 years of sales:

Figure 11.3 – 4 years of monthly sales for Canada

Looking at the chart, it appears that sales in Canada are not predictable. We can see that the peaks are in the following months:

- March 2011
- July 2012
- November 2013
- September 2014

With this information, we can say that there is no autocorrelation because the past data is not affecting the present data. The sales in Canada are sparse and difficult to forecast.

Let's look at the following linear regression error chart. This chart helps us to understand that there is no autocorrelation in the data:

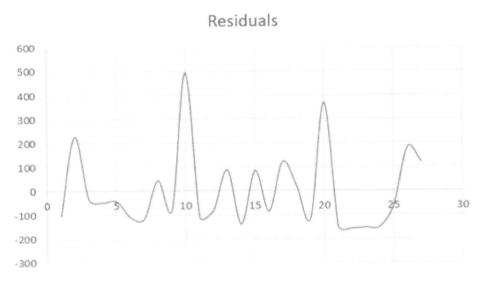

Figure 11.4 – The residuals of 4 years of monthly sales for Canada

The preceding residuals chart shows that there is no autocorrelation for Canada's sales data. The Durbin-Watson test will likely accept the `null` hypothesis that no autocorrelation exists. Note the peaks and see how they are not repeated regularly. The data after the peak in the **10** period is different from the data after the peak in the **20** period.

In this section, we learned why we need data autocorrelation relationships to design a predictive forecasting model. We need past data to correlate with present data in order to make accurate predictions. For example, to make inventory predictions, we first have to find the products that have autocorrelated data. This won't be all products. The autocorrelation statistical test deployed is Durbin-Watson. It uses linear regression errors to find out whether data has autocorrelation. In the next section, we will learn how to plot linear regression errors to give us an idea of autocorrelation. This knowledge is required to run the Durbin-Watson test, as we will see in the last section of this chapter.

Researching autocorrelation – past values' influence over present values

In this section, we will learn how to get data errors or residuals from the linear regression model that we want to use as a time-series model to do forecasts. The regression line indicates the trend of data. The Durbin-Watson test uses the errors to see whether there is periodic behavior in the time frame in order to decide whether there is autocorrelation or not.

First, we are going to use the regression function in Excel with the air passenger sales data, as shown in *Figure 11.5*. We have to enter the parameters in the regression function and specify that we want error results. To do this, go to the **Data** option in the **Data Analysis** upper menu and choose **Regression**.

If you cannot find the **Regression** option in **Data Analysis**, you will have to install the **Analysis** tool pack in Excel. To do this, follow these steps:

1. Click the **File** tab, and then go to the **Options | Add-ins** category.

2. In the **Manage** box, click on **Excel Add-ins | Go**.

3. In Excel for Mac, go to the **File** menu and then to **Tools | Excel Add-ins**.

4. In the **Add-Ins** box, check the **Analysis ToolPak** checkbox, and then click **OK**.

5. If **Analysis ToolPak** is not listed, go to **Browse…** to locate it.

6. Click **Yes** to install the Analysis ToolPak when prompted.

Now, you can input the values in the **Regression** window, as shown in the following screenshot. It's important to specify that the data contains labels if you have titles in your columns:

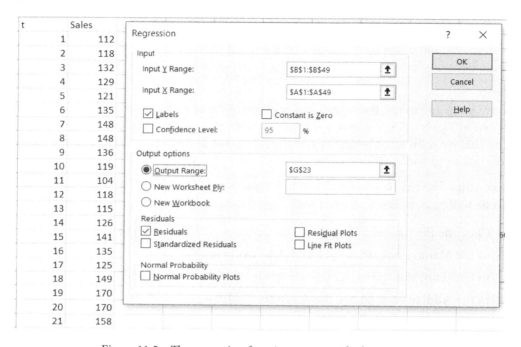

Figure 11.5 – The regression function to get residuals or errors

Referring to *Figure 11.5*, enter the sales data in the **Input Y Range** field regression. In the **Input X Range** field, enter the time period, or *t*; in this case, this is the month number of the data. Check the **Residuals** checkbox to get these results and click **OK**.

Do a plot of the residuals to get a chart like the one shown in the following screenshot. The residuals plot shows whether the data has periodic behavior and whether it is useful for making predictions:

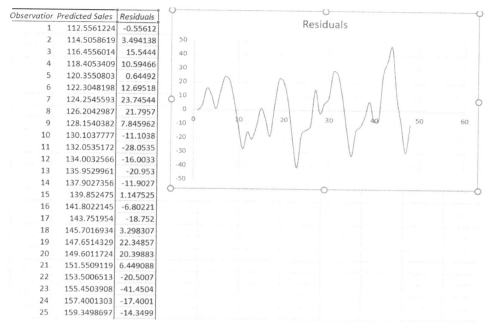

Observation	Predicted Sales	Residuals
1	112.5561224	-0.55612
2	114.5058619	3.494138
3	116.4556014	15.5444
4	118.4053409	10.59466
5	120.3550803	0.64492
6	122.3048198	12.69518
7	124.2545593	23.74544
8	126.2042987	21.7957
9	128.1540382	7.845962
10	130.1037777	-11.1038
11	132.0535172	-28.0535
12	134.0032566	-16.0033
13	135.9529961	-20.953
14	137.9027356	-11.9027
15	139.852475	1.147525
16	141.8022145	-6.80221
17	143.751954	-18.752
18	145.7016934	3.298307
19	147.6514329	22.34857
20	149.6011724	20.39883
21	151.5509119	6.449088
22	153.5006513	-20.5007
23	155.4503908	-41.4504
24	157.4001303	-17.4001
25	159.3498697	-14.3499

Figure 11.6 – The residuals of the air passenger sales' linear regression

Now, we are going to combine the air passenger sales data, the trend or regression line, and the residuals into one chart to have a complete idea of the data seasonality and whether the data appears to have autocorrelation.

In *Figure 11.7*, we've plotted the following elements to make a forecast:

- Air passenger sales
- Regression line
- Residuals

With these components, we will determine whether the seasonal and autocorrelation data is suitable to use as input to do a forecast with the time series. The output is shown in the following screenshot:

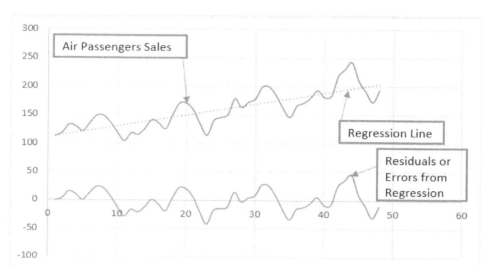

Figure 11.7 – Air passenger sales, regression line, and residuals

From *Figure 11.7*, we see how the residuals or errors reflect the periodic movement of the air passenger sales. Glancing at the chart, we can see that the data has autocorrelation and that past data can be used to predict a forecast.

We will do the same analysis for Canada's profits over 27 months. Use the regression function and data shown in the following screenshot. Define the **Y** and **X** values and choose the **Residuals** option. Go to **Data | Data Analysis** and choose the **Regression** option:

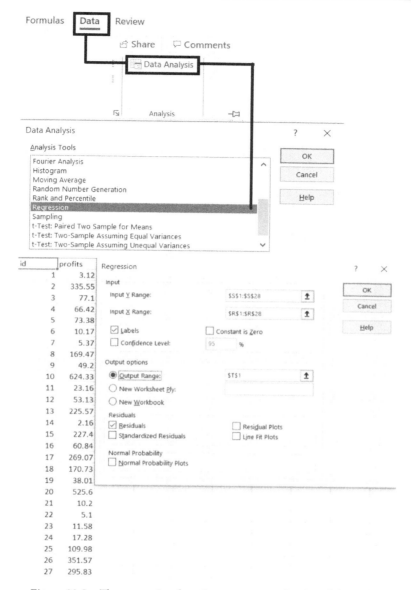

Figure 11.8 – The regression function parameters for Canada's profits

Using the settings shown in *Figure 11.8*, define the input for Canada's sales and then the input for the monthly `id` value, with a range of **S1** to **S27**. Choose the **Residuals** option to get the linear regression errors.

After the calculation, we get a data and residuals chart like the one shown in the following screenshot. From this **Residuals** chart, we can see that the sales are not periodic in the time frame:

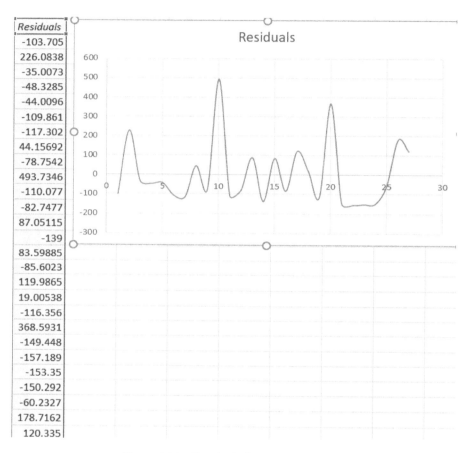

Residuals
-103.705
226.0838
-35.0073
-48.3285
-44.0096
-109.861
-117.302
44.15692
-78.7542
493.7346
-110.077
-82.7477
87.05115
-139
83.59885
-85.6023
119.9865
19.00538
-116.356
368.5931
-149.448
-157.189
-153.35
-150.292
-60.2327
178.7162
120.335

Figure 11.9 – Residuals for Canada's profits

We see from *Figure 11.9* that there is no periodic data in the time frame. Combining all the elements of the time series, Canada's profit, the regression line, and the residuals, we build a chart like the one shown here, which is enough to show that the past is not influencing the future:

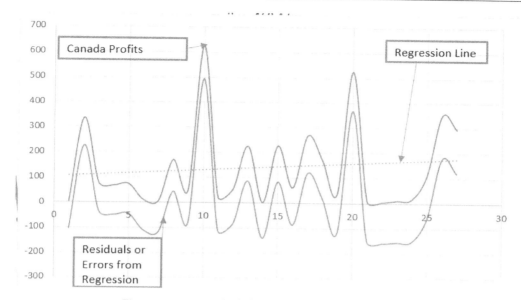

Figure 11.10 – Residuals for Canada's profits (continued)

If we look at the residuals or errors of Canada's profits, we can see that they have the same behavior as sales. They don't have regular behavior, so the Durbin-Watson test will probably return that the `null` hypothesis is valid. The values do not have autocorrelation, so it is not possible to do a forecast for Canada's sales. See that the trend line is far away from the expected values.

In this section, we explained how to use a regression function to make a chart of the errors or residuals of the linear model. Then, we charted those residuals, and we can see the probable outcome of the Durbin-Watson test – specifically, whether the data has autocorrelation or not. With this, we determined at the beginning of the analysis whether the data was useful for forecast prediction. In the next section, we will see how to use the Durbin-Watson test step by step, and we will also execute the Durbin-Watson test in the integrated add-in of Excel.

Performing the Durbin-Watson autocorrelation test

The Durbin-Watson autocorrelation test determines whether past data influences the present so that we can make predictions with it. This test returns a value interpretation, depending on its range. The function returns a value between 0 and 4. The interpretation is outlined here:

- The value is *2* – there is *no* autocorrelation.

- The value is *between 0 and 2* – it has *positive* autocorrelation, meaning that the relationship is growing over time. This is common in time-series data.

- The value is *between 2 and 4* – it has *negative* autocorrelation. The values are decreasing over time.

The test returns the following results:

- Accept the `null` hypothesis and that the data has no autocorrelation.

- Reject the `null` hypothesis and accept the alternative hypothesis that the data has autocorrelation.

We are going to perform the Durbin-Watson test step by step and analyze its value. The formula for the test is shown here:

$$W = \frac{\sum_{t=2}^{n}(e_t - e_{t-1})^2}{\sum_{t=1}^{n} e_t^2}$$

Here, e is the error or residual value for each row of data. We will explain step by step the calculation of the Durbin-Watson test, which you can see in *Figure 11.11*. The e_{t-1} term is one step forward from e_t. To calculate the sum of the upper term of the formula division, subtract e_t from e_{t-1} and square the result. Then, add all the results.

To get the sum of the lower term, square the e_t residual terms and then add all of them.

Calculating Durbin-Watson by hand in Excel

The Durbin-Watson test is the division of the two previously mentioned sums. Using it, we will find out whether the result rejects the `null` hypothesis that there is no autocorrelation in the air passenger data. Remember that the result is between 0 and 4. We will illustrate an example with the first line of the data shown in the following screenshot:

RESIDUAL OUTPUT		e_t Residuals	e_t^2	e_{t-1}^{2}	$(e_t - e_{t-1})^2$
Observation	Predicted Sales				
1	115.4731707	-3.473170732	12.06291493		
2	117.1963415	0.803658537	0.645867043	-3.47317073	18.29126859
3	118.9195122	13.0804878	171.0991612	0.80365854	150.7205369
4	120.6426829	8.357317073	69.84474866	13.0804878	22.30834176
5	122.3658537	-1.365853659	1.865556217	8.35731707	94.54004908
6	124.0890244	10.91097561	119.0493888	-1.36585366	150.7205369
7	125.8121951	22.18780488	492.2986853	10.9109756	127.1668783
8	127.5353659	20.46463415	418.8012507	22.1878049	2.969317371
9	129.2585366	6.741463415	45.44732897	20.4646341	188.3254149
10	130.9817073	-11.98170732	143.5613102	6.74146341	350.5571222
11	132.704878	-28.70487805	823.9700238	-11.9817073	279.6644393
12	134.4280488	-16.42804878	269.8807867	-28.704878	150.7205369
13	136.1512195	-21.15121951	447.3740869	-16.4280488	22.30834176
14	137.8743902	-11.87439024	141.0011437	-21.1512195	86.05956127
15	139.597561	1.402439024	1.966835217	-11.8743902	176.2741954
16	141.3207317	-6.320731707	39.95164932	1.40243902	59.64736615
17	143.0439024	-18.04390244	325.5824152	-6.32073171	137.432732
18	144.7670732	4.232926829	17.91766954	-18.0439024	496.2571222
19	146.4902439	23.5097561	552.7086318	4.23292683	371.5961466
20	148.2134146	21.78658537	474.6553019	23.5097561	2.969317371
21	149.9365854	8.063414634	65.01865556	21.7865854	188.3254149
22	151.6597561	-18.6597561	348.1864976	8.06341463	714.127854
23	153.3829268	-39.38292683	1551.014926	-18.6597561	429.4498052
24	155.1060976	-15.10609756	228.1941835	-39.3829268	589.3644393
25	156.8292683	-11.82926829	139.9315883	-15.1060976	10.73761005
26	158.552439	-8.552439024	73.14421327	-11.8292683	10.73761005
27	160.2756098	17.72439024	314.1540095	-8.55243902	690.4717564
28	161.9987805	1.001219512	1.002440512	17.7243902	279.6644393
29	163.7219512	8.27804878	68.52609161	1.00121951	52.9522442
30	165.445122	12.55487805	157.6249628	8.27804878	18.29126859
31	167.1682927	31.83170732	1013.257591	12.554878	371.5961466
32	168.8914634	30.10853659	906.5239753	31.8317073	2.969317371
33	170.6146341	13.38536585	179.168019	30.1085366	279.6644393
34	172.3378049	-10.33780488	106.8702097	13.3853659	562.7888296
35	174.0609756	-28.06097561	787.4183522	-10.3378049	314.1107808
36	175.7841463	-9.784146341	95.72951963	-28.0609756	334.0424881
37	177.5073171	-6.507317073	42.34517549	-9.78414634	10.73761005
38	179.2304878	0.769512195	0.592149018	-6.50731707	52.9522442
39	180.9536585	12.04634146	145.1143427	0.7695122	127.1668783
40	182.6768293	-1.676829268	2.811756395	12.0463415	188.3254149
			10796.31341		8117.005816

$$W = \frac{\sum_{t=}^{n} (e_t - e_{t-1})^2}{\sum_{t=1}^{n} e_t^2}$$

$$\sum_{t=1}^{n} e_t^2.$$

$$\sum_{t=2}^{n} (e_t - e_{t-1})^2$$

Figure 11.11 – Calculation terms for Durbin-Watson

We are going to do a step-by-step calculation of the Durbin-Watson formula with the values shown in *Figure 11.11*. Here, e_t is the residuals returned by the regression function. Here are the steps:

1. Getting e_{t-1}: Take the residuals and move all the terms to one row below.

2. Calculating e_t^2: Square the residuals.

3. Calculating $(e_t - e_{t-1})^2$: Subtract the residuals from the result calculated in *Step 1*. Then, square this result.

First, we get the e_{t-1} term by moving the e_t terms one row below. In the following screenshot, you can see an example of this for the first five terms:

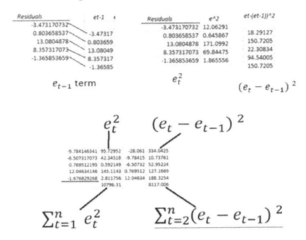

Figure 11.12 – Term calculation for Durbin-Watson

To calculate the e_{t-1} term, move the e_t term one row below. Refer to *Figure 11.12* for an example of how the first term, **-3.4731**, moves to the second row.

e_t^2 is the square of the e_t term. For example, in *Figure 11.12*, the square of **-3.4731** is **12.06291**.

For $(e_t - e_{t-1})^2$, we have to subtract $e_t - e_{t-1}$ and then square this result. For example, from *Figure 11.12*, we have calculated the first term like this:

$$e_t - e_{t-1} = (0.8036 - (-3.47317)) = 4.27677$$

Then, we square the result, *4.27677*, and we get *18.29127*.

We sum all the rows of $(e_t - e_{t-1})^2$ to get the result of the upper term of the $\sum_{t=2}^{n}(e_t - e_{t-1})^2$ Durbin-Watson formula. From *Figure 11.11*, we get the result of this sum – **8117.006**.

The denominator of the Durbin-Watson formula is the sum of e_t^2, using this formula – $\sum_{t=1}^{n} e_t^2$. From *Figure 11.11*, we can see the result is **10796.31**.

Finally, we are ready to calculate the Durbin-Watson formula, as follows:

$$W = \frac{\sum_{t=2}^{n}(e_t - e_{t-1})^2}{\sum_{t=1}^{n} e_t^2} = \frac{8117.006}{10796.31} = 0.7518$$

We see that Durbin-Watson falls in the range of 0 and 4. In this case, we have a value of *0.7518*, so we can reject the `null` hypothesis that there is no autocorrelation and conclude that the autocorrelation is positive. We accept the alternative hypothesis. There is autocorrelation in the air passenger sales data, so we can use this information to build a prediction model.

Calculating the Durbin-Watson test for the Canada sales, we confirm that there is no autocorrelation. The data and calculations are shown in the following screenshot. We used 27 observations for 4 years to get this data because we are missing some months, but we can explore the trends and conclude that we don't have periodic sales for Canada:

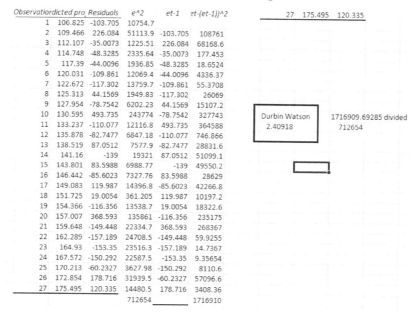

Figure 11.13 – Durbin-Watson calculations for Canada's sales

The result for the Durbin-Watson test of Canada's sales is **2.40918**. This value falls in the region of accepting the `null` hypothesis that there is *no* autocorrelation. This confirms the visual analysis that we did before. So, the sales data is not useful for building a forecast. We have to find autocorrelated data for other countries to improve our inventory and logistics management and predict when there is a high seasonal demand for products.

In this section, we learned how to calculate the Durbin-Watson formula by hand in Excel and interpret from the result whether the data has autocorrelation or not. We learned how to do the difficult task of forecasting inventories because we can have markets, such as Canada, that do not have a periodic demand, so there is no autocorrelation in their data. In the next chapter, we are going to learn how to build an ML time-series algorithm to make forecasts with autocorrelation probed by the Durbin-Watson test.

Summary

In this chapter, we learned that we have to produce a chart of time-series data as a first step to see whether our data is a good fit for forecasting. The data has to have autocorrelation (meaning that there is a relationship between past and present values) for us to be able to forecast with it. We can use the Durbin-Watson statistical test to see whether data has autocorrelation or not. The approach of Durbin-Watson is to research the periodicity of errors or residuals to see whether they have predictable behavior. Most products' sales probably do not have periodic behavior, making it difficult for planners to predict optimal inventory management.

In the next chapter, we will learn how to *smooth* time-series peaks with a **Moving Average (MA)**. We will combine the **Centered Moving Average (CMA)** with the residuals of linear regression to build a forecast model.

Questions and answers

Here are a few questions to test your understanding of this chapter:

1. What is autocorrelation?
2. What does a chart of data with autocorrelation look like?
3. What is the main requirement for doing a forecast?
4. What is the Durbin-Watson test value to accept positive autocorrelation?
5. The Durbin-Watson test uses what kind of linear regression to determine autocorrelation?

Answers

Here are the answers to the preceding questions:

1. It is where past data reflects present data.

2. It has periodic waves and appears to be predictable.

3. The data must be autocorrelated.

4. It has to be a value of less than 2. If it is near 2, we probably have to accept the `null` hypothesis, as the data has no autocorrelation.

5. This test uses residuals or errors to see whether the data has autocorrelation.

Further reading

To gain more insights into the Durbin-Watson test, you can refer to *Python for Finance – Second Edition* using the following link:

```
https://subscription.packtpub.com/book/big_data_and_business_
intelligence/9781787125698/8/ch21lvl1sec78/durbin-watson
```

12

Working with Time Series Using the Centered Moving Average and a Trending Component

The concept behind making a forecast with a time series is that a factor variable for each period determines whether a trend value goes up or down. The constraint of this prediction is that values must be autocorrelated, meaning that present values are dependent on past values. A prerequisite of making a forecast is a test of autocorrelation, such as the **Durbin-Watson probe** that we reviewed in the previous chapter.

Once we have validated the autocorrelation of data, we smooth the peaks of the periods using the moving average and the **Centered Moving Average** (**CMA**). The distance between the data and the CMA determines the factor that will give the forecast combined with the trend or linear regression of the data.

In this chapter, we will learn how to detect autocorrelation by reviewing the timeline data chart and determining whether it is worth using the Durbin-Watson statistical test to confirm that past data has an influence on the present to perform predictions. Also, we will learn how a seasonal trend directs the linear model to forecast the ups and downs of different seasons in a year.

To make our forecast, we will cover the following topics in this chapter:

- Calculating the CMA
- Producing the forecast – season and trend line

With this prediction calculation, we will get the future trend of the data based on the analysis of the past and present data. The forecast is a summary of what has happened before to the data. It gives a trend-based idea of what could happen in the future.

Technical requirements

Download the Excel file for this chapter here:

```
https://github.com/PacktPublishing/Data-Forecasting-and-
Segmentation-Using-Microsoft-Excel/blob/main/Chapter12/
chapterTwelveTimeSeriestoUPLOADSeries.xlsx
```

Calculating the CMA

The moving average of a value over a period of time helps to *smooth* the time-series lines and avoid the drastic peaks typical of this seasonal kind of data. The seasonal peaks that occur throughout are included in our analysis. They are part of the data behavior that will appear in the forecast, and they are *not outliers*. The moving average helps to direct the trend line of the forecast, including these peaks. We will use the distance of the data from the moving average line to determine the seasonal trend of the time series. This information helps to build the forecast curve of the data, taking the seasonal variations of the series into account.

The steps to produce a forecast from the moving average are as follows:

1. Calculating the moving average for the given period of time – for example, taking the moving average of all the quarters of the year.

2. Getting the CMA of your data. This is the middle of the calculating period. This CMA smooths the peaks of the time-series data. As we explained before, the moving average helps to factor in the trend information, including the seasonal peaks, to build the forecast model (see *Figure 12.1*).

3. Dividing the data by the CMA to get the **seasonal irregular** component. This is the distance from the data to the moving average line. This distance helps to calculate the seasonal trends for the forecast (see *Figure 12.1*).

4. Calculating the seasonal component by getting the average of all the periods of the season irregular data acquired in the last step. This information helps to calculate the forecast seasonal trends (see *Figure 12.1*).

5. Getting the regression line of the data or the trend line of *Figure 12.1*.

6. Multiplying the season component by the regression line to produce the forecast. The season component helps with the time-series peaks caused by the changing seasonal sales demand.

The general idea of the time-series algorithm is shown in *Figure 12.1*. The concept is to get the separation factor of the data between the moving average and the trend line. Then, we use these factors to produce a forecast. *Figure 12.1* has the airline passenger sales data for 7 years:

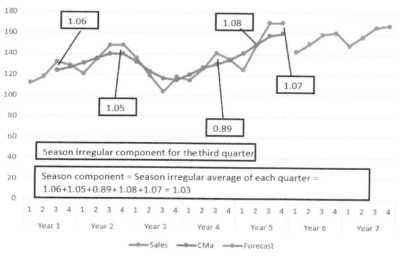

Figure 12.1 – The moving average, seasonal, and season irregular components

In *Figure 12.1*, the peaks in the air passenger sales over 5 years of data are smoothed out using the CMA. The seasonal irregular components are the separation of the sales across the CMA line. The season component is the average for each period of these distances. In *Figure 12.1*, we have the seasonal elements for the third-quarter distances. The third-quarter distances between the CMA and the data are **1.06 + 1.05 + 0.89 + 1.08 + 1.07**.

The average or season for these distances is **1.03**.

Let's calculate the average distances for each period. In this example, we use the first, second, third, and fourth quarters. For example, we have five third quarters for each instance of the 5-year data in *Figure 12.1*. Calculate the average distance for the third quarter's data:

```
Third quarter, year 1: 1.06
Third quarter, year 2: 1.05
Third quarter, year 3: 0.89
Third quarter, year 4: 1.08
Third quarter, year 5: 1.07
```

The average distance value for these third quarters is **1.03**, as shown in *Figure 12.1*.

The average results for each quarter over the 5 years are shown in *Table 12.1*:

Quarter	Season
1	0.947837
2	0.988296
3	1.034879
4	1.033587

Table 12.1 – Season results for each quarter

With these results, we get the **trend** line component by calculating the linear regression. From this, we can get the forecast information. These results are shown in *Figure 12.2*, which shows the airline passenger sales data for 7 years:

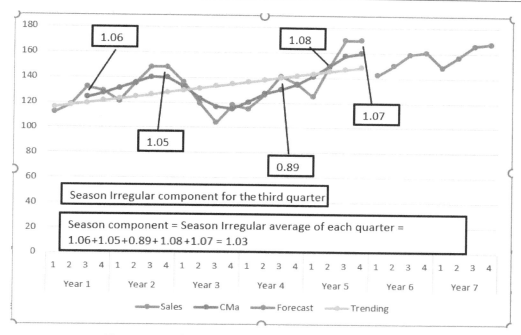

Figure 12.2 – The trend line and forecast of air passenger sales

We multiply the distance between the data and the CMA in the season component by the linear regression, and we get the forecast in *Figure 12.2*. The season element gives the trending movement of the linear regression to get the seasonal forecast. Note that time series have cyclical trends, which is what the algorithm is trying to predict.

Remember that the forecasts and linear regression predictions are just trends, not exact predictions of the future. Look at *Figure 12.2* and note the sales behavior decreasing in the first and second quarters and increasing in the third and fourth quarters. This trend of behavior is reflected in the forecast for **Year 6** and **Year 7** – we have low sales in quarters one and two, with incremental increases in quarters three and four.

In the next section, we will use the moving average and the CMA to smooth the top and bottom peaks of the time-series data. This will help us to calculate the forecast.

Calculating the moving average and CMA

A moving average is an approach to *smooth* the seasonal *peaks* in the time-series data, which is typical of these types of datasets. It helps to include the season peaks in the forecast model by following the trend's movements up and down over a time period. Choose the number of time periods to average. In this example, we will take the average of the four quarters per year from **Year 1** to **Year 5** (see the grouping of the moving average in *Figure 12.3*). Then, we calculate the CMA. Take the average of two quarters for this calculation, as shown in *Figure 12.3*:

Year	Quarterly	Sales	MA(4)	CenterMA(4)		t	Year	Quarterly	Sales	MA(4)	CenterMA(4)
1 Year 1	1	112				1	Year 1	1	112		
2	2	118				2		2	118		
3	3	132	122.75	123.875		3		3	132	122.75	123.875
4	4	129	125	127.125		4		4	129	125	127.125
5 Year 2	1	121	129.25	131.25		5	Year 2	1	121	129.25	131.25
6	2	135	133.25	135.625		6		2	135	133.25	135.625
7	3	148	138	139.875		7		3	148	138	139.875
8	4	148	141.75	139.75		8		4	148	141.75	139.75
9 Year 3	1	136	137.75	132.25		9	Year 3	1	136	137.75	132.25
10	2	119	126.75	123		10		2	119	126.75	123
11	3	104	119.25	116.625		11		3	104	119.25	116.625
12	4	118	114	114.875		12		4	118	114	114.875
13 Year 4	1	115	115.75	120.375		13	Year 4	1	115	115.75	120.375
14	2	126	125	127.125		14		2	126	125	127.125
15	3	141	129.25	130.5		15		3	141	129.25	130.5
16	4	135	131.75	134.625		16		4	135	131.75	134.625
17 Year 5	1	125	137.5	141.125		17	Year 5	1	125	137.5	141.125
18	2	149	144.75	149.125		18		2	149	144.75	149.125
19	3	170	153.5	157.625		19		3	170	153.5	157.625
20	4	170	161.75	159.75		20		4	170	161.75	159.75

Figure 12.3 – The moving average and CMA

In this example in *Figure 12.3*, we calculate the moving average in groups of four quarters. Remember that this number can change at your own discretion. The first moving average column is for the four quarters of **Year 1**:

```
112 + 118 + 132 + 129 = (491/4) = 122.75
```

The moving average for the next four quarters is calculated as follows:

```
118 + 132 + 129 + 121 = (500/4) = 125
```

Continue with the same month group calculations of four elements for the rest of the data in the **Sales** column to fill in the moving average column (**MA(4)**), as shown in *Figure 12.3*.

The CMA smooths the peaks and troughs of the dataset more.

In this case, we have four quarters, so the CMA is the average of two quarters. In *Figure 12.3*, the first two-quarters average is as follows:

```
122.75 + 125 = (247.75/2) = 123.87
```

The next average is as follows:

```
125 + 129.25 = (254.25/2) = 127.12
```

Continue until you finish all the calculations for the moving average and the CMA, and plot both, as shown in *Figure 12.4*, to see the smoothed data trend compared with the jagged up and downs of the original dataset:

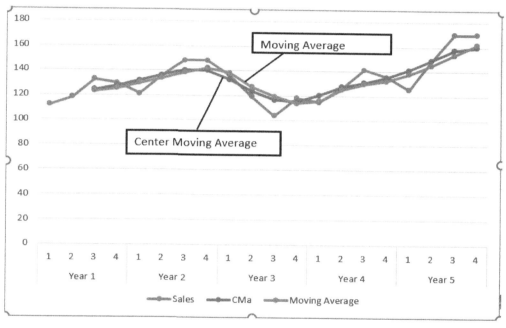

Figure 12.4 – The moving average and CMA smooth chart

Note how the CMA smooths the large peaks of the sales data in *Figure 12.4*. From the distance between the sales data and the CMA, we obtain a factor that helps to model the forecast, taking into account the up-and-down trends of the sales time series.

In this section, we learned how the CMA can be used to smooth the peaks of a dataset. In the next section, we will calculate the distance between a percentage of the data and the CMA to get a factor that will help the forecast follow the up-and-down trends of the time series.

Estimating the season irregular and season components

The season irregular component calculates the distance as a percentage between the data and the CMA. If the data line is above the CMA, the value is greater than 1. For example, a value of 1.10 means that the data is 10% above the CMA. If the value is 0.85, it means that the data is below 15% of the CMA. In *Figure 12.4*, we have the data for the CMA and the season irregular component, so we can see the distance between the data sales and the CMA as a percentage. We get this data by dividing the sales value by the CMA value:

Year	Quarterly	Sales	MA(4)	CenterMA(4)	St It
Year 1	1	112			
	2	118			
	3	132	122.75	123.875	1.06559031
	4	129	125	127.125	1.01474926
Year 2	1	121	129.25	131.25	0.92190476
	2	135	133.25	135.625	0.99539171
	3	148	138	139.875	1.05808758
	4	148	141.75	139.75	1.05903399
Year 3	1	136	137.75	132.25	1.02835539
	2	119	126.75	123	0.96747967
	3	104	119.25	116.625	0.89174705
	4	118	114	114.875	1.02720348
Year 4	1	115	115.75	120.375	0.95534787
	2	126	125	127.125	0.99115044
	3	141	129.25	130.5	1.08045977
	4	135	131.75	134.625	1.00278552
Year 5	1	125	137.5	141.125	0.88573959
	2	149	144.75	149.125	0.99916178
	3	170	153.5	157.625	1.07850912
	4	170	161.75	159.75	1.06416275

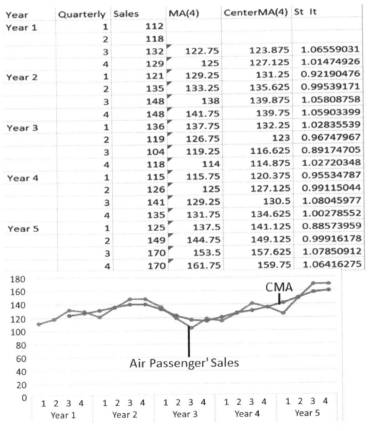

Figure 12.5 – The data and chart for the season irregular component and the CMA

For example, to get the season irregular component for the third quarter of the first year, divide the sales value by the CMA, as follows:

```
132(Sales) / 123.85 (CMA) = 1.06
```

That means that for this quarter, sales are above 6% of the CMA (see *Figure 12.5* and check for the chart for this quarter). For the first quarter of **Year 2**, the **Sales** value is below the CMA.

Calculating this seasonal irregular value, the **Sales** value is **121** and the **CMA** value is **131.25**. Since the CMA is greater than the **Sales** value, it means it is fewer than 1. This means that the **Sales** value is fewer than the **CMA**. The **Sales** line is below the **CMA** line, as you can see in *Figure 12.4*, for the first quarter of **Year 2**:

```
121(Sales)/131.25(CMA) = 0.92
```

That means that the **Sales** value is below 8% of the CMA (see *Figure 12.8* to see the **Sales** line below the **CMA** line).

With the seasonal irregular component, we get factors that help the forecast to take into account the direction of the trend. We need one more step to get this factor. We will look at the season alone, separately from the seasonal irregular calculation that we did before.

To get the season component, we take the values of each period. In this example, we have 4 quarters over each of the 5 years. But we can have bimonthly or trimester periods in some other data. The season component is the average of the seasonal irregular for each period. For example, the season component for the third quarter from **Year 1** to **Year 5** is shown in *Figure 12.6* (also refer to *Figure 12.4*):

Year	Quarter	Season Irregular	Season
Year 1	1		
	2		
	3	1.06559	1.03
	4		
Year 2	1		
	2		
	3	1.058088	1.03
	4		
Year 3	1		
	2		
	3	0.891747	1.03
	4		
Year 4	1		
	2		
	3	1.08046	1.03
	4		
Year 5	1		
	2		
	3	1.078509	1.03
	4		

Figure 12.6 – The seasonal irregular values for the third quarter – the season average of these values

To calculate the season component of the third quarter, we get the average of the third quarter seasonal irregular values and then write the result in the season rows for the third quarter of each year.

For this example, the seasonal irregular average of all third quarters is calculated as follows:

```
Season third quarter = (1.06 + 1.05 + 0.89 + 1.08 + 1.07) / 5 =
1.03
```

We do the same calculations for the other quarters, and we get results with the season components for all the periods, as shown in *Figure 12.7*:

Year	Quarter	Season Irr	Season		Quarter	St
Year 1	1	0.9478369	0.947837		1	0.947837
	2	0.9882959	0.988296		2	0.988296
	3	1.0348788	1.034879		3	1.034879
	4	1.033587	1.033587		4	1.033587
Year 2	1	0.9478369	0.947837			
	2	0.9882959	0.988296			
	3	1.0348788	1.034879			
	4	1.033587	1.033587			
Year 3	1	0.9478369	0.947837			
	2	0.9882959	0.988296			
	3	1.0348788	1.034879			
	4	1.033587	1.033587			
Year 4	1	0.9478369	0.947837			
	2	0.9882959	0.988296			
	3	1.0348788	1.034879			
	4	1.033587	1.033587			
Year 5	1	0.9478369	0.947837			
	2	0.9882959	0.988296			
	3	1.0348788	1.034879			
	4	1.033587	1.033587			

Season component for each quarter

Figure 12.7 – The season component for each quarter

The complete calculations for the season components of all quarters are shown in *Figure 12.7*. Let's have a quick look at the manual calculation for the first quarter.

The values of the seasonal irregular average of the first quarter to get the season component are as follows:

```
Season component first quarter = 0.92+1.02+0.95+0.88 = 0.94
```

The season component is the element that gives the up-and-down movements of the forecast. This *guide*, combined with the trend or regression line, allows us to build the prediction model.

In this section, we learned how to calculate the distance percentage and seasonal irregular between data and the CMA. The season component is the average of each period over the time frame. In this example, it is the average for each quarter of the 5 years of data. The season component directs the up-and-down position of the forecast. In the next section, we will calculate the trend line. Multiplying the trend line by the season component outputs the prediction.

Calculating the trend line

The trend line is the linear regression model of the data. With this line, the model takes the direction, up or down of the forecast. Then, multiplying this trend line by the season component gives a prediction that shows whether the forecast goes up or down.

We combine the data, the moving average, and the trend line to get the visualization of the possible forecast output. See *Figure 12.5* to research what the future values for **Year 6** and **Year 7** could be.

The values of the trend line are shown in *Figure 12.5* in the **Trend** column. Calculate the linear regression values using Excel's Data Analysis ToolPak, using **Sales** as the **Y** result variable and the correlative index as the **X** values (1 to 20):

Year	Quarterly	Sales	Trend t	CenterMA
Year 1	1	112	115.9868	
	2	118	117.6917	
	3	132	119.3965	123.875
	4	129	121.1013	127.125
Year 2	1	121	122.8062	131.25
	2	135	124.511	135.625
	3	148	126.2158	139.875
	4	148	127.9207	139.75
Year 3	1	136	129.6255	132.25
	2	119	131.3303	123
	3	104	133.0352	116.625
	4	118	134.74	114.875
Year 4	1	115	136.4448	120.375
	2	126	138.1497	127.125
	3	141	139.8545	130.5
	4	135	141.5593	134.625
Year 5	1	125	143.2641	141.125
	2	149	144.969	149.125
	3	170	146.6738	157.625
	4	170	148.3786	159.75

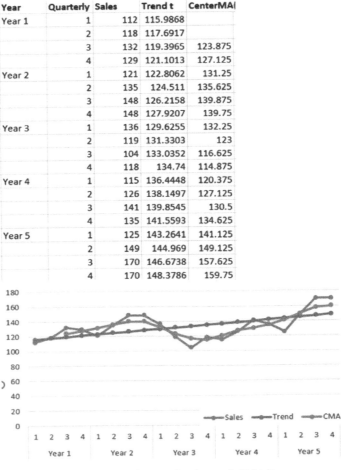

Figure 12.8 – The trend, sales, and CMA lines

The sales data in *Figure 12.8* shows an up-trending line through the period of **Year 1** to **Year 5**. Throughout each year of this period, the sales increase and decrease depending on the season of the year. In the first two quarters of each year, the sales decrease, and then increase in the third and fourth quarters. Based on this visualization, we expect that the forecast for the following years is that sales will grow in the direction of the trend line but with a cyclical behavior on an annual basis, decreasing during the first and second quarters and increasing during the third and fourth quarters of each year.

In this section, we calculated the trend line for sales using linear regression. This line gives the direction of the forecast and can be growing or decreasing values. In this case, we see that even with the cyclical effect of sales going up in the third and fourth quarters and going down in the first and second quarters, the trend line indicates that sales still grow over the years. In the next section, we are going to use the season component and the trend line (linear regression) to produce a forecast of future sales.

Producing the forecast – season and trend line

Now, we are ready to make the forecast. We are going to multiply the season component by the **trend** (**regression**) line to make a prediction for the following years. The concept behind this calculation is that every period of time (in this case, quarters) has an upper or lower inclination given by the seasonal component. The seasonal component moves up or down the trend line, depending on the predictive behavior for this lapse (we're using quarters in this example). The forecast for **Year 6** and **Year 7** is shown in *Figure 12.6*:

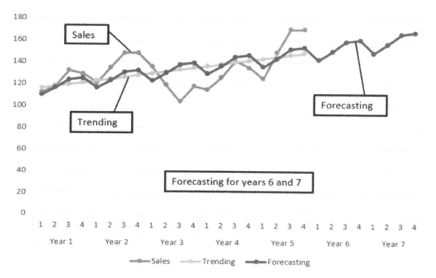

Figure 12.9 – Our forecast for years 6 and 7

A forecast is just an approximation of what could happen in the future based on past data. Visualize the sales by quarter for the 5 years of data we have, and note that the sales increase after the third quarter every year, despite sales suffering significant drops in **Year 3** and **Year 4**. This performance is reflected by the forecast line for **Year 6** and **Year 7**, where the third and fourth quarters of these years show increases in the sales volume.

This prediction model is the result of including the season component in the linear regression of the trend line. The first-quarter prediction for **Year 6** is the result of multiplying the season component by the linear regression, as follows:

```
Forecast First Quarter Year 6 = 0.94 (Season C.) * 115.98
(Linear Regression) = 109.93
```
```
Forecast Third Quarter Year 6 = 1.03 (Season C.) * 119.39
(Linear Regression) = 123.56
```

The complete forecast calculation demonstrating the multiplication of the season component by trend is shown in *Figure 12.7*. Remember that the season component has a four-quarter cycle. It repeats every four quarters across all of the years.

Index	Year	Quarterly	Sales	Season	Trend t	Forecasting
1	Year 1	1	112	0.947837	115.9868	109.9366
2		2	118	0.988296	117.6917	116.3142
3		3	132	1.034879	119.3965	123.5609
4		4	129	1.033587	121.1013	125.1688
5	Year 2	1	121	0.947837	122.8062	116.4002
6		2	135	0.988296	124.511	123.0537
7		3	148	1.034879	126.2158	130.6181
8		4	148	1.033587	127.9207	132.2171
9	Year 3	1	136	0.947837	129.6255	122.8638
10		2	119	0.988296	131.3303	129.7932
11		3	104	1.034879	133.0352	137.6753
12		4	118	1.033587	134.74	139.2655
13	Year 4	1	115	0.947837	136.4448	129.3274
14		2	126	0.988296	138.1497	136.5327
15		3	141	1.034879	139.8545	144.7324
16		4	135	1.033587	141.5593	146.3139
17	Year 5	1	125	0.947837	143.2641	135.791
18		2	149	0.988296	144.969	143.2723
19		3	170	1.034879	146.6738	151.7896
20		4	170	1.033587	148.3786	153.3622
21	Year 6	1	158	0.947837	150.0835	142.2547
22		2	133	0.988296	151.7883	150.0118
23		3	114	1.034879	153.4931	158.8468
24		4	140	1.033587	155.198	160.4106
25	Year 7	1	145	0.947837	156.9028	148.7183
26		2	150	0.988296	158.6076	156.7513
27		3	178	1.034879	160.3125	165.904
28		4	163	1.033587	162.0173	167.459

Figure 12.10 – The season component for each quarter

The season component values reflect the fact that the first and second quarters have lower sales than the third and fourth quarters. As a result, the season components for the first and second quarters are less than one, while for the third and fourth quarters, the figures are above one. Remember that for this example, we used a four-quarter cycle length, but we can change this time period and use, for example, five bimonthly periods. The trend or linear regression gives the direction of the data if it goes up or down. With this information, we can produce a sales forecast for the forthcoming 2 years based on the data of the past 5 years.

In this chapter, we learned how to smooth the *peaks* and *troughs* of the time series using the CMA to get the seasonal component that directs the trend regression line to the up-and-down course of the sales forecast. In the next chapter, we are going to train the model with 80% of known data, and then we will test it with the remaining 20% of the dataset. Finally, we will use the time-series prediction model to calculate future values.

Summary

The forecast calculation depends entirely on the quality of autocorrelation in the data. If present values are dependent on past data, then the data will give good future predictions for the time series. The Durbin-Watson probe to check the level of autocorrelation of the time series tells us how good the prediction will be by measuring the influence of past data on the current values.

The season component depends on the CMA distance to the data. The season component is determined by the forecast as a factor to move the trend (linear regression) up or down, depending on the cycles of the time series. Comparing the forecast time-series line chart with the original data gives us an idea of how accurate the model's prediction is.

In this chapter, we learned to use the CMA to smooth the peaks and troughs of the seasonal values over the years. The CMA helps to calculate the seasonal trend weight that leads the regression line up and down for the monthly dependable forecasting model.

In the next chapter, we will test and run the time-series model to research how well it conforms with reality.

Questions

Here are a few questions to help you recall what you learned in this chapter:

1. How many time periods can we use to calculate the moving average?
2. Can we use data in which the Durbin-Watson autocorrelation equals `false`?
3. What does the seasonal component show about the trend of the data?

4. What is the forecast formula?

5. What does the seasonal irregular component indicate?

Answers

Here are the answers to the preceding questions:

1. The number is up to the researcher – for example, we can use a bimonthly, quarterly, or semester time period when calculating the moving average.

2. No. Autocorrelation is a key factor in calculating future values because our forecast depends on past data to make predictions.

3. The cyclical seasonal component shows the increasing and decreasing values of the forecast based on the past data.

4. Multiply the season component by the trend of linear regression.

5. It shows the distance between the data and the CMA line.

Further reading

Here are a few sources you can refer to for more information on a time series:

- *Practical Time Series Analysis*:

  https://www.packtpub.com/product/practical-time-series-analysis/9781788290227

- *Time Series Analysis with Python 3.x [Video]*:

  https://www.packtpub.com/product/time-series-analysis-with-python-3-x-video/9781838640590

13
Training, Validating, and Running the Model

In this chapter, we will apply the forecast time-series model to a real-life dataset to predict automobile sales in the US, using Kaggle retail sales data.

We have quarterly data for the years 2012 to 2019. We will design, train, and test the model and see whether it does a good job of making predictions.

In **Machine Learning** (**ML**), when working with statistical groups, linear regression, or time series, you have to apply your experience to do an initial quality check of data with a chart. In a time-series forecast, you use your judgment to see whether the data has autocorrelation. That means that the past has influence over the present and is useful to predict the future using a forecast.

Many time-series datsets have two components that need prediction – a season component and a growing decreasing trend. The season component is when data has cycling peaks depending on a year's seasons.

After these calculations, you chart the forecast and decide whether it makes sense with the past data and represents the seasonal cycling of the data. Remember that the forecast just gives an idea of what the future could be. It is not an exact prediction.

In this chapter, we will be looking at the following topics:

- Training the model
- Building and training the forecast model
- Testing the forecast model
- Doing the forecast

Let's begin with the prerequisites of this chapter in the next section.

Technical requirements

For the exercises of this chapter, you will need an Excel file that you can download at the following link:

```
https://github.com/PacktPublishing/Data-Forecasting-and-
Segmentation-Using-Microsoft-Excel/blob/main/Chapter13/
chapterThirteenTimeSeriestoUPLOADSeries.xlsx
```

Now that we have the requirements, let's get started!

Training the model

We are going to use sales data of quarters for the years 2012 to 2015 to design and train the forecast time-series model. With this design, we will test the predictions with a group of known sales for 2016 to 2017. Finally, we will make a forecast for 2018 to 2019.

The model has to take both of these components (known sales and forecast) to make a good prediction. The steps to develop a forecast, as we will see in this chapter, are as follows:

1. Look at the data chart to decide whether it has autocorrelation or not.
2. Test the autocorrelation with the Durbin-Watson test.
3. Calculate the moving average (explained in *Chapter 12, Working with Time Series Using the Centered Moving Average and a Trending Component*) to smooth the peaks of the data.
4. Design the model, calculating the seasonal trends.
5. Test the forecast by multiplying the seasonal trend by the regression line.
6. Use the model to make forecasts.

In this chapter, we will design a time-series forecast using the data of car sales found in the Kaggle US retail sales dataset (`https://www.kaggle.com/ryanholbrook/linear-regression-with-time-series/data?select=us-retail-sales.csv`).

The steps to make the forecast are as follows:

1. Perform the Durbin-Watson test for the 2012 to 2015 sales to see whether the data has autocorrelation and is useful to make a forecast.

2. Take the quarterly sales for the years 2012 to 2015 to train the time-series model.

3. Test the forecast model with the sales of the years 2016 and 2017. Review the forecast chart to check the accuracy of the prediction.

4. Use the model to predict the sales for the years 2018 and 2019.

Before we design the model, we have to test whether the data is useful to do forecasts as we did with the linear regression relationship among variables in *Chapter 8*, *Finding the Relationship between Variables*. The data is useful if the present data depends on the past and has autocorrelation. We will see this test, Durbin-Watson, in the next section.

Conducting the Durbin-Watson test

This test uses regression model errors to see whether past data influences the present (autocorrelation). This is necessary to build the forecast. The steps to run the Durbin-Watson test are as follows:

1. Select the **Sales** column as the **Y** series and the row number as the **X** series in the **Regression** function under the **Data** option of Excel.

2. Select the **Errors** option in the regression function.

3. Do the Durbin-Watson calculations using the errors as input data.

4. Verify that the Durbin-Watson value falls in the autocorrelation range.

Drawing a chart of the data can give an idea of whether past data has influence over the present and then confirm our interpretation using the Durbin-Watson test. *Figure 13.1* shows the monthly sales of cars for the years 2012 to 2015:

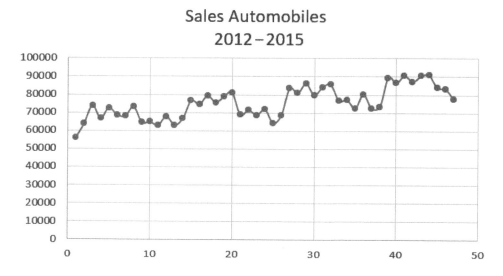

Figure 13.1 – Monthly automobile sales for the years 2012–2015

The monthly automobile sales for the 2012–2015 chart in *Figure 13.1* shows two pieces of information:

- The season-cycling trend, depending on the month of the year
- The sales-growing trend year after year

With this visual information, we can interpret that past data has influence over the present because it appears to be cycling. We will test this fact using the Durbin-Watson test.

We can get another sense of the data autocorrelation by plotting the errors of the regression model of the monthly automobile sales from 2012 to 2015. The errors plot is shown in *Figure 13.2*:

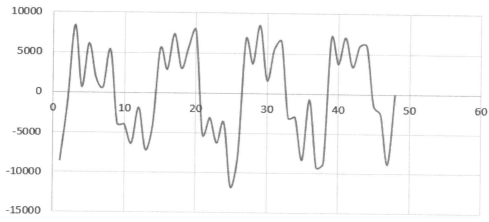

Figure 13.2 – Errors for the regression of monthly automobile sales for the years 2012–2015

The error plot of *Figure 13.2* confirms our idea that the data has a predictable cycle, so the past has influence over the present. We will confirm this by doing the calculations of the Durbin-Watson test.

The Durbin-Watson formula is as follows:

$$W = \frac{\sum_{t=2}^{n}(e_t - e_{t-1})^2}{\sum_{t=1}^{n} e_t^2}$$

We will use the calculations of the regression errors from *Figure 13.3* as parameters for the formula:

Observation	Predicted Automobiles	Residuals e_t	e_t^2	$e_{t-1}{}^2$	$(e_t - e_{t-1})^2$
1	64509.64371	-8564.6	73353121.84		
2	64984.57554	-1362.6	1856612.09	-8564.6437	51869785.95
3	65459.50736	8354.49	69797547.21	-1362.5755	94421413.86
4	65934.43919	657.561	432386.2167	8354.49264	59242759.57
5	66409.37102	6079.63	36961888.54	657.560808	29398823.26
6	66884.30285	1773.7	3146001.588	6079.62898	18541048.91
7	67359.23468	645.765	417012.854	1773.69715	1272230.209
8	67834.1665	5339.83	28513821.77	645.765324	22034276
9	68309.09833	-3841.1	14754036.4	5339.8335	84289509.23
10	68784.03016	-3929	15437278	-3841.0983	7732.006384
11	69258.96199	-6384	40754970.66	-3929.0302	6026690.28
12	69733.89382	-1871.9	3503986.459	-6383.962	20358759.19
13	70208.82564	-7209.8	51981585.82	-1871.8938	28493516.2
14	70683.75747	-4059.8	16481630.73	-7209.8256	9922929.488
15	71158.6893	5482.31	30055730.61	-4059.7575	91051065
16	71633.62113	2913.38	8487776.45	5482.3107	6599410.737
17	72108.55296	7339.45	53867482.91	2913.37887	19590079.46
18	72583.48478	3034.52	9208282.594	7339.44704	18532438.04
19	73058.41661	5750.58	33069209.3	3034.51522	7377026.315
20	73533.34844	7727.65	59716598.63	5750.58339	3908798.557
21	74008.28027	-5183.3	26866394.34	7727.65156	166692160.7
22	74483.2121	-3088.2	9537053.953	-5183.2803	4389310.645
23	74958.14392	-6280.1	39440207.71	-3088.2121	10188428.79
24	75433.07575	-3641.1	13257432.64	-6280.1439	6964680.816
25	75908.00758	-11792	139051442.8	-3641.0758	66437689.67
26	76382.93941	-7701.9	59319870.66	-11792.008	16728657.65
27	76857.87124	6655.13	44290738.85	-7701.9394	206125406.5
28	77332.80306	3685.2	13580676.45	6655.12876	8820495.063
29	77807.73489	8459.27	71559166.15	3685.19694	22791726.91
30	78282.66672	1620.33	2625479.935	8459.26511	46770988.55
31	78757.59855	5486.4	30100600.88	1620.33328	14946483.11
32	79232.53038	6476.47	41944658.78	5486.40145	980234.9851
33	79707.46221	-2992.5	8954830.049	6476.46962	89660669.96
34	80182.39403	-2926.4	8563782.037	-2992.4622	4365.003345
35	80657.32586	-8294.3	68795841.49	-2926.394	28814692.11
36	81132.25769	-744.26	553919.508	-8294.3259	57003529.4
37	81607.18952	-9235.2	85288725.42	-744.25769	72095923.31
38	82082.12135	-8660.1	74997701.72	-9235.1895	330703.4024
39	82557.05317	6903.95	47664481.78	-8660.1213	242240218.1
40	83031.985	3707.01	13741960.2	6903.94683	10220373.11
41	83506.91683	7055.08	49774198.54	3707.015	11209560.48
42	83981.84866	3361.15	11297338.35	7055.08317	13645132.35
43	84456.78049	5986.22	35834824.07	3361.15134	6890982.907
44	84931.71231	6032.29	36388494.73	5986.21951	2122.276467
45	85406.64414	-1367.6	1870450.498	6032.28769	54758991.06
46	85881.57597	-2549.6	6500337.626	-1367.6441	1396962.846
47	86356.5078	-8780.5	77097317.19	-2549.576	38824511.45
. 48	86831.43963	-67.44	4548.103135	-8780.5078	75917556.97
			1570699435		**1847790850**

Figure 13.3 – Regression error calculations for the Durbin-Watson formula

We divide the summation results highlighted by black boxes in *Figure 13.3* to calculate the Durbin-Watson test values:

$$W = \frac{\Sigma_{t=2}^n (e_t - e_{t-1})^2}{\Sigma_{t=1}^n e_t^2} = \frac{1847790850}{1570699435} = 1.176412755$$

The resulting test result is *1.17*, meaning that it has a positive autocorrelation. It is far from the rejection region of 2, so we accept the alternative hypothesis that the past data has influence over the present. With this result, we can use the automobile sales data from 2012 to 2015 to make forecasts.

In this section, we reviewed how to do a Durbin-Watson test and interpret the result to be sure that the data is useful to do a forecast.

Once we are sure that the car sales data has autocorrelation, we can proceed to build and train the model, as we will explain in the next section.

Building and training the forecast model

We are going to use the car sales for the years 2012 to 2015 to design and train the time-series forecast model. We saw in the previous section that this data has autocorrelation. The steps for designing the model are as follows:

1. Calculate the moving average for two quarter periods.
2. Get the center moving average of the preceding step.
3. Calculate the separation between the quarter sales and the center moving average for each record. This separation between the quarter sales and center moving average is the fluctuation of sales over time.
4. Get the seasonal trend for each record by averaging the fluctuation for each quarter.
5. Compute the trend with the regression line of the quarterly sales.
6. Calculate the forecast by multiplying the season trend by the regression for each record.

Calculate the moving average and the center moving average for the data to get the chart shown in *Figure 13.4*. The center moving average is useful to smooth the ups and downs of sales peaks:

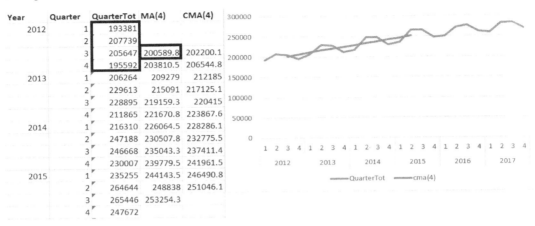

Figure 13.4 – The moving average and center moving average chart for 2012–2015

The center moving average (the center moving average of four periods – **CMA(4)** in the figure) in *Figure 13.4* represents the smooth quarterly sales of automobiles from 2012 to 2015. In the next step, we are going to calculate the separation between the quarter total (**QuarterTot** in *Figure 13.4*) to the center moving average, and this distance will give us the seasonal trend of the data, which will be useful to make the forecast.

We calculate the seasonal trend for each quarterly period using the distance from the sales to the center moving average given by the season iterator value for each record. If the sales are above the center moving average, the seasonal trend is greater than one. If the sales are below the center moving average line, the seasonal trend is less than one. See *Figure 13.5* to understand this relationship:

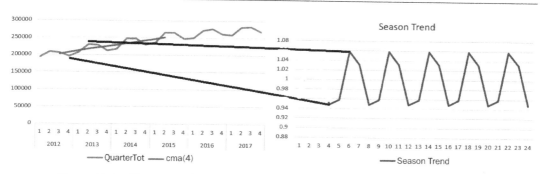

Figure 13.5 – The seasonal trend chart for quarterly and center moving average sales

The fourth-quarter sales of 2012 are below the center moving average line. *Figure 13.5* shows the seasonal trend, where you can see that data number 4 is below one. The third-quarter sales of 2013 are above the center moving average line. In *Figure 13.5*, the seasonal trend for record number 6 corresponding to the third quarter of 2013 is greater than one.

The seasonal trend value in *Figure 13.5* guides the up-and-down hills of the regression line to do the forecast. The forecast is the multiplication of the seasonal trend by the regression value shown in *Figure 13.6*. For this example, we use the data sales from 2012 to 2015:

Year	Quarter	QuarterTot	MA(4)	CMA(4)	SeasonTrend	Regression	Forecast
2012	1	193381			0.958017077	195232.69	187036.2521
	2	207739			1.057865125	199469.88	211012.232
	3	205647	200589.8	202200.1	1.031503181	203707.07	210124.4943
	4	195592	203810.5	206544.8	0.947983363	207944.26	197127.7033
2013	1	206264	209279	212185	0.958017077	212181.46	203273.4581
	2	229613	215091	217125.1	1.057865125	216418.65	228941.7391
	3	228895	219159.3	220415	1.031503181	220655.84	227607.199
	4	211865	221670.8	223867.6	0.947983363	224893.03	213194.8503
2014	1	216310	226064.5	228286.1	0.958017077	229130.22	219510.6641
	2	247188	230507.8	232775.5	1.057865125	233367.41	246871.2462
	3	246668	235043.3	237411.4	1.031503181	237604.6	245089.9037
	4	230007	239779.5	241961.5	0.947983363	241841.79	229261.9972
2015	1	235255	244143.5	246490.8	0.958017077	246078.99	235747.8702
	2	264644	248838	251046.1	1.057865125	250316.18	264800.7533
	3	265446	253254.3		1.031503181	254553.37	262572.6084
	4	247672			0.947983363	258790.56	245329.1442

Figure 13.6 – The forecast multiplying the season trend by the regression model

The forecast is positively designed according to *Figure 13.6*. The sales represented by **QuarterTot** and **Forecast** are on the same curve line. The straight line is the trending regression model. So, the forecast is giving almost the same results as the sales from 2012 to 2015. You can verify the numbers on the table to the right of *Figure 13.6*. With this design, we are ready to test the model with the known data from 2016 to 2017.

In this section, we built the model using the data from 2012 to 2015. Verify how well the forecast fits with this known data. In the next section, we will use the data from 2016 to 2017 to test the model.

Testing the forecast model

We will see the forecast fit using the car sales from 2016 to 2017. This data is known from the dataset, so we will be able to check whether the model works well or not.

Follow these steps to test the model:

1. Copy and paste from the previous data the seasonal trend for each quarter from 2016 to 2017.
2. Calculate the trend for 2016 to 2017 using the regression line.
3. Test the forecast by multiplying the seasonal trend by the regression.

Use the known data of sales for the years 2016 and 2017 to test the forecast model, as mentioned in *step 3* of the previous list. The automobile sales are in the highlighted **QuarterTot** column in *Figure 13.7*. We use this data to see whether the model is useful to predict this information.

The season trend per quarterly period for the years 2016 and 2017 is the same past data we have seen before. Calculate the regression trend for the 2016–2017 quarters. This data is highlighted in *Figure 13.7*. Test the forecast model by multiplying the season trend by the regression trend. The data for the quarters' periods of the years 2016 and 2017 is shown in *Figure 13.7*:

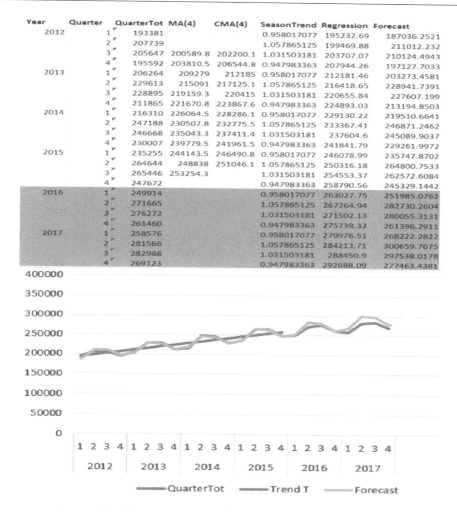

Year	Quarter	QuarterTot	MA(4)	CMA(4)	SeasonTrend	Regression	Forecast
2012	1	193381			0.958017077	195232.69	187036.2521
	2	207739			1.057865125	199469.88	211012.232
	3	205647	200589.8	202200.1	1.031503181	203707.07	210124.4943
	4	195592	203810.5	206544.8	0.947983363	207944.26	197127.7033
2013	1	206264	209279	212185	0.958017077	212181.46	203273.4581
	2	229613	215091	217125.1	1.057865125	216418.65	228941.7391
	3	228895	219159.3	220415	1.031503181	220655.84	227607.199
	4	211865	221670.8	223867.6	0.947983363	224893.03	213194.8503
2014	1	216310	226064.5	228286.1	0.958017077	229130.22	219510.6641
	2	247188	230507.8	232775.5	1.057865125	233367.41	246871.2462
	3	246668	235043.3	237411.4	1.031503181	237604.6	245089.9037
	4	230007	239779.5	241961.5	0.947983363	241841.79	229261.9972
2015	1	235255	244143.5	246490.8	0.958017077	246078.99	235747.8702
	2	264644	248838	251046.1	1.057865125	250316.18	264800.7533
	3	265446	253254.3		1.031503181	254553.37	262572.6084
	4	247672			0.947983363	258790.56	245329.1442
2016	1	249914			0.958017077	263027.75	251985.0762
	2	271665			1.057865125	267264.94	282730.2604
	3	276272			1.031503181	271502.13	280055.3131
	4	261460			0.947983363	275739.32	261396.2911
2017	1	258576			0.958017077	279976.51	268222.2822
	2	281566			1.057865125	284213.71	300659.7675
	3	282988			1.031503181	288450.9	297538.0178
	4	269123			0.947983363	292688.09	277463.4381

Figure 13.7 – The testing forecast for automobile sales for 2016–2017

Review the forecast and the automobile sales curves in *Figure 13.7* and check that both lines are almost fixed. That means that the model is working well. The model predicts that the peak of sales is in the second quarter in both years and also that the sales fall in the fourth quarter in both years. This is exactly the same as the trend of the known data used to test the forecast. Also, the model follows the growing trend of sales. The sales grow year after year, as the regression trending line suggests.

In this section, we reviewed the forecast model and saw that it fits well in the 2016 and 2017 quarters. So, we can approve the model application and move forward to the next section to do a forecast for the years 2018 to 2019.

Doing the forecast

To build the forecast, we follow the same steps that we saw earlier when testing the model:

1. Get the seasonal trend for each quarter from 2018 to 2019.

2. Calculate the trend for 2018 to 2019 using the regression line.

3. Forecast by multiplying the seasonal trend by the regression.

The forecast chart reveals that car sales keep growing, following the trend with a season fall in the fourth quarter. We see that the data has two components:

- A seasonal component with the sales fluctuation amount quarters

- A trend component that indicates the sales growth each year

To do the forecast, we calculate the seasonal trend and the regression trend. The highlighted data in *Figure 13.8* shows the calculations to apply the model to make a forecast for the years 2018 and 2019:

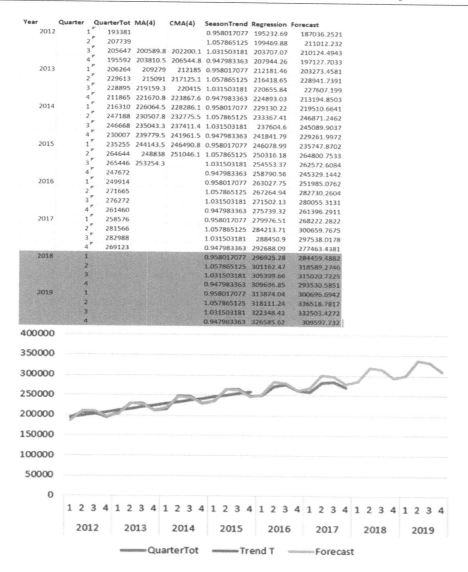

Year	Quarter	QuarterTot	MA(4)	CMA(4)	SeasonTrend	Regression	Forecast
2012	1	193381			0.958017077	195232.69	187036.2521
	2	207739			1.057865125	199469.88	211012.232
	3	205647	200589.8	202200.1	1.031503181	203707.07	210124.4943
	4	195592	203810.5	206544.8	0.947983363	207944.26	197127.7033
2013	1	206264	209279	212185	0.958017077	212181.46	203273.4581
	2	229613	215091	217125.1	1.057865125	216418.65	228941.7391
	3	228895	219159.3	220415	1.031503181	220655.84	227607.199
	4	211865	221670.8	223867.6	0.947983363	224893.03	213194.8503
2014	1	216310	226064.5	228286.1	0.958017077	229130.22	219510.6641
	2	247188	230507.8	232775.5	1.057865125	233367.41	246871.2462
	3	246668	235043.3	237411.4	1.031503181	237604.6	245089.9037
	4	230007	239779.5	241961.5	0.947983363	241841.79	229261.9972
2015	1	235255	244143.5	246490.8	0.958017077	246078.99	235747.8702
	2	264644	248838	251046.1	1.057865125	250316.18	264800.7533
	3	265446	253254.3		1.031503181	254553.37	262572.6084
	4	247672			0.947983363	258790.56	245329.1442
2016	1	249914			0.958017077	263027.75	251985.0762
	2	271665			1.057865125	267264.94	282730.2604
	3	276272			1.031503181	271502.13	280055.3131
	4	261460			0.947983363	275739.32	261396.2911
2017	1	258576			0.958017077	279976.51	268222.2822
	2	281566			1.057865125	284213.71	300659.7675
	3	282988			1.031503181	288450.9	297538.0178
	4	269123			0.947983363	292688.09	277463.4381
2018	1				0.958017077	296925.28	284459.4882
	2				1.057865125	301162.47	318589.2746
	3				1.031503181	305399.86	315020.7225
	4				0.947983363	309636.85	293530.5851
2019	1				0.958017077	313874.04	300696.6942
	2				1.057865125	318111.24	336518.7817
	3				1.031503181	322348.43	332503.4272
	4				0.947983363	326585.62	309597.732

Figure 13.8 – Using the forecast for automobile sales for 2018–2019

The forecast model makes a good prediction for the years 2018 and 2019. Look how it fits with the seasonal trend by predicting the ups and downs of sales for each quarter. Also, it's a good fit for growing trends year after year using the regression line as a guide.

In this chapter, we applied almost all the concepts that we have learned in this book:

- Testing the data to see whether it is useful to build a prediction model
- Using a regression model to check the data trend
- Using a model application to predict the future

Let's summarize the learnings of this chapter in the next section.

Summary

This book covered the basic statistic concepts to use ML models. We can group our data to research the segments that are more important for our activity. Then, we can apply the regression model to these segments and see what the most influential variables are to build predictions using them. Finally, we forecast the values of these important segments and have an idea of what the behavior of our research variables can be in the future.

In this chapter, we applied the three general steps of the ML algorithm by designing a forecast model with known data, testing the model, also with known data, and finally, doing a prediction. As with any other ML function, we need to observe and ensure quality control of the data source to be sure that it is useful to do forecasts. In the case of time series, we know that the Durbin-Watson test checks for data autocorrelation to see whether the past has an influence on the present and whether it can predict the future. Then, we test the model to see whether it fixes the seasonal and regression trends. The seasonal trend is the up-and-down cycle of data. The regression is the growth or decline of data values along with the time series. In this chapter, we used a real-life example from the Kaggle car sales dataset. This example gives assurance that ML concepts are valid for practical problems. With these topics, we have reached the end of this book.

Questions

Here are a few questions and their answers to revisit the concepts we learned in this chapter:

1. What are the first two steps before designing and training a forecast model?
2. What element of regression is the input for the Durbin-Watson test?
3. What is the input value for seasonal trending?
4. What are the elements to calculate the forecast?
5. What are two possible elements of time-series data?

Answers

Here are the answers to the preceding questions:

1. The following are the two steps:

    A.   Review the data chart and decide whether the past has an influence on the present.

    B.   Confirm the influence using the Durbin-Watson test.

2. The Durbin-Watson test uses the regression errors' fluctuation to see whether the past has an influence over present data.

3. The distance from the medium moving average to the Y value. In this example, the Y value is the quarterly car sales.

4. The season and the regression trend value.

5. Here are two elements of time-series data:

    A.   A season component

    B.   A trend component

Index

Packt.com

Subscribe to our online digital library for full access to over 7,000 books and videos, as well as industry leading tools to help you plan your personal development and advance your career. For more information, please visit our website.

Why subscribe?

- Spend less time learning and more time coding with practical eBooks and Videos from over 4,000 industry professionals

- Improve your learning with Skill Plans built especially for you

- Get a free eBook or video every month

- Fully searchable for easy access to vital information

- Copy and paste, print, and bookmark content

Did you know that Packt offers eBook versions of every book published, with PDF and ePub files available? You can upgrade to the eBook version at packt.com and as a print book customer, you are entitled to a discount on the eBook copy. Get in touch with us at customercare@packtpub.com for more details.

At www.packt.com, you can also read a collection of free technical articles, sign up for a range of free newsletters, and receive exclusive discounts and offers on Packt books and eBooks.

Other Books You May Enjoy

If you enjoyed this book, you may be interested in these other books by Packt:

Hands-On Machine Learning with Microsoft Excel 2019

Julio Cesar Rodriguez Martino

ISBN: 9781789345377

- Use Excel to preview and cleanse datasets
- Understand correlations between variables and optimize the input to machine learning models
- Use and evaluate different machine learning models from Excel
- Understand the use of different visualizations
- Learn the basic concepts and calculations to understand how artificial neural networks work
- Learn how to connect Excel to the Microsoft Azure cloud
- Get beyond proof of concepts and build fully functional data analysis flows

Forecasting Time Series Data with Facebook Prophet

Greg Rafferty

ISBN: 9781800568532

- Gain an understanding of time series forecasting, including its history, development, and uses
- Understand how to install Prophet and its dependencies
- Build practical forecasting models from real datasets using Python
- Understand the Fourier series and learn how it models seasonality
- Decide when to use additive and when to use multiplicative seasonality
- Discover how to identify and deal with outliers in time series data
- Run diagnostics to evaluate and compare the performance of your models

Packt is searching for authors like you

If you're interested in becoming an author for Packt, please visit `authors.packtpub.com` and apply today. We have worked with thousands of developers and tech professionals, just like you, to help them share their insight with the global tech community. You can make a general application, apply for a specific hot topic that we are recruiting an author for, or submit your own idea.

Share Your Thoughts

Now you've finished *Hands-On Financial Modeling with Microsoft Excel 365*, we'd love to hear your thoughts! Scan the QR code below to go straight to the Amazon review page for this book and share your feedback or leave a review on the site that you purchased it from.

https://packt.link/r/1-803-23114-9

Your review is important to us and the tech community and will help us make sure we're delivering excellent quality content.

Made in the USA
Middletown, DE
09 July 2023

34780940R00183